THE REAL PATRIOTS
OF EARLY SCOTTISH INDEPENDENCE

THE REAL PATRIOTS OF EARLY SCOTTISH INDEPENDENCE

ALAN YOUNG

AND

GEORGE CUMMING

First published in Great Britain in 2014 by
John Donald, an imprint of Birlinn Ltd

West Newington House
10 Newington Road
Edinburgh
EH9 1QS

www.birlinn.co.uk

ISBN: 978 1 906566 65 4

The publishers gratefully acknowledge the support of the Strathmartine Trust

THE
STRATHMARTINE
TRUST

towards the publication of this book

British Library Cataloguing-in-Publication Data
A catalogue record for this book is available on request from the British Library

Typeset by Hewer Text UK Ltd, Edinburgh
Printed and bound in Britain by Bell and Bain Ltd, Glasgow

Contents

Illustrations and Tables

Maps and Plans

Tables

Preface and Acknowledgements

When my research on the Comyn family started in 1970, I did not think that I would still be exploring new angles on the family's history over forty years later especially after bringing together, in 1997, all of my research on the family to that date in *Robert the Bruce's Rivals: the Comyns, 1212–1314* (Tuckwell Press). Some comments from reviewers of this book gave me food for thought. Fiona Watson[1] confirmed my own slight misgivings about a title (chosen, perhaps, too much for commercial reasons than historical ones!) which seemed to *keep* the Comyns in Robert Bruce's shadow. She also suggested, quite rightly, that more could be done to 'push the case for the Comyns and the implications of their leadership of the community of the realm of Scotland, and the patriotic party during the first phase of the wars with England'. At last, I am grasping that nettle after further reflection following my own recent work and that of others.

Like others before me, I was drawn, like a moth to a flame, to Scotland's two most famous medieval icons, William Wallace and Robert Bruce, in the hope of shining new light on these famous figures. Work on *In the Footsteps of Robert Bruce* (Sutton Publishing, 1999 and History Press, 2000) and *In the Footsteps of William Wallace* (Sutton Publishing, 2002 and History Press, 2010), both with the landscape photographer Michael J. Stead, may have added to the narrow concentration of Scottish medieval history on these two figures but it also convinced me that certain members of the Comyn family deserve to share the accolade of these 'Patriot Heroes' for their contribution to Scottish independence in the thirteenth century. My initial thought was to bring to public attention the remarkable (and greatly underestimated) fifty-year career of Alexander Comyn, Earl of Buchan (d.1289), surely one of the 'unsung' heroes of Scottish medieval history. However, long and stimulating discussion with the barrister Dr George Cumming about the circumstances surrounding the murder of John

Comyn III, Lord of Badenoch, in 1306 by Robert Bruce (the future king), persuaded me to widen the scope of my study to include not only the murdered John Comyn but also Walter Comyn, a key national figure for the significant (but underestimated) period of Scotland's development from c.1230 to 1258. It also persuaded me that after so much pro-Wallace and pro-Bruce propaganda on behalf of their heroes in the fourteenth and fifteenth centuries, a Comyn/Cumming perspective by a member of that family was long overdue. I was, therefore, pleased that Dr Cumming accepted my invitation to participate in the book by contributing a chapter on the murder of John Comyn. Dr Cumming, as a barrister, looks at the murder of John Comyn from a distinctively legal perspective (a medieval canon law perspective), forensically examining, as in a legal case, only facts as far as they can be ascertained and eschewing speculation, i.e. the biased narratives, created after the event, which have been the main focus of historical discussion of the murder.

In 2014 there was a natural concentration on Bannockburn celebrations, Robert Bruce and the issue of the Scottish Independence referendum but it should be remembered that Bannockburn was as important a defining moment for the Scottish civil war as it was for the Anglo-Scottish war. Bannockburn gave Scotland a hero but robbed the country of three patriot heroes from the Comyn family. As Dr Cumming's examination of John Comyn's murder makes even clearer, the dubious actions of Robert Bruce in 1306 necessitated a very robust defence, subsequently, to preserve his reputation (even after Bannockburn). Historians in the centuries since have tended to follow the pro-Bruce propaganda of the fourteenth and fifteenth centuries. This has had the effect of writing the Comyns out of the century of Scottish history (before Bannockburn) which they dominated. This was 'the Comyn century' and 'the Comyn century' deserves Comyn heroes.

Since 1997 there has been excellent editorial work on major sources for the study of this period. Good examples are Professor Duncan's excellent edition of John Barbour's *The Bruce* and his work on the *Melrose Chronicle* and the marvellous work of Professor D.E.R. Watt and his editorial team in providing illuminating examination of the sources behind that major Scottish narrative in their new edition of Walter Bower's *Scotichronicon*. Particular mention should be made of Professor Dauvit Brown's work on *Liber Extravagans* appended to *Scotichronicon* and his important findings on *Gesta Annalia* (formerly attributed to John of Fordun). Also valuable is Andy King's new edition of an important English source for the period, Thomas Gray's *Scalacronica*. All the above have been of great benefit in reviewing traditional values on Scottish heroes and villains as well as traditional views on Scotland's image and identity prior to 1306. Thought-provoking writings by Edward Cowan, Alexander Grant, Amanda Beam, Fiona Watson and James Fraser have already shed much new light on the roles of John Comyn, William Wallace and John Balliol as well as on general issues of nationhood and identity. I have been greatly stimulated by their work and am much in their debt. Professor Cowan's refreshingly forthright views on John Comyn in his *'For Freedom Alone': The Declaration of Arbroath* (Tuckwell Press, 2003) have, in particular, influenced me to try to assess the 'patriot' credentials of other members of the Comyn family too.

Tim Jeal's new biography of David Livingstone, revised forty years after the publication of his first biography (in 1973) also struck a chord especially with his comment that even after the publication of his findings 'Livingstones' reputation as a near-saint survives'[2]. Old propaganda has had a powerful impact in all historical periods in sealing the reputations of historical figures and making it difficult to update them. I am grateful to my former colleague, Dr David Powell, of York St John University for reading Chapter 1 and making several valuable comments from a modern historical perspective. I am, similarly, grateful for comments on Chapter 1 from Paul Brunyee.

I owe thanks to the staff of a number of record offices, libraries and museums for their help and advice in the course of my research for this book – the National Records of Scotland, the National Library of Scotland, the British Library, Historic Scotland, the Royal Commission on the Ancient and Historical Monuments of Scotland, and the Cambridge University Collection of Aerial Photography. In particular, I would like to thank Mrs G.C. Roads, Lyon Clerk and Keeper of the Records of the Court of the Lord Lyon, for most valuable assistance with research on seals. I am also grateful for the ready assistance of Joanne Turner of Dumfries Museum. Research in Edinburgh over a number of years has been made even more enjoyable by the hospitality so generously offered by Geoff and Janet Bone who have made Edinburgh a second home – my appreciation of good malt whisky has also been enhanced considerably! The final drafts of the book have been prepared on disk by Joanne Ripley whose meticulous and efficient work is much appreciated. I have also been grateful for the good advice and patience of Mairi Sutherland at Birlinn for seeing this project to completion and to Jacqueline Henrie for her careful copy-editing. My wife Heather has always been ready to advise on phraseology and grammar and I owe special thanks to my daughter Alice Rosamund, whose co-ordination of picture research and computer skills has been of invaluable assistance. As her birthday, on St Andrew's Day, is always a reminder of Scottish history and Scottish friends, I dedicate this book to her. In addition, I would like to dedicate the book to all those successors of the thirteenth-century Comyns who have had to endure for centuries the vilification of their ancestors instead of celebrating the outstanding contributions of 'the Real Patriots of Early Scottish Independence'.

I am grateful to the Strathmartine Trust and the Marc Fitch Fund for their help towards the cost of illustrations in this book.

Alan Young
Malton, North Yorkshire

The Comyn Family Tree: featuring the Badenoch and Kilbride lines

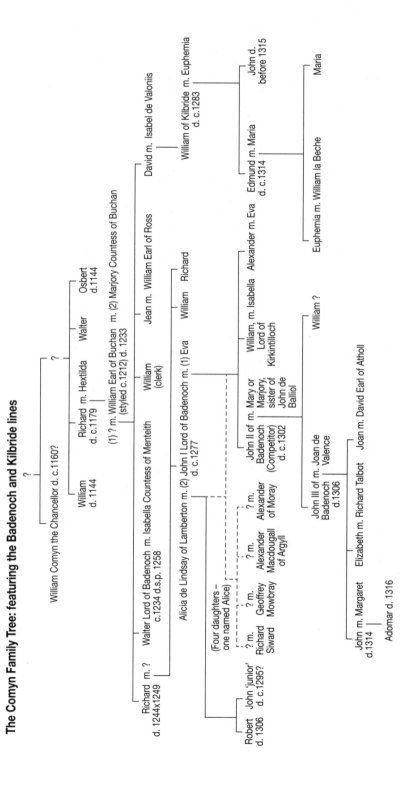

The Comyn Family Tree: featuring the Buchan line

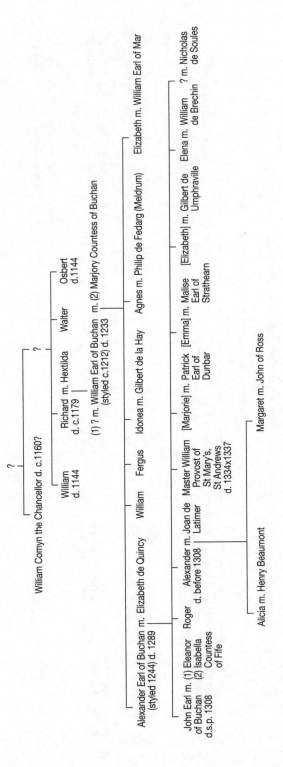

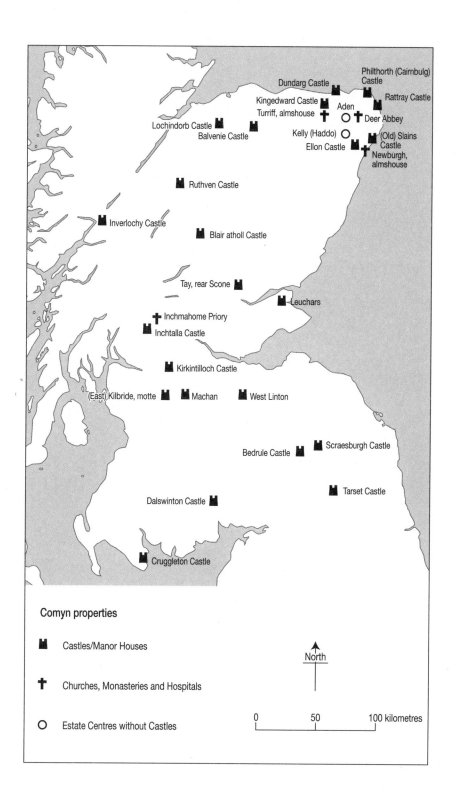

Philthorth (Cairnbulg)
Castle

Dundarg Castle

Rattray Castle

Kingedward Castle
Turriff, almshouse   Aden

Deer Abbey

Lochindorb Castle
Kelly (Haddo)

(Old) Slains
Castle

Balvenie Castle
Ellon Castle

Newburgh,
almshouse

Ruthven Castle

Inverlochy Castle

Blair atholl Castle

Tay, rear Scone

Leuchars

Inchmahome Priory

Inchtalla Castle

Kirkintilloch Castle

(East) Kilbride, motte   Machan   West Linton

Scraesburgh Castle

Bedrule Castle

Tarset Castle

Dalswinton Castle

Cruggleton Castle

Comyn properties

Castles/Manor Houses

Churches, Monasteries and Hospitals

Estate Centres without Castles

North

0   50   100 kilometres

I

Heroes, Villains and Patriots

PROPAGANDA, LITERATURE AND THE
RETELLING OF NATIONAL HISTORY

Who knows whether the best of men be known? Or whether there
be not more remarkable persons forgot, than any that stand
remembered in the known account of time?
Sir Thomas Browne, *Urn Burial* (1658)[1]

How are patriot heroes made? It would be reasonable to assume that
clear historical evidence naturally throws up achievements worthy of
hero status and that time helps to cement such achievements into a
nation's traditions. However, history is more than just a record of past
events, it is how those events are recorded and interpreted; tradition,
in turn, passes on beliefs (rather than truth) from generation to generation. There can be no simple transition from factual history to tradition – there is plenty of scope for ambiguity. This is particularly true
where national history and the study of a nation's patriot heroes are
concerned. Powerful traditions can develop over time, bolstered by
propaganda, literature and the media, and these can defy historical
evidence from the continuing exploration of the past.

The ambiguities and distortions between history and tradition are,
perhaps, best illustrated by the influence which William Shakespeare
has had in forging public perceptions of medieval British kings.[2]
Shakespeare was not an historian and was naturally more interested in
the dramatic potential offered by characters from history. He was also
'influenced' by the politics of his time. Few people can forget his image
of Richard III as an evil, crook-backed king. This image, largely based
on the Tudor propaganda of his time, has been successfully recycled
with dramatic effect over centuries and to a world-wide audience due
to the success and circulation of Shakespeare's works. It is an image
which has 'lived on' to the present day despite the best work of historians and the Richard III Society to update this negative stereotype.

The tradition of Richard III also illustrates a truism that history is written by the winners and that a civil war engenders particularly savage indictments for the losers. Heroes of one side can be easily turned into villains by the very partial views of the other side.

In Scotland, national heroes are publicly acknowledged in modern opinion polls and nineteenth-century monuments and memorials. A report in the *Scotsman*, 18 December 1999, gave the results of a survey on the greatest Scots in history as conducted by *Who's Who in Scotland*[3]. Robert Burns was the comfortable winner, with William Wallace in second place, Robert Bruce in third place and Walter Scott down in seventh place. The nineteenth century saw a spate of monuments and memorials recognising Scotland's patriot heroes. Victorian regard for William Wallace as 'the Scottish hero'[4] was apparent when the foundation stone for the 220-foot high National Wallace Monument was laid at Abbey Craig, near Stirling, in 1861. The monument's status as a national monument for Scottish heroes is confirmed by the 'hall of [Scottish] heroes' at its foot. This acknowledges the national status of Bruce, Buchanan, Knox, Burns and Livingstone. William Hole's famous late nineteenth-century frieze at the Scottish National Portrait Gallery depicts a painted procession of famous Scots from all periods of Scotland's history. For the more modern period people such as Scott, Burns, Macauley, Telford, Watt and Livingstone are celebrated. For the medieval period, kings feature strongly as well as William Wallace; Robert Bruce, Bruce's family and key supporters such as James Douglas are particularly prominent. An interesting feature of the frieze is the figure of Isabella, Countess of Buchan, half-hidden behind the figures of William Wallace and Robert Bruce. Isabella, Countess of Buchan, was the wife of John Comyn, Earl of Buchan, cousin and right-hand man of John Comyn III, Lord of Badenoch, murder victim of Robert Bruce in the Greyfriars Church at Dumfries on 10 February 1306. (Referred to as John Comyn 'the Younger' for most of his career, he became John Comyn III, Lord of Badenoch, in 1302.) As the aunt of the earl of Fife, Isabella had fulfilled the traditional leading role of that earldom in the enthronement of a new king. She had, however, betrayed the cause of her husband and the Comyn family in seeking justice for their murdered leader. The frieze commemorates her value to the new (and illegal) Bruce kingship – she is the only member of the Comyn family depicted despite their dominant role in thirteenth-century Scotland as pillars of the Scottish monarchy.

Opinion polls and memorials reflect the enduring, somewhat static, positions of Scottish heroes (and villains, for that matter) in the popular imagination. Do they, however, simply recycle old images and reputations in the same way that the enduring popularity of William Shakespeare's works have repeated and cemented the image of Richard III in the popular mind to the present day? In the modern period, the cult and celebrity of David Livingstone as the great Victorian missionary explorer remain strong despite new evidence and conclusions about his achievements. Tim Jeal, whose revised and expanded biography of David Livingstone, updates his earlier biography written forty years previously has reflected on the distortions caused by 'old' propaganda.[5] Having shown forty years ago that Livingstone, the great missionary, had only made one convert (and even this one had lapsed) and that the great explorer's geography was faulty and had led traders and missionaries into unsuitable and dangerous regions, Jeal concedes that 'Livingstone's reputation as a near-saint survives'. He notes the power of Henry Stanley's famous interview with Livingstone and his idealised portrait of the man leading to a general observation: 'Enduring celebrity may therefore sometimes owe almost as much to the creative ingenuity of its journalist begetter as to the achievements of the celebrated person.' The strength of *this* image was no doubt bolstered by Livingstone's own book *Missionary Travels* which sold extremely well (70,000 copies) and the reporting of his adventures (complete with pictures) in the cheap newspapers rapidly expanding in mid nineteenth-century Britain. If the strength of early propaganda and the longevity of its recycling has proved such a barrier to new public perceptions of a nineteenth-century Scottish hero, the problem of changing perceptions of medieval heroes of early Scottish independence is magnified.

For over 700 years the names of Robert Bruce and William Wallace have formed an exclusive club of Scottish heroes of the early Scottish independence movement. Modern writers acknowledge the relevance of Wallace and Bruce (and their reputations) to Scottish politics today:

Where would Scotland be if it were not for the Wars of Independence and the two medieval leaders, William Wallace and Robert Bruce?[6]

and:

Without the actions of people 700 years ago, like William Wallace, Robert Bruce and their supporters, the idea of Scotland as an independent country might not exist now. Understanding the time of Wallace and Bruce is part of what it means to be Scottish today.[7]

Modern politics itself seems to recognise this too. In 1997, the date 11 September (undoubtedly chosen to stir memories of William Wallace and his victory on that date at Stirling Bridge 1297) was deemed appropriate for the great majority of the Scottish people to vote for a Scottish parliament (which they did). In 2014, the Referendum vote on Scottish Independence is unlikely to take place without major reference to Robert Bruce, the 700th anniversary of the Battle of Bannockburn (23–24 June 1314) and much playing of 'Flower of Scotland', adopted as an 'unofficial' national anthem in celebration of Bruce's victory at that battle.

It is clear that the names William Wallace and Robert Bruce were already deeply etched into the Scottish psyche by the nineteenth century when 'an increasing emphasis on the emotional trappings of the Scottish past'[8] saw the raising of monuments to Wallace and Bruce as patriot heroes. Fittingly, at least to Scottish tradition, both William Wallace and Robert Bruce look down from the walls on either side of the entrance to Edinburgh Castle as if united in the patriot cause. Elsewhere Wallace statues and memorials, in particular, were enthusiastically set up – the Wallace Monument at Wallacestone (1810), the 21-foot memorial at Dryburgh (1814), the Wallace Tower in Ayr (1834), which contained a statue of Wallace high up on the front, one of two statues of Wallace in the town, and the Wallace Memorial Window in Paisley Abbey (1873) among many. Chief among them all, however, was the National Wallace Monument, Abbey Craig, Stirling – constructed between 1861 and 1869 and built by public subscription, the magnificent 220-foot monument attracted much public interest from the outset. A crowd of over 50,000 people attended the ceremony for the laying of the foundation stone. It is noteworthy that the monuments and memorials of this time represent William Wallace with a seniority of years and a certain 'gravitas' – in keeping with the Victorian era, but also in keeping with Wallace's perceived military leadership of the early Scottish independence movement. He had become *the* national symbol for that movement by the nineteenth century but not only in Scotland. At Ballarat, Victoria, their Wallace monument (1889) also became the focal point for Scottish national sentiment. Monuments and memorials reflect the views of Thomas Smith Hutcheson (1858) that William Wallace was 'the most perfect model of the Patriot Hero the world has ever beheld'.[9]

Robert Bruce, by comparison, never attracted the cult status and the plethora of monuments associated with William Wallace despite the high regard in which he was held by Scottish historians by the nine-teenth century.[10] Robert Bruce was portrayed by them in heroic terms. P.H. Tytler (d. 1849) described Bruce's military record against England: 'Bruce stood alone, and shared the glory with no-one', while P. Hume-Brown (d. 1918) saw Bruce as 'the greatest king that ever sat on the Scottish throne'. There are significant late-nineteenth/early-twentieth-century statues of Bruce on the esplanades of Stirling and Edinburgh castles but nothing equivalent to the National Wallace Monument. The most noted modern biographer of Robert Bruce, G.W.S. Barrow, is in no doubt about the significance of Bruce to the Scottish independence movement: 'As far as the independence and survival of the kingdom of Scotland are concerned, it would be hard to exaggerate the importance of his role, even allowing for the fact that he was able to build upon the achievement of Wallace.' Again, Bruce and Wallace are tied together as heroes of the Scottish independence movement, with Bruce taking over the leadership role from Wallace. William Wallace's biographer, Andrew Fisher, firmly concluded that Wallace 'remains not merely the first but the most durable and heroic of Scottish patriots'.[11]

Modern notions of Scottish patriot heroes have all looked to the medieval period to establish their authority, credibility and justifica-tion. The major Scottish narratives of the fourteenth and fifteenth centuries – the *Gesta Annalia* (formerly known as the work of John of Fordun) of the 1380s, Walter Bower's *Scotichronicon* (c.1440) and Andrew Wyntoun's *Oryginale Cronykil of Scotland* (c.1420) – have laid the foundation for Scottish history and tradition for the Middle Ages. In particular, *Gesta Annalia* has formed the main strand in the standard narrative account of Scottish medieval history – the source is acknowledged as invaluable for the century up to the Battle of Bannockburn because of the use of some original thirteenth-century material not found elsewhere. Are these well-used Scottish narratives the solution to the problem of identifying Scotland's patriot heroes of the early Scottish independence movement, their respective leadership roles and their interrelationship? Or are they part of the problem with their narrow focus on William Wallace and Robert Bruce? Is Sir Thomas Browne's enquiry, '[are] the best of men ... known' and 'more remarkable persons forgot'[12] applicable to the early Scottish independence movement?

Adulation of William Wallace and Robert Bruce first occurred in *Gesta Annalia*, and was then bolstered by Walter Bower and Andrew of Wyntoun. In *Gesta Annalia*, William Wallace had five chapters devoted to his role between 1297 and 1298, he was mentioned in two further chapters for his role in 1304 – his continuing resistance stressed when 'all the magnates' submitted to the English – before a short chapter was devoted to his execution and death. His introduction was suitably powerful and his leadership role emphasised:

> From that time there flocked to him all who were in bitterness of spirit and were weighed down beneath the burden of bondage under the unbearable domination of English despotism, and he became their leader. He was wondrously brave and bold, of goodly mien and boundless liberality and by dint of his prowess brought all the magnates of Scotland under his sway, whether they would or not.[13]

Walter Bower added further praise for Wallace:

> rightly striving until his death for faithfulness and his native land, a man who never submitted to the English.[14]

Bower compared Wallace to Mattathias who initiated the revolt in Israel as dramatically as Wallace (according to *Gesta Annalia* and Bower) 'led' the fight for Scotland's liberty in 1297. Most memorable of all was the assessment of Wallace given by Andrew Wyntoun:

> In all England there was not then
> As William Wallace so true a man
> Whatever he did against their nation
> They made him ample provocation
> Nor to them sworn never was he
> To fellowship, faith or loyalty[15]

Gesta Annalia introduced Robert Bruce earlier when describing his father's elevation to the earldom of Carrick (1272):

> Of Martha, by God's providence, he begat a son, who was to be the saviour, champion and king, of the bruised Scottish people, as the course of the history will show forth.[16]

Subsequently, Robert Bruce was mentioned unflatteringly in the chapter on the Battle of Falkirk (1298), is absent for ten chapters (the years

1298–1305) before a succession of six chapters out of seven justified his murder of John Comyn III, Lord of Badenoch, his coup and coronation in 1306. Interestingly, the chapter here in which Robert Bruce was omitted concerned the torture and death of William Wallace in 1305. Bruce is seen as Wallace's natural successor. Before describing Wallace's death, Robert Bruce was introduced into the narrative as Scotland's champion against English oppression:

> The English lorded it in all parts of the kingdom of Scotland ruthlessly harrying the Scots in sundry and manifold ways, by insults, stripes and slaughter, under the awful yoke of slavery ... But God, as is the wont of his fatherly goodness, had compassion ... so He raised up a saviour and champion unto them – one of their own fellows, to wit, named Robert Bruce.[17]

Naturally, Robert Bruce, as king, dominates the narrative after 1306 with twelve chapters devoted to his struggles against his enemies within Scotland before the relatively short chapter on the Battle of Bannockburn (1314). Concern with enemies within Scotland explains the need for Robert Bruce and his supporters to vilify his enemies.

Walter Bower in his *Scotichronicon* added a biblical flourish in his expansion of *Gesta Annalia*'s narrative on Robert Bruce as he had done with William Wallace:

> He was to become the stick which beat the English; indeed he was to become the champion and the king of Scots, born as he was of royal stock.[18]

and:

> like a second Maccabeus adopting forceful measures in order to free his own fellow-countrymen ... He happily faced up to plots and weariness, hunger and danger arising not only from his enemies but also from false fellow-countrymen.

> ... whoever has learned to recount his individual conflicts and particular triumphs – the victories and battles in which the help of the Lord, by his own strength and his energetic valour as a man, he forced his way through the ranks of the enemy without fear ...

he will find, I think, that he will judge none in the regions of the world to be his equal in his own times in the art of fighting and in physical strength.[19]

The focus on William Wallace and Robert Bruce as Scottish patriot heroes was understandable given the context of the continuing military conflicts of the fourteenth and fifteenth centuries to preserve Scottish independence and resist English interference and tyranny. This was the context in which *Gesta Annalia* and Walter Bower were compiling their narratives. The biblical references by Bower to the Book of the Maccabees and the plight of Israel in danger at the hands of Syria, its more powerful neighbour, must have felt very natural to church writers in Scotland.

It is important to note the significance of the much wider coverage given to these heightened views of William Wallace and Robert Bruce in the *Gesta Annalia*, Walter Bower and Andrew Wyntoun. This occurred through the poems specifically dedicated to these two Scottish heroes – *The Brus*,[20] written in 1375 by John Barbour, Archdeacon of Aberdeen, and *The Wallace*, written in the 1470s by Henry the Minstrel, better known as 'Blind Harry'. The effect of these two works, further heightening the images of Bruce and Wallace to epic proportions, was comparable to the impact of Shakespeare's works on the reputations of Richard III and other British monarchs. *The Brus* was a very full account of Robert Bruce's life, in fact the most comprehensive life of any medieval king in the west – it portrayed Robert Bruce as the hero of an epic poem. The vernacular poem *The Wallace* fulfilled a similar purpose for William Wallace. *The Brus* had been written to be a popular work with the widest possible audience, but *The Wallace* soon outstripped *The Brus* in popularity and influence. *The Brus* was written with a purpose and undoubtedly Barbour wrote the poem to please Robert II and allow him to indulge in the achievements of Robert Bruce, his grandfather. It proved to be such a success that it provoked Sir William Wallace of Craigie, a descendant of William Wallace and probably very familiar with the history and traditions associated with Wallace, to be patron to Henry the Minstrel (Blind Harry) in the writing of *The Wallace*. The purpose was to prevent William Wallace's career and achievement as a patriot hero being completely overshadowed by that of Robert Bruce. In effect, a media war and popularity contest were being fought in the fourteenth and fifteenth centuries between rival supporters of Bruce and Wallace.

Rivalry led to further distortion in favour of Wallace's place in Scottish history over Bruce. Cheekily, Blind Harry added some of Robert Bruce's military activities to William Wallace's military record – the Battle of Loudoun Hill was taken from Bruce's career, as was the invasion of Bruce's army into Yorkshire to threaten the English war capital at York.

This internal popularity contest in Scotland also occurred during a period when the search for heroes (and the embellishment of their achievements) was rife in European literature. While Robert Bruce was seen in 1375 as the chivalric hero of an epic poem, William Wallace came to be seen as a hero in the mould of popular heroes of the time such as Robin Hood. By the end of the fourteenth century, Robin Hood's reputation was already widespread and it is important to note that both Walter Bower and Andrew Wyntoun, both influences on Blind Harry's writing, were familiar with the ballads of Robin Hood. Blind Harry's *The Wallace* followed the conventions of these ballads and it is not surprising that they share common features and that William Wallace came to be seen as a Scottish Robin Hood – both were proud outlaws, expert archers, skilful users of inaccessible wood and forests from which to engage in guerrilla-type warfare. In *The Wallace* and the ballads of Robin Hood, the arch-enemy is a sheriff, chief representation of their oppressors. No doubt such 'embellishments' enhanced the particularly 'popular' element in Wallace's reputation as a Scottish patriot hero. It is interesting to note that at about the time Blind Harry was writing, the tale of William Tell was being embellished. Rather more established stories were also gaining new life – in 1485 Malory's *Le Morte D'Arthur* was published in England, giving greater prominence to this long-lived saga.

The Wallace succeeded in the patron's ambitions. Between 1508 and 1800 there were thirty-seven printings of *The Wallace* compared with twelve of *The Brus*; twelve 'Wallaces' appeared between 1700 and 1750 compared with one 'Bruce'.[21] Only the Bible was found more often in Scottish households than *The Wallace*. The popularity of the book was increased further, no doubt, with the translation of William Hamilton of Gilbertsfield in 1722, *A New Edition of the Life and Heroik Actions of the Renoun'd Sir William Wallace, General and Governor of Scotland*. The many editions of this translated version ensured that *The Wallace* retained its ascendancy in the eighteenth and nineteenth centuries. It outstripped Barbour's *The Brus* in popularity and was the most renowned work in Scotland before the era of Robert Burns and Walter Scott. Robert Burns was, like others, influenced by the life of William Wallace and ranked him alongside Hannibal as one of his chief heroes. His passion for his hero is evident:

> The story of Wallace poured a Scottish prejudice in my veins which will boil along there, until the floodgates of life shut in eternal rest.[22]

It is appropriate that Robert Burns' verses 'Scots wha hae wi Wallace bled' was in effect the Scottish national anthem for two centuries. Wallace remained a popular Scottish patriot hero to the working classes and middle classes in the nineteenth century and a symbol of twentieth-century democracy as *The Wallace* continued to exert its influence on Scotland's living culture. As Andrew Fisher concluded: 'Harry's poem established a national stereotype of such remarkable force that Wallace remains not merely the first but the most durable and heroic of Scottish patriots.'[23] This stereotype and Harry's poem was notably reinforced by the film *Braveheart* (1995) which was based on Randall Wallace's novel *Braveheart* (London, 1995), which in turn used Blind Harry's *The Wallace* as its main source. Both have combined to produce a powerful image of violent resistance to English imperialism. Indeed, both show such relish in Wallace's violent anti-English acts of vengeance that Wallace's cause itself seems to become revenge against the English rather than defence of John Balliol's right to the Scottish throne, which is barely mentioned in *The Wallace*. The book, which blends fact with much fiction, distortions of earlier chroniclers and incorrect chronology, has had a massive circulation and therefore a wide influence. 'The legacy of Wallace has obscured too many facts. This should be accepted as the history of the nation, not the search for truth.'[24] Yet this also means the acceptance of William Wallace as a 'symbolic' patriotic hero – as legendary as Robin Hood – rather than a true historic hero. It also means that real historic achievements – the 'facts' – behind other 'patriot heroes' are obscured.

It is ironic that *The Brus*, written with the widest possible audience in mind, was overtaken by *The Wallace* to make William Wallace *the* 'popular' Scottish patriot hero. Robert Bruce came to be acknowledged as the great 'political' patriot hero who restored an independent Scottish monarchy. Based on the works of *Gesta Annalia*, Walter

Bower, and the popularity of *The Brus*, the image of Robert Bruce as a patriot hero was further burnished by historians to the present day. John Mair (Major) in his *Historia Majoris Brittaniae* (1521) even rated Robert Bruce more highly than William Wallace as a national patriot leader. There is, however, an occasional discordant note which hints at the reason Robert Bruce never became such a cult figure as William Wallace. It is notable as Professor Barrow points out[25] that Andrew Lang in his *History of Scotland* (1900) paints a picture of Bruce as an 'evershifting politician ... unscrupulously and perfidiously self-seeking' *before* his murder of the leader of the Scottish political community, John Comyn III, Lord of Badenoch, in 1306; then suddenly after his successful 'coup' he became, to Lang, a man of 'unflinching resolution, consummate generalship, brilliant courtesy ... and wisdom'. Lang displays here the need for a rewriting of Bruce's contribution to the Scottish independence movement after the events of 1306. Was the murder of John Comyn (re-examined in Chapter 5) and the role of Robert Bruce before 1306 the pre-eminent Scottish example of the memorable phrase of G. Morton about the writing of national histories?

All nations of the world are made up from half-remembered stories, of myths and legends and *convenient forgetfulness about history that is uncomfortable.*[26]

There has been a lot of 'convenient forgetfulness' about Robert Bruce's role before 1306 and his murder of John Comyn is certainly 'history that is uncomfortable'. As a result, the history of the early Scottish independence movement has been distorted. The key part of literature in deliberate distortion has been the invented meeting of William Wallace and Robert Bruce at the Battle of Falkirk (1298). This is mentioned for the first time by Walter Bower (c.1440), but was dramatised (and publicised) much further in Blind Harry's *The Wallace*, and still further in the film *Braveheart*. The episode has been described as 'perhaps the most dramatic scenes in the whole of old Scottish literature'.[27] Walter Bower's significant elaboration (c.1440) of *Gesta Annalia* (1380s) was an inventive attempt to improve Robert Bruce's image for 1298. *Gesta Annalia*, though solidly pro-Bruce on the whole, had blamed Robert Bruce for causing William Wallace's loss at the Battle of Falkirk:

> It is commonly said that Robert Bruce – who was afterwards king
> of Scotland, but then fought on the side of the king of English –
> was the means of bringing this victory.[28]

While it is unlikely that Robert Bruce was at the battle, his father may
have been with the army and it is certainly true that the Bruce family
(including the future king) were on the English side at the outbreak of
the war in 1296. At this time the Bruces were more intent on gaining
Edward I's support for the family's dynastic ambition for the Scottish
Crown than supporting the national cause (until 1306, the cause was
represented by the Balliol dynasty).

As William Wallace was perhaps the most fervent upholder of the
kingship of John Balliol, Walter Bower's ingenious (but wholly ficti-
tious) story of a meeting between Wallace and Bruce, after the Battle
of Falkirk was lost, satisfied a need (in the fifteenth century) to bring
Robert Bruce and William Wallace together in a common national
cause:

> Robert de Bruce . . . is said to have called out loudly to William,
> asking him who it was that drove him to such arrogance as to seek
> so rashly to fight in opposition to the exalted power of the king of
> England . . . It is said that William replied like this to him: 'Robert,
> Robert, it is your inactivity and womanish cowardice that spur
> me to set authority free in your native land . . .
>
> . . . On account of all this Robert himself was like one awakening
> from a deep sleep, the power of Wallace's words so entered his
> heart that he no longer had any thought of favouring the views of
> the English. Hence, as he became every day braver than he had
> been, he kept all these words uttered by his faithful friend, consid-
> ering them in his heart.[29]

This well-known story, linking William Wallace and Robert Bruce to
the national cause, with Robert Bruce taking on William Wallace's
achievement and leadership of the Scottish cause in 1306, is a purely
literary device which distorts the history of the early Scottish independence movement and the role of Robert Bruce (and others) in it.
There is no contemporary evidence hinting that Wallace had any role
in rousing Robert Bruce's dormant nationalism, the episode is not
mentioned in *Gesta Annalia* (c.1380s) (which does use some

contemporary material). Significantly, *The Brus* does not mention William Wallace in any context linking him with Robert Bruce; indeed, he does not get a mention at all! Historically, the pricking of Robert Bruce's conscience in 1298 is not apparent in Robert Bruce's behaviour after 1298. He rejoined the English side c.1301 and even took action for Edward I against Wallace in 1304.[30] As Goldstein points out, 'historical narrative, whether medieval or modern, necessarily 'forges' the past'.[31] Robert Bruce had to be 'forged' or grafted onto William Wallace's upholding of the national cause – represented by John Balliol since 1292 – despite his being in bitter opposition to John Balliol's kingship apart from a brief period in 1297 and between 1298 and 1300.

The Scottish narratives of the fourteenth and fifteenth centuries – the basis of Scottish tradition on medieval patriot heroes – were written in a particular political context that required the 'forging' of the past within a strict framework and within strict themes. The political context was the instability of a divided country. After Robert Bruce's death in 1329, Scotland suffered from another minority period as well as civil war and Edward III's support of Edward Balliol's attempt to gain the Scottish Crown (and regain it for the Balliol dynasty) was a strong reminder of Edward I's earlier interference. Scottish government and kingship was further weakened following David II's capture by the English at the Battle of Neville's Cross (1346) and his subsequent long captivity. One historian has suggested that 'Perhaps, indeed, the whole of *Gesta Annalia* II was designed to support David II's anti-magnate policy of the later 1350s and 1360s which was at its peak when the chronicle was being written.'[32] Walter Bower's elaboration of *Gesta Annalia* in the 1440s took place against a background of further political instability, the country being once more divided, following the murder of James I, and another minority period.

Fourteenth- and fifteenth-century anxieties and preoccupations naturally affected interpretations of Scottish history for the century before Bannockburn, and the themes they chose to highlight in their narratives. The century was viewed in a strongly monarcho-centric way, and unsurprisingly emphasis was placed on the threat posed to the monarchy by the faction and lawlessness of the nobility acting as overmighty subjects. The importance of the monarchy – the reign of Alexander III was used to create an ideal for the kind of kingship to be aimed at – was emphasised as the key to the attainment of a strong independent nation. The dangers of a minority period (Alexander III's minority 1249–1258), the uncertainty of the succession after Alexander III's death (1286–1292) and the weakness of John Balliol's kingship (1292–1296) were emphasised as a lesson to their audience in similarly unstable periods in the fourteenth and fifteenth centuries.

William Wallace and Robert Bruce, in this context, were raised as patriot heroes. Wallace was used to demonstrate the strong leadership required of good kingship (in the absence of the king, John Balliol). He was an ideal figurehead for the anti-English party – in late-fifteenth-century Scotland, the pro-English policies of James III of Scotland provoked hostile anti-English sentiment. Robert Bruce returned Scotland to the kingship of the 'Golden Age' of Alexander III but the patriot narratives of the fourteenth and fifteenth centuries were left with a dilemma – how could they justify his violent seizure of the Scottish throne and his sacrilegious murder of the man acknowledged at the time as leader of the Scottish political community, John Comyn III, Lord of Badenoch, in 1306?

There was a need for pro-Bruce propaganda to support Robert Bruce's illegal usurpation of the Scottish throne in 1306. Violent civil war had been unleashed *by* Robert Bruce in 1306 after twenty years of Bruce family opposition (incipient civil war) to the Scottish political establishment, i.e. the Guardianship (1286–1291)[33] and the John Balliol kingship (1292–1296). Opposition to Robert Bruce's usurpation in 1306 was natural from the Scottish political establishment prior to the coup. The fact that John Balliol was still alive (he died in 1314) – and he had a son and heir, Edward – meant that Bruce had to *justify* his position. The king of France still acknowledged John Balliol as king in April 1308. By 1309, Robert Bruce had defeated most of his opposition within Scotland and could begin to use his control over the machinery of Scottish government to strengthen the national and international acceptance of his kingship. There is a conscious attempt by Bruce in the first 'acta' of his kingship to refer to himself as successor to Alexander III and completely ignore any reference to John Balliol.[34] Bruce himself, of course, had issued 'acta' in the name of King John during his joint-guardianship with John Comyn 1298–1300, but in 1309 it was still politic either to ignore the Balliol kingship completely or explain it away. The declarations of Bruce's first parliament at St Andrews in 1309 attempted to do this – the St Andrews parliament solemnly upheld Robert Bruce's right to the throne and saw declarations of support for Bruce from both magnates and clergy. The Declaration of the Clergy was, above all, a propaganda document for

Bruce and against Balliol. The complaint against 'the divers stratagems and tricks of Robert's rivals'[35] was an obvious ploy to divert attention from his illegal usurpation. The 1309 Declaration turned Balliol into a villain – for the first time it was declared that Balliol was imposed by English force on the Scots, a belief perpetuated and strengthened by the powerful patriotic narratives of the fourteenth and fifteenth centuries. The Declaration of Arbroath (1320) was the most famous propaganda document for Robert Bruce.

The fourteenth and fifteenth-century patriotic narratives made a powerful case, albeit an artificial one, for linking Robert Bruce to William Wallace's 'leadership' of the patriotic cause with the famous meeting at the Battle of Falkirk. One historian has argued further, that there was a rewriting of Wallace's story in these narratives to give Robert Bruce's violent seizure of the throne a greater acceptance.[36] This argument is that there was a deliberate attempt to mould Wallace's career into a mirror image of Bruce's. Thus *Gesta Annalia's* description of William Wallace imposing his authority on the Scottish magnates by force in 1297 is not an accurate account of Wallace's role then (see Chapter 4), but it mirrors exactly Robert Bruce's need for violent campaigns between 1306 and 1314 to impose his authority in Scotland after his *illegal* coup in 1306. Fraser's argument concludes that the rewriting 'made Bruce no greater a villain or less worthy a candidate to lead the Scots than Wallace had been and no less worthy of the adulation of those who remembered Wallace fondly'. As with the invented 1298 meeting, Bruce and Wallace were seen as 'soulmates' or kindred spirits, Wallace providing the precedent for Bruce's actions. The dubious actions of Robert Bruce between 1296 and 1306 were effectively covered up and Wallace and Bruce seen as equally worthy patriotic heroes, Bruce bringing Wallace's efforts to completion.

A more obvious way to bolster the images of William Wallace and Robert Bruce was to vilify their enemies and this was a notable feature of Scottish narrative accounts of the fourteenth and fifteenth centuries. It is well known that winners write history in their favour, but, as the much recycled Lancastrian propaganda against Richard III has shown, the winners of civil wars rewrite history much more vitriolically against their enemies. Certainly civil war or faction-fighting was a real present fear for Scottish writers of the fourteenth and fifteenth centuries and therefore one of their main themes for their moralistic history writing was the need to strengthen monarchy (or authority figures such as William Wallace) and suppress revolt and internal dissension. Thus in their reflections on the century before 1306, they roundly condemn the role of the nobility and the threat posed by faction-fighting to the strength (and independence) of the monarchy.

Unsurprisingly, the noble family principally blamed for weakening royal authority before 1306 were the Comyns – this was another good way to exonerate Robert Bruce for his sacrilegious murder of John Comyn III, Lord of Badenoch, in the Greyfriars Church at Dumfries. Thus the Comyns were vilified for weakening royal authority during Alexander III's minority and kidnapping the king in 1257:

> these councillors were so many kings,[37]

and

> the Comyns were in the lead among those who rose against the king.[38]

At the Battle of Falkirk in 1298, the Comyns were principally blamed by *Gesta Annalia* for the defeat of Wallace through their desertion. His plea to his fourteenth-century audience is general: 'And it is remarkable that we seldom, if ever, read of the Scots being overcome by the English, unless through the envy of lords, or the treachery and deceit of the natives, taking them over to the other side',[39] but one family is specifically targeted – 'the glaring wickedness of the Comyns and their abettors'.

Similarly, the Comyns, seen as almost representative of the over-mighty subjects threatening royal authority, were blamed for betraying Robert Bruce to Edward I in 1306. John Comyn had 'such a strong sense of greed and such a great and culpable intensity of ambition that he broke his agreement'.[40] As for John Balliol (vilified in a similar manner) he was accused of 'submitting to thraldom unto him for ever'[41] and showing a lack of authority: 'stripped of his kingly ornaments, and holding a white wand in his hand'.[42] Scotland was regarded as 'abnormal in the time of this disastrous King John'.

The vilification of the enemies of Robert Bruce, in particular, and the nobility in general, was propaganda, but has had a long-lasting impact on the popular mind because of repetition in later histories. It has certainly affected the perception of Scotland's patriot heroes. Historians from the sixteenth century to fairly recent times have reflected the narratives of *Gesta Annalia* and Bower closely. In the late 18th century,

David Dalrymple (Lord Hailes) wrote: 'There is scarcely one of our writers who has not produced an invective against Comyn or an apology for Wallace . . .'[43] For Thomas Carlyle 'the nobles of the country have maintained a quite despicable behaviour since the days of Wallace downwards – a selfish, ferocious, famishing, unprincipled set of hyenas, from whom at no time, and in no way, has the country derived any benefit'.[44] Similar sentiments were expressed by P.H. Tytler and Joseph Stevenson. Tytler (1841) wrote that: 'the patriotic principle . . . entirely deserted the highest ranks of the Scottish nobles, whose selfish dissensions had brought them and bondage upon their country'.[45] Tytler saw Wallace in 1298 and, indeed, Robert Bruce as standing alone against treacherous nobles. 'Bruce stood alone, and shared the glory with no-one.'[46] The narrow focus on only two patriot heroes by the nationalist writers of the fourteenth and fifteenth centuries has been extended to modern times. The anti-noble theme was further emphasised by Joseph Stevenson (1841): 'The truth is, and it must be confessed with shame and sorrow, that the Scottish nobility as a body were not true to Scotland',[47] but was still forcibly voiced in the mid twentieth century:

> The Scots Crown to the Commons, was not tyranny but a shield against tyranny, as for the nobles, if they wished to revolt, they did so without squaring of conscience . . . the major problem before a medieval administrator was the curbing not of the King but of the nobles . . . the inveterate hostility of great houses to the Crown and to each other.[48]

The repercussions of these consistently held views for the leading noble family of thirteenth-century Scotland, the Comyns, is obvious and can be traced through major works on Scottish history from the sixteenth century onwards. Thus Mair (Major), Buchanan, and Hailes do not have a good word for any of the Comyns. According to Hailes, describing their capture and kidnapping of Alexander III in 1257, the Comyns 'flew to arms, strengthened with a hypocritical pretext, they seized the King and Queen at Kinross, and detained them in separate confinement . . .'[49] Even writers describing Comyn sites such as Kirkintilloch are damning of the Comyns:

> The property of an Anglo-Norman race who held lands in Scotland and England both, and were void of anything in the shape of national sentiment . . . taking sides almost alternately with the

different factions who struggled for ascendancy in Scotland, the
Comyns finally flung in their lot with the party favourable to the
English supremacy, and consequently the fortresses in their
possession became obstacles in the path of the Scottish
patriots . . .[50]

There can hardly be found a more wholehearted swallowing of fourteenth and fifteenth-century propaganda. Even distinguished medieval
historians have found it difficult to move away from the entrenched
Comyn stereotype with statements about 'The Challenge of the House
of Comyn' and the family performing 'the more fearful role of overmighty subjects'.[51]

Historians have started to acknowledge the distortion of medieval
Scottish history prior to 1306 and explore the consequences for the
reputations of the medieval nobility in general and the enemies of
Robert Bruce (and William Wallace) in particular.[52] Some are more
reluctant than others to 'celebrate' the 'patriot hero' pedigree of John
Comyn III, Lord of Badenoch, murdered by Robert Bruce at Greyfriars
Church at Dumfries on 10 February 1306. Professor Barrow acknowledged the lengthy leadership of the 'patriotic' party in Scotland by the
Comyns in the second half of the thirteenth century as well as John
Comyn's 'natural . . . prescriptive right to leadership of the community
of the realm', but still concluded: 'the harsh fact remains that he was
an almost total failure'.[53] Professor Cowan has been more forthright
and positive:

> John the Red Comyn has suffered at the hands of posterity one of
> the great betrayals in all Scottish history . . . it is easier to believe
> that Comyn would have been readier to die 'for freedom alone'
> than Bruce.[54]

Alexander Grant stated that: 'His [John Comyn's] military record was
far better than Bruce's . . . the youngest Robert Bruce's anti-English
record much weaker than John Comyn's' and argued that John
Comyn's status in the Scottish political community was such that a
claim for the Scottish throne could be contemplated.[55] There has been
much progress in uncovering Scotland's medieval past from the centu-
ries-long acceptance of Bruce propaganda since Professor Frame's
remark in 1990 that:

Those Scots who did not at once accept the Bruce version of the past deserve a more sympathetic hearing than they have often been granted.[56]

His comment on 'the impudent success of the Bruce and Stewart dynasties in seizing the national past for themselves' may have caused more academic scrutiny of the Bruce version of Scotland's past. However, as Professor Gordon Donaldson sagely noted: 'It takes a long time for the findings of scholars to filter through to the popular mind . . . a good error never seems to die.'[57] This certainly seems to be true when the 700th anniversary of Robert Bruce's key victories over the Comyns in 1308 was celebrated in Aberdeen with the commissioning of a new statue of King Robert.[58] In patriot history, especially in northern Scotland, it *should* seem strange to declare a celebration after a Comyn defeat by a usurper king. The Comyns *led* Scotland into war with England in 1296 (see Chapter 4); it was from northern and north-eastern Scotland that the Comyns (John Comyn III, Lord of Badenoch, murdered by Robert Bruce in 1306, and his cousin John Comyn, Earl of Buchan) ran their war government against the English on behalf of the legitimate Scottish ruler, John Balliol, symbol of the Scottish patriot cause. Is there commemoration of Comyn leadership of the patriot cause in north-east Scotland not only between 1296 and 1306 but after 1212 when the family were pillars of the Scottish monarchy and key contributors to the growth and development of an independent Scottish kingdom? Seeing, and acting upon, pro-Bruce propaganda and only seeing the Wars of independence from a Bruce (or Wallace) perspective limits the Comyns only to the role of English collaborators and distorts not only their role in Scottish history but the role of northern (and north-eastern) Scotland itself in national (and patriot) history.

How can a true roll call of patriot heroes of medieval Scotland be achieved when the 'official' history from Scottish nationalist narratives of the fourteenth and fifteenth centuries limits the choice to two – William Wallace and Robert Bruce? It has been easy to criticise these nationalist writings for their black and white portraits of individuals based on either their enmity or friendship with William Wallace and Robert Bruce. Recent research[59] has demonstrated, however, that the *Gesta Annalia* and Walter Bower's *Scotichronicon* did include sections praising the Comyns and giving some criticism of Robert Bruce during the war period. Dauvit Broun's research has established that *Gesta Annalia* (formally attributed to John of Fordun) contained a contemporary *St Andrews Chronicle* for the period 1285–1363. This section, now dubbed *Gesta Annalia* II, includes an interesting pro-Comyn section for the period 1298–1304, a vital period for the Wars of Independence and for the role of John Comyn III, Lord of Badenoch.

Another source[60] which is mainly anti-Bruce has been uncovered in the generally very pro-Bruce *Scotichronicon* of Walter Bower (c.1440). 'The Scottish poem' within *Liber Extravagans* (Supplementary Book) of *Scotichronicon* may have been written c.1304–6 and contains material supportive of Balliol's candidature for the throne in 1292 but is rather ambivalent for the period 1304–6 – it has been interpreted as supportive of a contemporary Comyn claim to the throne by one historian.[61] The *Gesta Annalia* (supplemented by Walter Bower's *Scotichronicon*) has also provided the main narrative for pre-1286 Scottish medieval history of the thirteenth century. Again there is a pro-Bruce interpretation of the period c.1240 to 1286 especially with regard to the role of the Bruces' historic enemies, the Comyns. The recent re-editing of Bower's *Scotichronicon* has shed interesting light on Bower's use of sources and the use of earlier contemporary Scottish source material in both *Gesta Annalia* and *Scotichronicon*. This can explain some of the apparent contradictions in the narrative. There is some evidence of a relationship with the *Melrose Chronicle*, the most significant contemporary Scottish source (and also a pro-Comyn source) of the thirteenth century, but naturally the pro-Bruce compilations in the *Gesta Annalia* and Bower have largely removed the pro-Comyn elements. There is, however, more extensive pro-Comyn (and contemporary) narrative material contained in the separate, accessible *Melrose Chronicle* which gives an alternative view of the Comyns' role in the growth and development of an independent Scotland in the difficult political years 1242–58. There is more scope, therefore, to examine the Comyns' role as patriot heroes before 1286 than after.

There is no equivalent of John Barbour for Robert Bruce and Blind Harry for William Wallace for any of the families who also made a big contribution to the growth and defence of an independent Scotland. Maximum use needs to be made of those contemporary narrative sources which have escaped the seemingly all-enveloping coverage of the pro-Bruce and pro-Wallace *Gesta Annalia*. In addition, contemporary or near-contemporary English sources such as Matthew Paris, the *Guisborough* and *Lanercost Chronicles* and Thomas Gray's *Scalacronica* should also be used as a guide from the 'enemies' perspective' on who were 'Scottish heroes'.

Some work has already started, using non-Bruce sources, to rebalance historical opinion on two historic villains in Scottish tradition – John Comyn III, Lord of Badenoch,[62] (d. 1306) and King John (John Balliol[63]). Both studies point to the fact that *Gesta Annalia* and Bower's *Scotichronicon* cannot be given total responsibility/blame for the bias of Scottish tradition towards William Wallace and Robert Bruce as *the* Scottish patriot heroes. The clear bias *Gesta Annalia* and Bower demonstrated did not lead them to exclude all non-Wallace/Bruce sources, some of which, remarkably, found their place in their compilations by accident more than design. It has been the further censuring of anti-Bruce and Wallace-biased material by historians from the sixteenth century onwards that has led to such a distorted picture of Scotland's patriot heroes.

Recent historians have recognised that there are 'unsung heroes' in Scottish medieval history, that not all belong to the period covered by the Wars of Independence'[64] and that there was not just one patriotic route in the medieval period[65] (despite the power and longevity of the *Gesta Annalia* and Bower, and the stamp they have had on medieval Scottish history). The following chapters will examine the omissions and contradictions within the narrowly-focused Scottish narratives of the fourteenth and fifteenth centuries. They will also point out those areas where later histories have been guilty of 'convenient forgetfulness about history that is uncomfortable'.[66]

There is no denying the importance of wars in the making of patriot heroes in all eras. Famous victories against external threats have raised, in English tradition, patriot heroes such as Alfred the Great, Francis Drake, Horatio Nelson, the Duke of Wellington and Winston Churchill. Undoubtedly, the Falklands War has added considerably to Margaret Thatcher's reputation as a great political leader in more recent times. Has Scottish tradition recognised all key Scottish military achievements in the wars with England in the Middle Ages and the war records of Scottish leaders other than William Wallace and Robert Bruce? It will also be asked whether the Wars of Independence have been given too much credit in creating the Scottish national cause. Historians for many years have thought that 'Scottish nationalism was the product rather than the cause of the War of Independence'[67] but more recently R. James Goldstein has put forward an argument which 'challenges the received views concerning the historical significance of the war of national liberation'.[68] As he has noted, the process of developing a national consciousness in Scotland was already well developed before the war began. Historians of patriot heroes must acknowledge those who contributed to the growth, definition and preservation of Scotland's separate identity and political integrity before 1296.

Scottish tradition and the fourteenth and fifteenth-century narratives behind it have painted Alexander III's kingship as an 'ideal' for strong leadership and an independent kingship:

> How worthy of tears, and how hurtful, his death was to the kingdom of Scotland is plainly shown by the evils of aftertimes . . . and if, at any time, any of his people rebelled, he curbed their madness with discipline . . . he was looked upon with equal fear and love, both far and near, not only by his friends but also by his adversaries – and especially by the English.[69]
>
> *Gesta Annalia*

This was the type of strong, ruthless leadership to be aimed at – and ultimately achieved – by Robert Bruce according to the fourteenth and fifteenth-century narratives. Alexander III has been given all the credit by *Gesta Annalia* as the symbol of patriot leadership, but Walter Bower adds an interesting new dimension which points to the importance of nobles in government:

> And so that he might put down all civil discord and insubordination everywhere within his realm, he had this habit of travelling all over his kingdom almost every year with a strong company of picked knights and nobles . . . He had his justiciar with him to administer justice to anyone at all . . . and justice promptly meted out to everyone.[70]

This contradicts the constant theme of fourteenth and fifteenth-century narrative sources – the nobility as disruptive threats to an independent monarchy (and to William Wallace and Robert Bruce personally). Recent research[71] has emphasised the interdependence of Alexander III's kingship and a number of key noble families who were instrumental in the growth and definition of an independent Scottish kingdom. Families such as the Comyns, Stewarts and Morays had a vested interest in an independent Scottish monarchy, but their contribution to the national cause has been seriously underestimated. This has been particularly the case with the Comyn family whose occupation of the chief political office, the justiciarship of Scotia, for no fewer than sixty-six out of the hundred years between c.1205 and 1304, meant that they stood closely in support of Scottish kingship during formative developments.

Despite the political need to blacken the name of Comyn and paint the whole family as villains after Robert Bruce's sacrilegious murder of John Comyn in the Greyfriars Church at Dumfries on 10 February 1306, there is an historical need to understand the significance of John Comyn's leadership of the national cause in 1306 and the contribution of two other members of his family to the kingship of Alexander III and the definition of the national cause by 1289 – Walter Comyn, Earl of Menteith (d. 1258) and Alexander Comyn, Earl of Buchan (d. 1289). They were key contributors to the territorial definition of the Scottish kingdom, establishment of royal authority within the kingdom, the defence of the kingdom from external threats from Norway and England, and the maintenance of the kingdom's integrity during periods of political instability – Alexander III's minority (1249–1258) and the uncertain years after Alexander III's sudden death in 1286. The Scottish cause was defined in these years and the Treaty of Birgham (1290) summed up the nature of a politically mature, independent kingdom, ready to defend itself against external threats. It provided an important and underestimated articulation of Scottish nationalism. The Scottish cause was thus defined before William Wallace and Robert Bruce appeared on the political scene. Therefore the search for 'patriot heroes' should be extended to the noble families who helped Alexander III to define that Scottish cause.

As well as the need to look for the definition of the Scottish cause before the Wars of Independence started in 1296, the wars themselves need closer scrutiny. Nationalist writers of the fourteenth and fifteenth centuries rewrote Scottish history 'to make Bruce a stalwart for independence from the very start'[72] and to place him with William Wallace as kindred spirits in the early Scottish independence movement. Historians, however, now accept that the war was the 'war of the Comyns'.[73] They rejected the overlordship of Edward I first and were the first to lead Scotland into military action against the English. The role of John Comyn the Younger of Badenoch (murdered by Robert Bruce on 10 February 1306) has been seriously underestimated for his leadership (and military activities) in the war effort. His absence as a patriot hero is perhaps the best example of what G. Morton described as 'convenient forgetfulness about history that is uncomfortable'.[74] The Comyns' role in defending the Scottish cause in war – especially the role of John Comyn the Younger of Badenoch – has been largely written out of Scottish history, but there is a contemporary pro-Comyn source for the period 1298 to 1304 which gives insight into an important period in the conflict. This source also acknowledges a Comyn-led Scottish victory over the English at Roslin in 1303 – the pro-Bruce framework in *Gesta Annalia* II even allows this victory to be given more precedence and space in the compilation than Bannockburn. Why have subsequent histories not given this great victory as much kudos as the Battles of Stirling Bridge and Bannockburn? Behind the pro-Bruce propaganda of Scottish tradition can be discovered Comyn words as well as deeds that are fitting for patriot heroes. Even Barbour provides words to John Comyn fitting for a patriot leader: 'For there is neither man nor boy in all this land who does not yearn to make himself free.'[75]

The murder of John Comyn III, Lord of Badenoch, by Robert Bruce in 1306 has caused a vital period of Scottish history to be seen mainly through pro-Bruce propaganda over many centuries. Propaganda has been recycled and retold. There is a need for the murder to be re-examined, and the details accurately relayed and the implications of it analysed critically. There should be a retelling of this period of Scottish history to see if the 'best of men be known' in the early Scottish independence movement.

2

Real Patriot 1

WALTER COMYN, EARL OF MENTEITH (d. 1258)

To be regarded as the leader of the 'native' party in Scotland of the 1250s by the contemporary English chronicler Matthew Paris[1] is perhaps reason enough for Walter Comyn, Earl of Menteith, to be taken seriously as a true Scottish patriot. The 1250s have been given surprisingly little attention in Scottish history as a period when Scotland's independence was being threatened by England. The 1250s have, in fact, a number of common features with the period from 1286 to 1296 when an increasingly interventionist approach by Edward I eventually led to the outbreak of war. The chief feature, however, was that Scotland was without an adult ruler and in danger of political interference from England in *both* periods. In the period after 1296 when war broke out, contemporary and vitriolic English narrative accounts targeted William Wallace for abuse as, with ferocious resistance, he became a constant thorn in the side of English forces. Undoubtedly, this helped to establish Wallace's contemporary reputation as a 'patriot hero' before Scottish nationalist writings of the fourteenth and fifteenth centuries elevated him to legendary hero status. A contemporary English perspective on the 1250s can be useful in uncovering individuals who were considered principal enemies to English interests at that time.

The reputation and image of Water Comyn, Earl of Menteith, in Scottish tradition is based on *Gesta Annalia*, c.1380s, (formally attributed to John of Fordun). This has formed the main strand in the standard narrative account of Scottish medieval history and, together with the supplements and elaborations provided by Walter Bower's *Scotichronicon*, has provided the most memorable descriptions of Walter Comyn. It should be noted that these comments (principally anti-Comyn) relate to these narratives' main theme for the 1250s – the threat to kingship caused by bad counsellors and overmighty subjects during a minority period. Thus Walter Comyn as head of the Comyn family and leader of the king's counsellors between 1251 and 1255 was roundly criticised in *Gesta Annalia*:

> these councillors were so many kings. For he who saw the poor crushed down in those days the nobles ousted from their inheritance, the drudgery forced upon citizens, the violence done to churches, might with good reason say 'Woe unto the kingdom where the king is a boy' . . . judgement and righteousness were slumbering.[2]

and, after their replacement in 1255:

> Walter Comyn, Earl of Menteith, and his accomplices were more than once summoned before the king and his councillors, upon many grave charges; but they did not appear. But as they durst not await their trial according to the statutes of the kingdom they took counsel together, and with one accord, seized the king, by night, while he was asleep in bed at Kinross, and before dawn, carried him off with them to Stirling.[3]

Walter Bower repeated these charges but added new ones against the Comyns' disruptive behaviour between 1242 and 1244:

> the common report rang in everyone's ears that the kingdom was being undermined by the Comyns' reign of terror.[4]

Commenting on the Comyns' kidnapping of the king in 1257, Bower added to *Gesta Annalia*'s charges:

> This group, who did nothing in accordance with the law but everything in accordance with their own wishes, ruled the people regardless of right or wrong.

and

> As I said earlier these Comyns were in the lead among those who rose against the king: as a consequence their name is, so to speak, obliterated in the land.[5]

Despite the fact that sections *contradictory* to such views on Walter Comyn and his party are to be found in both *Gesta Annalia* and Walter

Bower (see pages 47–8, 56, 58, 64–5), it is the above opinions that have become ingrained in Scottish tradition. The black picture of the Comyns under Walter's leadership was seized upon by writers such as George Buchanan:

> The power of all things were mostly in the Faction of the Cumins. For they turned the Public Revenue to the enrichment of themselves, oppressed the Poor, and, by false Accusations, cut off some of the Nobles, who were averse to their humours and desires, and dared to speak freely of the State of the Kingdom.[6]

and on Walter Comyn's death in 1258:

> When the king took the government into his own hands, he pardoned the Cumins upon their humble submission, as if their crimes had been expiated by the death of [Earl] Walter.[7]

In the late eighteenth century, Lord Hailes' *Annals of Scotland* reflected Walter Bower's more extreme opinions – Walter Bower had become to historians of later centuries the most widely used source for Alexander III's reign:

> They flew to arms; strengthened with a hypocritical pretext, they seized the King and Queen at Kinross, and detained them in separate confinement, until the friends of the English interest dispersed.[8]

Historical debate in the late twentieth century has still been largely based around 'The Challenge of the House of Comyn 1242–1258' and the Comyns in their 'more fearful role of overmighty subjects'.[9]

Thus for a very long time, Walter Comyn has been seen in a narrow focus limited by the historical framework and agenda of *Gesta Annalia* and Walter Bower. The dangers to kingship in periods of political instability, political division and minority government in the fourteenth and fifteenth centuries caused both sources to highlight the role of the King's counsellors when reflecting on similar circumstances in mid thirteenth-century Scotland. This was particularly apparent in Walter Bower who devoted several chapters to the qualities needed for king's counsellors,[10] before targeting the Comyns and their head, Walter Comyn, Earl of Menteith, as mid thirteenth-century examples of bad counsellors. No doubt, this was natural in an age when Robert

Bruce's reputation as patriot hero had been secured and the temptation to vilify his enemies, the Comyns, must have been overwhelming. Such was the emphasis on the threat to kingship that even the intervention of Henry III in Scottish political affairs during Alexander III's minority was regarded as beneficial for Scottish political stability and Scottish kingship. There is little coverage given to the potential dangers of English interference; there was no reflection, with fourteenth and fifteenth-century hindsight, on this precedent for Edward I's interventionist role from 1289 (in circumstances very similar to those in 1249 in Scotland). The preoccupation of *Gesta Annalia* and especially Walter Bower with the dangers of internal political disorder have not allowed full discussion of Walter Comyn's role from the 1230s to 1258 as Scottish king's agent in the process of defining the Scottish kingdom geographically and politically and resisting Henry III's attempts at political interference in Scotland.

Walter Comyn's contribution to the development of an independent Scottish monarchy should be judged in the light of closer scrutiny of *Gesta Annalia* as well as the contemporary nationalist (and pro-Comyn) chronicle, the *Melrose Chronicle*. The new edition of Walter Bower's *Scotichronicon* (with its excellent editorial notes) has revealed the contemporary material hidden behind the fourteenth and fifteenth-century framework and agendas of *Gesta Annalia* and Bower's *Scotichronicon* and exposed some of the contradictions within these two major sources. The *Melrose Chronicle*, the principal Scottish narrative source between 1171 and 1263, gives invaluable insight into the mid thirteenth-century political issues and vital commentary on national issues and political figures then. Contemporary English sources such as Matthew Paris add another element to analysis of mid thirteenth-century Scottish politics. This is a vital period in Scottish political development, an underestimated period and one deserving of a Scottish patriot hero. There are enough contemporary Scottish and English sources not to have to rely on a pro-Bruce fourteenth and fifteenth-century overview of the period. The sources have different emphases, but they all recognise Walter Comyn as the most powerful nobleman in Scotland in the 1240s and 1250s.

The Wars of Independence have become, in Scottish tradition, Scotland's finest hour with William Wallace and Robert Bruce seen as the founding fathers of a Scottish nationalist cause which was the product of the wars. Increasingly, however, historians are acknowledging that a sense of national consciousness and national identity was already well-developed in thirteenth-century European countries, including Scotland.[11] Such views support James Goldstein's argument which 'challenges the received views concerning the historical significance of the war of national liberation'. He has seen how the 'resistance to English attempts to limit the power of two ancient Scottish institutions, the monarchy and the Church, provides the earliest evidence for habits of thought and expression that we should be justified in describing as Scottish national consciousness'.[12] This process was gathering momentum during the thirteenth century and not just at the end of it. It is true that the unexpected death of Alexander III in 1286, the absence of an adult succession and the rule of a Guardianship between 1286 and 1291 accelerated 'the theory of sovereignty and nationhood which were being developed' during these years of crisis.[13] This led to the Treaty of Birgham/Northampton (1290) 'the single most valuable indication of the idea of Scottish nationhood shared at this time by Scotland's ruling classes'.[14] Undoubtedly, the Guardians of Scotland must have been conscious – in negotiating on behalf of the Scottish kingdom with Edward I – of the recent precedent of Edward I's subjugation of Wales. However, a member of the Scottish Guardianship of 1286–91, Alexander Comyn, Earl of Buchan (d. 1289), was old enough to remember the 1240s and 1250s when Scotland was faced with a remarkably similar set of circumstances to those in 1286–9 – lack of an adult heir to the Scottish throne, negotiations for a marriage alliance with the English royal family, the issue of English overlordship over Scotland and Border issues. The practical politics of this period must have helped to formulate a clearer idea of nationhood and independence well before the new crisis of 1286.

It is also increasingly apparent that a number of factors were involved in the development of a national cause in Scotland and elsewhere. Michael Clanchy mentions a number of issues which contributed to national identity in thirteenth-century England – 'royal government (and misgovernment), the effects of war, xenophobic prejudices, hostility to papal imperialism and reactions to stronger senses of 'Scottishness' and 'Welshness'.[15] In turn Henry III's assertion of his rights towards the Welsh and Scots in the 1240s and 1250s had a major effect on both those countries. The definition of the geographical kingdom, the focus on the issues of independence and political integrity and reaction to Border disputes were key contributors to the growth of national consciousness in Scotland in the 1230s, 1240s and 1250s. This period shows that the Wars of Independence that started in 1296 have been overestimated in the development of the Scottish national cause. The pressures (i.e. the consequences) of peaceful marriage unions involving the royal families of Scotland and England in 1251 (as in 1289) were as important in focusing attention on national identity as the direct impact of warfare and invasion. The success in overcoming internal resistance to royal, i.e. national, authority was also important in the development of national consciousness. Walter Comyn, Earl of Menteith, was involved in all of these issues vital to the development of a national cause.

The Political Inheritance of Walter Comyn

The Comyn family had established a very solid power base by 1233 through a combination of royal patronage and good marriages.[16] Royal patronage from David I (1124–1153), Earl Henry and William the Lion (1165–1214) ensured that the Comyns established a firm territorial base in Tynedale (Northumberland), southern Scotland (Peeblesshire and Roxburghshire) and central Scotland (north and south of Glasgow) through Walter's grandfather, Richard Comyn (d. c.1179) and Walter's father, William (d. 1233). Complementary to Richard Comyn's growing importance as a landowner in southern Scotland was his increasing significance in royal service. By his death c.1179, he had become a counsellor of long experience to the Scottish monarchy as shown by his prominence in royal witness lists. He had been involved in the Scottish invasion of northern England in 1174 to further Scottish royal claims to the English northern counties. Richard Comyn's close association with royal interests was clearly demonstrated by William the Lion's bestowal of the office of justiciar of Lothian on him in the 1170s. The office was an important one and an early sign of the Comyn family's burgeoning role as members of the new aristocracy of royal service. The justiciar was the chief judicial officer of the Crown in the area and a significant administrative and political adviser to the king.

Walter Comyn's father, William Comyn, increased both the landed power and political influence of the family. Royal patronage was behind grants of the lordship of Lenzie (to the north of Glasgow) and the right to have a burgh at Kirkintilloch (another lordship also north of Glasgow). He also acquired further lands in the Glasgow area – Machan (in the Clyde valley) and land around Lesmahagow, both south of Glasgow. A frequent witness to the royal charters of William the Lion, it is probable that William Comyn became sheriff of Forfar by c.1195. The sheriff was the right hand of the king in the localities and his duties were all embracing, encompassing military, financial, judicial and administrative matters. The office of sheriff was crucial in defining and controlling the country for the king. William was sheriff of Forfar between c.1195 and 1212, but his role as a royal servant entered a new level when he was promoted to the office of justiciar of Scotia, i.e. the area north of the Forth, c.1205. This office, the premier justiciarship in Scotland, represented the most senior royal administrative post for the north.[17] Promotion to this office was the first major sign of a deliberate royal policy to involve the family in the consolidation of royal authority in the north.

There was a real need for Scottish kings to assert greater authority in northern Scotland. Lack of royal demesne in the north meant that the royal authority of William the Lion was 'conspicuously absent'[18] from the region. This was particularly significant as the region (especially Moray and Ross) formed the base for the alternate claimants to the Scottish throne, the MacWilliam dynasty. Moray was a consistently troublesome area to control. Donald MacWilliam claimed the Scottish throne from the 1160s until 1187 and rebellions continued from Moray and Ross under Guthred son of Donald MacWilliam until 1230. There was a need to seek a permanent solution to the lack of royal authority in the north. Despite the planned settlement of Moray in David I's time, and the establishment of sheriffdoms such as Aberdeen and Banff, Highland rebellions continued to be both a danger to the throne itself but also to all royal attempts to define Crown authority in the north. It was probably in his role as justiciar – described as the 'most significant bridge between the king's court and the localities'[19] – that William Comyn was in charge of the operation between 1211 and 1212 to suppress the rebellion of Guthred son of Donald MacWilliam who landed in Ross in January 1211 to lead a rebellion through Ross and Moray. The rebellion was met by a large royal force under the leadership of William Comyn, Earl of Atholl, and the representatives of the two families claiming the earldom of Mar – Malcolm son of Morgrund and Thomas Durward. The expedition was successful and Guthred MacWilliam captured.

It seemed that Comyn was then given the post of 'warden of Moray' perhaps on a short-term, temporary basis, but the fact that the rebellion had some support from the nobility in the north meant that the Scottish king needed a greater permanent presence in the north. This

was achieved by William Comyn's elevation to the earldom of Buchan
c.1212 on marriage, his second, to Marjorie, the only child and heiress
of Fergus, Earl of Buchan. Probably a reward for his successful efforts
against the MacWilliam rebels in 1211–12, William's promotion to
the status of earl in Buchan seems to be further evidence of a royal
intention to use the Comyn family (and Buchan) as permanent (i.e.
hereditary) representatives of royal interests in the north. It was more
than a little convenient for the Crown to introduce a powerful royal
agent – his justiciar since c.1205 – into north-eastern Scotland, next to
an area of uncertain loyalty. This was a bold, indeed an historic, move
– William Comyn became the first 'Norman' earl in Scotland.

As earl of Buchan, after c.1212, William Comyn was very well positioned to counter further threats to royal interests in the north from
the Moray and Ross areas. The earldom of Buchan covered a vast area
in north-east Scotland.[20] Visible signs of Comyn power in Buchan were
probably soon present in their architectural patronage, though the
very thorough 'herschip' of Buchan by Robert Bruce (1308) has
destroyed much visible evidence of thirteenth-century building. The
scant remains of Deer Abbey, a Cistercian monastery on the banks of
the river Ugie, founded by William Comyn, Earl of Buchan, c.1219 are
a useful starting point. It is possible that ecclesiastical patronage here
was matched by signs of secular lordship at the same time though the
sparseness of documentary, architectural and archaeological evidence
makes this difficult to confirm. It seems that there were thirteenth-
century inland castles in Buchan at Ellon and Kingedward and as befit-
ting a coastal earldom, Buchan was defended by an impressive grouping of well-sited castles along its coastline – Dundarg (New Aberdour),
Cairnbulg (originally known as Philorth), Rattray and Slains. These
were also established in the thirteenth century though it is difficult to
say how many were started by William Comyn, Earl of Buchan (d.
1233).[21]

William Comyn's military presence in Buchan was certainly required
c.1229–30 when the peace of Moray was again disturbed by the rebel-
lious MacWilliam family, this time represented by Gilleasbuig. Wooden
fortifications were burned in the vicinity of Inverness and a baron,
Thomas de Thirlestane, (Lord of Abertarff at the south end of Loch
Ness), killed. The increasing dependence on strong baronial support in
the north was revealed here after the king himself campaigned unsuc-
cessfully against Gilleasbuig. Given his previous success against the
MacWilliams between 1211 and 1212, William Comyn was appointed

to the wardenship of Moray as 'a special emergency office', given a large force of troops and made responsible for Gilleasbuig's capture.[22] Comyn was successful – Gilleasbuig and his two sons were killed and their heads brought to the king. In c.1229 the replacement of the temporary expedient of a warden of Moray by a more permanent hereditary lordship, the lordship of Badenoch, represents a further extension of royal influence in the north through the Comyn family. The lordship of Badenoch, perhaps part of the estates forfeited by Gilleasbuig because of his rebellion (or at least lands under his influence), was in the highest part of Moray and probably the most difficult for the Crown to control. It was a region of great strategic value. It dominated the principal passes from both the North and West Highlands into the basin of the Tay. The lordship of Lochaber went with the lordship of Badenoch and this meant that Comyn power extended across northern Scotland from Buchan in the east to Loch Linnhe on the west coast. It amounted virtually to vice-regal power in northern Scotland.[23]

The success of royal policy in the north in countering the threat from the MacWilliam dynasty and, at the same time, consolidating royal authority in that region, was proven by the fact that there were no more challenges to the established royal line from the MacWilliams. Success had repercussions for the Comyn family – it consolidated the family's prestige as royal trouble-shooters in the north. This was Walter Comyn's inheritance. He appeared as lord of Badenoch (and Lochaber) c.1229 and it was probable that Alexander II granted it to him so that he could vigorously continue his father's successful defence of royal interests in this key area. Walter Comyn's grandfather Richard and father William – Walter Comyn was the second son of William Comyn by his first marriage – had built up a considerable legacy of landed and political power through royal service and 'good' marriages. It gave their successors the means to dominate the Scottish political scene on a national basis from the 1230s onwards. Walter Comyn was the first member of the family to benefit from this legacy.

Walter Comyn: Royal Trouble-shooter

It is a testament to the political influence of his father that Walter Comyn appeared regularly at the royal court from c.1211. By 1221 Walter not only attended Alexander II on his marriage at York to Joan, sister of King Henry III, he was one of twelve Scottish noblemen who swore on the Scottish king's behalf to observe the terms of the treaty with the king of England. From 1220 to 1229, Walter Comyn appeared with increasing regularity and prominence in the witness lists of Alexander II's charters.

It was to be in the period between 1229 and 1235 that Walter Comyn rose to the fore as a key royal trouble-shooter in areas where royal authority was weak. It was probably shortly after his father's successful campaign against Gilleasbuig MacWilliam's rebellion in Moray in 1229 that Walter Comyn became lord of Badenoch by the gift of Alexander II, thus continuing his father's role in the area since c.1211 – his father was probably regarded as too old for this additional responsibility. The establishment of Badenoch (with Lochaber) as a hereditary lordship was undoubtedly a military response to the revolt centred on Ross and Moray in 1229. This suggests that castle-building within his new lordship took place under Walter Comyn shortly after its creation, i.e. in the 1230s and 1240s. Walter Comyn was certainly known to have been involved in building activity elsewhere in this period, for example the foundation of the Augustinian priory at Inchmahome in Menteith, Perthshire (in 1238) and at Tarset castle in Northumberland (before 1244).[24] In Badenoch (and Lochaber) Alexander II wanted Walter to control the vitally important passes from both the north and west Highlands into the basin of the Tay. The key Comyn castles of Badenoch and Lochaber – Ruthven and Inverlochy, supplemented by Lochindorb in the hill country between Badenoch and the Moray coast, and Blair in Atholl – are strategically sited. Ruthven commanded the northern end of two passes over the Mounth, Drumochter and Minigaig. Blair Atholl controlled the southern end of Drumochter and the southern end of the Glen Tilt route from Deeside; Lochindorb, although not in Badenoch but integrally related to it, was strategically situated on a loch between Forres and Grantown and fully occupied its island site one acre in extent. Inverlochy, the principal castle of Lochaber, commanded the entrance to the Great Glen, securing its southern sea outlet, and the scarcely less important overland route to the Spey by way of Glen Spean.

The lordship of Badenoch (and Lochaber), initially founded to protect and defend royal interests in the north, would become a key area of Scottish resistance to English attempts at conquest after war broke out in 1296. Walter Comyn started the process of building up this area as a Scottish fortress. Ruthven, regarded as the caput of Badenoch, was a possible early motte site, situated on a prominent hill artificially scarped, rising from the flat floor of the Spey valley. The site, now unfortunately covered by the eighteenth-century Ruthven Barracks, is thought to have had a castle on it before 1269. It is known that John Comyn I of Badenoch had built a castle at Blair in Atholl at that time. Professor Barrow has argued that 'a fortress to guard the southern outlets makes little sense unless it can be matched by one to keep the northern outlets also'.[25] This makes practical sense and makes it probable that Ruthven was already established by 1269 and started in the time of Walter Comyn (d. 1258). A combination of documentary and architectural evidence points to a concentrated programme of castle-building and strengthening of the major castles of Badenoch and Lochaber, i.e. Inverlochy (Lochaber), Lochindorb, Blair Atholl and Ruthven, from c.1260 to c.1280. John Comyn I, head of the Badenoch branch of the family, c.1258–c.1278, almost literally built on the foundations left by his uncle, Walter Comyn.

That the north of Scotland was a priority for the Scottish king and Walter Comyn, a key agent for royal policy in the north, is reflected in Walter Comyn's brief appearance as earl of Caithness in 1235. Scottish kings had found Caithness a consistently difficult region in which to establish their authority in the twelfth and thirteenth centuries.[26] The family of de Moravia (Moray) had been promoted into territorial, administrative and ecclesiastical offices to promote royal interests and loosen the grip of the earls of Caithness – the situation in Caithness was complicated by the fact that it was under the jurisdiction of the earls of Orkney, nobles who were bound by allegiance to the kings of Norway. They also, however, owed allegiance to the kings of Scotland in their role as earls of Caithness. The authority of the Morays was in need of supplementing if Scottish kings were to have much greater authority in Caithness. As rebellion against royal authority in Caithness was connected to rebellion in Moray, so the Scottish king sought a more permanent solution to the problem there as he had done in Moray. It is in this connection that Walter Comyn's role in Caithness as well as Moray is not surprising.

After rebellion in Moray was dealt with c.1211–12 (largely through the efforts of Walter Comyn's father), King William the Lion, in 1214, took as hostage the daughter of John Haraldson, Earl of Caithness – this strongly implied that rebellion in Moray had support in Caithness. The Scottish king consolidated the treaty of peace with Caithness by tying the earldom's family through marriage with one of his own vassals, a member of the house of Angus. After the murder of Earl

John in 1231, the title to the earldom of Caithness and Orkney would eventually (after 1239) come to the house of Angus. The Comyn family were to play a significant role in the political settlement of Caithness. Walter Comyn himself briefly held the title to the earldom of Caithness in 1235 – he witnessed a charter with the title 'comit' [de] Katany [Caithness] on 7 July 1235[27] – probably in a temporary role to establish some stability in the area. The Comyn family's involvement (perhaps under Walter's supervision) did not end there. One heiress was married to a member of the Comyn family, John Comyn, Earl of Angus (he was killed in 1242), while another heiress was married to Freskin de Moray, a Comyn ally. Comyns and Morays together played key roles, on behalf of the Scottish Crown, in the establishment of a new regime in Caithness. William de Moray became earl of Sutherland in 1235 and it was probably intended that William's nephew, Freskin, would become earl of Caithness. The Morays and Comyns were linked through marriage – a daughter of John Comyn I, Lord of Badenoch, married Alexander de Moray – and this alliance helped further consolidate royal interests in northern Scotland. By the mid thirteenth century the Moray family held the earldom of Sutherland, the lordships of Duffus (near Elgin) and Petty (near Inverness) as well as lands in Strathspey. This complemented Comyn landholding in the north.

After the death of Walter Comyn's father, William Comyn, Earl of Buchan, c.1233, the Comyns did not have the status of earl to be in keeping with their role as key royal trouble-shooters (Alexander Comyn, heir to Buchan, did not have the title and status of earl of Buchan until c.1244). It was probably not coincidental that shortly after 1233 Walter Comyn, Lord of Badenoch, gained the earldom of Menteith on marriage to Isabella, Countess of Menteith, c.1234. Undoubtedly, Alexander II would have favoured this further enhancement of status for one of his most important royal trouble-shooters. This increased status was displayed prominently in the foundation of Inchmahome Priory in 1238 on the largest of the three islands in the Lake of Menteith. Inchmahome is the finest visible symbol of Comyn ecclesiastical lordship, and its foundation c.1238 a fitting monument to Walter Comyn's status in 1237 as the leading baron in Scotland.[28] There is no physical evidence of Earl Walter's main residence in Menteith but it would seem that there was a hall on an island adjacent to Inchmahome, Inchtalla.[29]

Walter Comyn's elevation to the earldom of Menteith coincided with an extension of his royal trouble-shooter's role. He was not just royal trouble-shooter in northern Scotland, Moray and Caithness. In 1235 he was directly involved in another trouble spot for royal authority, Galloway. Alexander II, having obtained a victory over rebels in Galloway in 1235, found that business in other parts of his kingdom demanded his presence. He turned, therefore, to Walter Comyn, Earl of Menteith, for the task of tranquilling Galloway and bringing it to order. The king departed the district: 'but he entrusted the earl of Menteith with the duty of reducing it to order'.[30] Earl Walter was thus performing a similar role to that he performed in Moray and Caithness. It is possible that Walter Comyn may have been given a more formal involvement in this troublesome south-western corner of Scotland – perhaps as a temporary warden of Moray, or even more formally as justiciar of Galloway or equivalent.

There is no definite evidence of Walter Comyn having such a formal title but there is plenty of evidence of Walter having an active role in the south-west in this period. Contemporary English chroniclers, for instance, accused Walter of fortifying a castle in Galloway sometime before 1244. Walter was also implicated by the English in the harbouring of English outlaws and pirates, the de Marisco family, who were attacking English shipping in the Irish Sea – this again implies an involvement from the Galloway area.[31] It is also worth noting that Walter Comyn's nephew and heir, John Comyn I, Lord of Badenoch, was known to hold the office of justiciar of Galloway in 1258 (Walter died in 1258), in the period 1266x1272 and also in 1275. Interestingly, as had been pointed out,[32] there is a grave paucity of records relating to Galloway generally and in particular there does not seem to be any record of a justiciar for this region between 1200 and 1258. Given the tendency of the Scottish Crown to confer hereditary titles and offices on the Comyn family in the thirteenth century, and the favour shown particularly to Walter Comyn after c.1229, it does seem probable that Walter Comyn's role in Galloway could have been an official one, 'justiciar' or quasi-'justiciar' after 1235.

Walter Comyn was perhaps the leading trouble-shooter of the Crown in northern and south-western Scotland in the 1230s – in practice he was in the vanguard (with the Scottish king) of those defining the Scottish kingdom in Moray, Caithness and Galloway. Walter Comyn's influence on the national scene was recognised in 1237 at the Treaty of York when it was he alone who took the formal diplomatic oath on the king's soul to keep the agreement whereby the Scottish king formally renounced the centuries-old Scottish claims to the counties of Northumberland, Cumberland and Westmoreland. This treaty, in retrospect, has been credited with providing the definitive solution to Anglo-Scottish tensions on the Border yet the period up until 1244 shows that Anglo-Scottish relations remained fraught for longer. While the major source behind Scottish tradition for this period, Walter Bower, dwells on the internal conflicts within Scotland, 1242–4, between the Bissets and the Comyns, very much in line with his fifteenth-century theme, i.e. the danger to kingship of internal discord, the contemporary English and Scottish narratives, Matthew Paris and the *Melrose Chronicle* focus on the Border issues which almost led to an armed confrontation between the English and Scottish armies in 1244. The period c.1235 to 1244, as seen by Matthew Paris and the *Melrose Chronicle*, is better regarded as another attempt by the Scottish Crown (again with the aid of Walter Comyn) to define its authority in the Border areas as it had tried to do in Caithness, Moray and Galloway.

The Treaty of York (1237) provided only temporary stability to the Border and Anglo-Scottish relations.[33] Financial constraints and Henry III's Continental ambitions caused him to compromise with northern security in 1237 and the years afterwards. Henry III, like his predecessor, King John, begrudged spending money on Border defence. On 28 February 1237, for example, he ordered expenditure on the castles of Bamburgh and Newcastle to be reduced. In 1242 Henry III crossed the sea to pursue his ambitions on the Continent. Contemporary chroniclers noted that he had prepared for this attempt by establishing good relations with Scotland '. . . and the side of England which borders upon Scotland was intrusted to the Scottish king for keeping while king [Henry] was engaged abroad'.[34] Given Alexander II's determination to define royal authority in all parts of his kingdom, Henry III's policy was risky as the events of 1242 to 1244 showed. According to the contemporary English chronicler Matthew Paris, Alexander II fortified the castles which border England but specifically accused Walter Comyn: 'Walter Cumin [Comyn] a noble and prominent baron of Scotland, and certain others of the kingdom of Scotland had fortified two castles in Galloway and Lothian suspiciously to the prejudice of the king of England, and contrary to the charters of [Alexander's] predecessors'.[35] The two castles mentioned were probably Caerlaverock (by the mouth of the Nidd) and Hermitage in Liddesdale, the work of John or Aymer Maxwell and Nicholas de Soules respectively. These two nobles were in the following of Walter Comyn in the 1240s and

1250s so the co-ordinating role of Walter Comyn in these activities is highly probable. The mention of Caerlaverock indicates that Walter Comyn could have been involved in his capacity as 'justiciar', or quasi-'justiciar' of Galloway. Official evidence from the English Close Rolls proves that Walter Comyn was personally involved in arming and strengthening his family's castle in Tarset[36] (Tynedale, in Northumberland). Walter Comyn himself was not known to own land in Tynedale, but his elder brother Richard, and Richard's son John (Walter's heir), had inherited the family's Tynedale lands (including Tarset).[37] Another castle in Northumberland, Dally in Tynedale, was constructed by the Lindsays. The English attitude to Dally castle was that 'once it is finished and furnished with weapons ... [de Lindsay] plans to garrison it with men who wish evil to the kingdom of England, especially Northumberland. If such men come from the north, this house will be an excellent refuge for them and a great nuisance to the king's land.'[38]

The seriousness of the 1244 crisis – and the prominent role in it of Walter Comyn – has been underestimated in Anglo-Scottish relations. It led to a major confrontation between English and Scottish armies at the Border. Henry III's aggressive assertion of English military superiority at the Border in 1244 had a number of causes. Despite the strong vested interests on both sides of the Border for the maintenance of peace in Anglo-Scottish relations – powerful social, economic and religious networks bound the north of England to the south of Scotland in the twelfth and thirteenth centuries[39] and played a part in preventing the Border confrontation breaking out into war[40] – the years 1242–4 revealed a number of tensions especially on the English side. The real fear of a French marriage alliance with the Scots had been a preoccupation of Henry III since 1238 when his sister Joan, Queen of Scotland, died and Alexander II married the daughter of a French nobleman. Henry's aggressive stance in 1244 forestalled another French marriage alliance with the future Alexander III. Instead, such an alliance was made between the young Alexander and Henry's daughter Margaret. Henry also feared, as English reaction to the building of Dally Castle in Tynedale has shown, disloyalty amongst northerners, real or imagined. The fundamental relationship between England and Scotland itself was a cause of tension – according to Matthew Paris:

The king of Scots had saucily sent a message to him that he did not hold the least particle of Scotland from him, the king of

England. The friendship between the two kings had become very much lessened since the king of Scotland had formed a matrimonial alliance with the daughter of Engelram de Courcy who, as also all the French, was discerned to have been the chief, or one chief, enemy of the king of England ... And not to reply lukewarmly to the announcement and insolence of the king of Scotland [Henry] wrote confidently to the count of Flanders as his vassal and one in many ways obliged to him, to come with an armed band to his aid against the king of Scotland.[41]

Anxiety about his enemies was fundamental to Henry III's attitude in 1244 and showed itself in the bond of good behaviour he forced the king of Scots and the two main political groups in Scotland to sign – those led by Earl Walter Comyn (his named following was forty in number) and Patrick, Earl of Dunbar. Both groups had to swear that they were not linked with attacks on the English king's lands in Ireland or had given shelter to the English king's enemies.[42] Walter Comyn, indeed, as well as fortifying Border castles, was implicated by the English in harbouring English outlaws and pirates, the de Marisco family, who were attacking English shipping in the Irish Sea.[43] What is clear is that on a number of fronts, Walter Comyn was a major concern for the English king. William Wallace was similarly deemed to be a nuisance by English sources in the late 1290s.

Another cause for the English king's intervention in 1244 also involved the Comyn family (and by implication, Walter Comyn, the family's political leader at the time). The suspicious death of Patrick, heir to the earldom of Atholl (and a relative of the Comyns) in 1242 – Patrick was killed in his lodging at Haddington and the crime covered up by a fire – caused a political crisis in Scotland which according to contemporary England and Scottish sources (as well as the fifteenth-century Walter Bower) contributed to Henry III's military invention in 1244. The episode, however, was used primarily by Bower (and in turn Scottish tradition) to paint the Comyns as unprincipled aggressors, a danger to Scottish kingship itself: 'the common report rang in everyone's ears that the kingdom was being undermined by the Comyns' reign of tyranny'.[44] Such a view, aimed largely at Bower's fifteenth-century audience because of the political instability of the 1440s, has retained its influence until the 1970s when, to an eminent historian, the episode (1242–4) sparked a period (1242–58) he referred to as 'The Challenge of the House of Comyn' in which the Comyns under the leadership of Walter Comyn, Earl of Menteith, were criticised for indulging in the 'more fearful role of overmighty subjects'.[45] However, for the 1240s, it is a misleading view of the Comyns' place in Scottish politics.

The events of 1242–4 marked a challenge to the family's pre-eminent position in Scotland as the 'pillars' of the Scottish monarchy and prime trouble-shooters for that monarchy in rooting out opposition to its authority. The death of Patrick of Atholl, heir to the earldom of Atholl, effectively removed that earldom from Comyn influence in a year when the Comyns also lost influence over the earldom of Angus. The violent reaction to the suspicious death of Patrick of Atholl, which contemporary English and Scottish sources laid at the door of the Bisset family,[46] was the harrying of Walter Bisset's lands at Aboyne by Alexander Comyn, heir to Buchan, and John Comyn, nephew of Earl Walter. This was perhaps a hot-headed overreaction by two young members of the Comyn family to the 'murder' of a relative of similar age. However, this was not just the reaction of *one* 'overmighty' family. The Comyns did not act alone in 1242 – *two* well-defined and powerful groups launched separate attacks on the Bissets.[47] Apart from the Comyns, led by Earl Walter, another group was led by Patrick, Earl of Dunbar, the king's cousin. Moreover, the decision reached at the royal court – the disinheritance and exile of the two principal members of the Bisset family, Walter and John – was advocated by the majority of the Scottish political community.

The 1242–4 episode – not reported, incidentally, in *Gesta Annalia*, usually the most reliable of Scottish sources factually – is of significance. It demonstrates some of the 'growing pains' of a Scottish kingdom expanding and defining its areas of authority – that growth involved more than just the Comyns acting as agents of royal authority and being rewarded for their efforts. As has been seen, the Morays in the north of Scotland also played a role in establishing royal authority in the north. They acted in harmony with the Comyns and the two families became more closely associated through marriage. However, two other royal agents in the north, the Bissets and the Durwards, were to be involved in very acrimonious rivalry with the Comyns in the 1240s and 1250s. The Durwards and Bissets were neighbours (and allies) in both Mar and Moray and both families had reason to be jealous of the seemingly pervasive territorial influence of the Comyns who held land in Mar close to Coull and Aboyne. Durward rivalry with the Comyns over the earldom of Mar and Atholl exacerbated this territorial rivalry and continued into the minority of Alexander III after 1249. The festering territorial rivalries and competing ambitions of Bissets, Durwards and Comyns were set in train by the 'suspicious' death of Patrick, heir to the earldom of Atholl, with the Bissets strongly implicated in the 'murder'. Matthew Paris believed that Walter Bisset was the murderer in hot-headed revenge for the fall he had received at the hands of the young Patrick at a tournament only the previous day. Another English chronicle, the *Lanercost Chronicle*, added another twist to the motive, stating that the inheritance of Thomas of Galloway was at the root of the murder. In 1233 Walter Bisset married the sister of Alan of Galloway and thus became Patrick of Atholl's uncle by marriage. It is in keeping with the Bisset's rivalry with the Comyns over land that an inheritance was at the heart of the trouble in 1242.[48]

Both Matthew Paris and the *Melrose Chronicle*, contemporary English and Scottish narrative sources respectively, put great emphasis on an aspect of the dispute which Walter Bower tends to gloss over, the impact of the dispute on Anglo-Scottish relations. While Walter Bower gives little emphasis to this aspect – instead spending three chapters on the dangers of faction-fighting (and especially the turmoil caused by the 'overmighty' Comyns) to the kingdom – the *Melrose Chronicle* gives a nationalistic interpretation very much in favour of the Comyns:

> In the same year [1244, i.e. after his sentence of exile] *the most abominable traitor*, Walter Bisset, with his accomplices desisted not from pouring the poison of discord into the ears of Henry, the king of England, until [Henry] collected his army, and caused [it] to come as far as Newcastle against lord Alexander, king of Scotland.[49]

A nationalistic interpretation from the English side corroborates this story but adds a sinister contemporary edge to how the 'English' viewed the Scottish king and kingdom at the time:

> [Walter Bisset] hastened to the king of the English, to make serious complaint before him of so great an injury inflicted upon him . . . For he asserted that the king of Scotland had disinherited him unjustly, and could not otherwise allay the presumption of some of his rebels who rose in fury against him . . . He added moreover that since the king of Scotland was the liegeman of the

lord king of England he could not disinherit or irrevocably exile from his land one so noble, especially unconvicted, *without the king of England's assent*. He added moreover that the said king of Scotland, in violation of the vassalage and fealty by which he is bound to the king of England, had received in his land Geoffrey Marsh when he fled from Ireland . . . and having received him had protected him and was still protecting him. And hence the lord king of England was violently provoked against the king of Scotland but reserved his anger for a fitting time of retribution, as the sequel shall declare . . . Moreover, the lord king [Henry] heard other news in addition to the foregoing . . .[50]

In 1244, Henry III had a great number of motives for interfering in Scottish affairs and the issue of the jurisdictional rights of the English king in Scotland was certainly raised as one of them. The 1244 confrontation has been seriously underestimated in the history of Anglo-Scottish relations. 1244 rather than 1237 and the Treaty of York marked a key stage in Anglo-Scottish relations as Henry III gave closer attention to Scottish affairs through the 1240s and 1250s. Walter Comyn's role should be cast in this light. Contemporary English sources and the English king saw Walter Comyn as a major presence in Scotland and as a significant threat to English interests in 1244. Together with the contemporary Scottish source, the *Melrose Chronicle*, contemporary English records paint Walter Comyn as an upholder of Scottish national interests, a patriot hero. Of course, this was in keeping with his role during the 1230s as the 'enforcer' of Scottish royal authority. This is a view much closer to reality than the view of Walter Comyn seen by the fifteenth-century narrative of Walter Bower – Walter Comyn, the leader of a Comyn family guilty of fomenting internal disorder to the detriment of the kingdom. Unfortunately this is the view that has been passed down by repetition through the ages to be lodged in Scottish tradition.

It would seem that Henry III achieved his aim in stifling the influence of Walter Comyn principally through the bond of good behaviour which he forced Walter and his forty main supporters to swear to in 1244. He also ordered Hugh de Bolbec, sheriff of Northumberland, to take charge of the Comyn castle of Tarset in Tynedale and force Walter to 'demilitarise' the castle.[51] In Scotland too, Walter Comyn's political influence seemed to have waned. From 1244 Alan Durward took over from Walter Comyn as Alexander II's chief adviser, justiciar of Scotia and head of a totally non-Comyn government. Durward was not involved in either of the two political groups who had hounded the Bissets out of the country and had to swear an oath of good behaviour to Henry III. Was Walter Comyn's demotion due to Henry III's military influence over the Scottish king in 1244? Or was Alexander II himself alarmed by the power of the Comyns in the north (which he had helped to create!) and his own lack of power in bringing the personal feud between Comyns and Bissets under control? Matthew Paris noted that 'the king with difficulty curbed their [the Comyns'] fury'.[52] Certainly, Alexander II seems to have replaced the two co-justiciars of Scotia, Robert Mowat and Philip de Melville who had been ineffective as royal officers for the north in bringing order to northern Scotland when the Comyns sought vengeance against the Bissets in Aboyne during 1242. Their ineffectiveness was hardly surprising as both were under the influence of the Comyn family. The fact that this change in the justiciarship seems to have taken place before Alexander II's confrontation with Henry III's army at the Border in 1244 seems to suggest that Alexander II himself wanted to reassert his personal control, though undoubtedly the move would have been backed by the English king.

Alan Durward, the new justiciar, may have come to Alexander II's notice because of his involvement with the army of Mar in the king's attempt to rescue the Bissets from Comyn attacks at Aboyne in 1242. Durward was a neighbour of Walter Bisset in Mar but he was already a territorial rival of the Comyns in Mar and Moray and the families had clashed before 1242 when the Durwards sought to remove the earldoms of Atholl and Mar from Comyn influence. Walter Comyn must have resented the fact that Durward, who had little political influence before 1244, had such an important position in Scottish government. Such resentment must have been exacerbated by Alan Durward's marriage to Alexander II's illegitimate daughter Marjory – this entrenched him even more firmly in the royal circle. The return of Walter Bisset to the Scottish royal court by November 1247 must have caused anger among the Comyns. Durwards and Bissets had been allies in the north before 1242 (and afterwards). However, Walter Comyn's decline in influence was more apparent than real judging by his prominence in the witness lists of Alexander II's charters between 1244 and 1249. The clue to Walter Comyn's continuing influence in Scottish politics in the late 1240s and, in fact, until his death in 1258 is contained in the list of forty names in his following in 1244.[53] This group who swore to uphold a bond of good behaviour to Henry III gives a good cross-section of his 'party' at that time. It contained a tightly-knit family with all three branches of the Comyn family (the Badenoch, Buchan and Kilbride lines) with their connections, represented. Names in the list connected to the Comyns through marriage were members of the de la Hay, de Soules and de Valloniis families. Families regularly associated with the Comyns were the de Erths (Airth, near Stirling), Mountfichets or Muschets (Latinised 'de Monte Fixo') who held land in Cargill on Tay and Kincardine in Menteith (west of Stirling), Bonekils, de Boscos, Grahams and Uvieth or Eviots. The 1244 list does not give a complete list of those in Walter Comyn's following. His cousin Alexander Comyn (he would become earl of Buchan c.1244) was not in the list but certainly active in the Comyn cause in 1242 and always a prominent member of Earl Walter's following until Walter's death in 1258. The Mowat (or Monte Alto) family were also in the Comyn following in this period. The list showed that Walter Comyn inherited support as well as landed power from his father, William Comyn, Earl of Buchan.

Alexander II's sudden death in 1249 meant that Scotland was faced with a minority crisis, its kingship (and symbol of its independence) in jeopardy with the young Alexander III a minor, aged eight. Walter Comyn used his support within Scotland to rescue the Scottish monarchy and resist English interference in Scottish political affairs. Political groups in Scotland, England and France were eager to influence the new king. Shortly after the 1244 confrontation at the Border and perhaps to secure a continued influence on Scottish affairs, Henry III agreed to give his eldest daughter, Margaret (then aged five) in marriage to the even younger Alexander (future Alexander III). This Alexander was the offspring (in 1241) of Alexander II's marriage to the French noblewoman Marie de Courcy. No doubt Henry III feared a future Franco-Scottish alliance if another French marriage was arranged for the young Alexander. However, the first major pressure on the young Alexander III and the Scottish monarchy itself came from Alan Durward.

As has been seen, Alan Durward had entrenched himself in the royal circle by marrying Alexander II's illegitimate daughter Marjory. There is no evidence that there were any formal arrangements made in Scotland with regard to its government if Alexander II died before his son and heir reached adulthood. Soon after Alexander II's death, Durward appears to have sought to formalise and make secure his position as head of the Scottish government. This can be seen in the change of government seals on Alexander III's letters in 1250. There were two seals in operation in 1250 – the small seal, or seal of minority, and the great seal (with the enthroned monarch on one side, the monarch as a mounted knight on the other). Two authorities on the seal of minority agree that the great seal was 'a token that the king was now considered of age to grant secure titles and to be represented as exercising government' and that 'this change of seal [in 1250] ... represents a decisive shift of power into the hands of Alan Durward'.[54] Although chroniclers are not the most reliable sources for exact titles given to officials, evidence from the change of seals seems to add veracity to *Gesta Annalia's* description of Alan Durward as 'justiciar of all Scotia'[55] in 1249. Durward was seeking, by various means in 1249 and 1250, to enlarge his political authority. He was seeking a post with equivalent status to the English justiciar, the English king's representative in his absence. The contemporary Scottish chronicle, the *Melrose Chronicle*, strongly nationalist and therefore very protective of the legitimate Scottish monarchy and its succession, suggested even more sinister motives for Alan Durward:

> lord Alan, the Doorward of Scotland, and also at that time justiciar, had along with his accomplices sent envoys, with gifts, to the lord pope in order that he should in such a manner legitimize his daughters (whom he had by the king's sister), that if any accident should happen to the king of Scotland they should succeed him in the kingdom as the lawful heirs. And if he had obtained this, none doubted that he would have turned traitor to the king and queen.[56]

The attempt by Alan Durward to bolster his status was also demonstrated by his attempt to knight the young Alexander before he was enthroned. In similar circumstances in England in 1216, Henry III had been knighted by William Marshal who was then asked by the English knights to take the office of 'rector regis et regni'.[57] However, it soon became apparent that Durward did not have enough authority over the Scottish nobility, the majority of whom were suspicious of him and his motives. It was Walter Comyn, Earl of Menteith, who seems to have been accepted as leader of the Scottish political community in 1249 by *all* sources as he thwarted Durward's scheme and 'rescued' the Scottish monarchy:

there arose a dispute among the nobles . . . While they were argu-
ing, the lord Walter Comyn, Earl of Menteith, a man of foresight
and shrewdness in counsel, answered and said that he had seen a
king consecrated who was not yet a knight . . . and he went on to
say that a country without a king was beyond doubt, like a ship
amid the waves of the sea without a rower or steersman. For he
had always loved king Alexander, of pious memory now deceased
– and this boy also for his father's sake. So he moved that this boy
be raised to the throne as quickly as possible . . . and by his advice,
the said bishops and abbot [of Scone], as well as the nobles, and
the whole clergy and people, with one voice, gave their consent
and assent to his being set up as king.'[58]

Gesta Annalia

Walter Bower repeated and elaborated on this account describing
Walter Comyn as 'a man far-seeing in his counsel and steadfast in
spirit [who] wisely set about urging the two sides towards an agreement. He said that he ought to have a voice in their deliberations
because he himself as earl of Menteith had learned a great deal from
experience.'[59] Such words of praise for Walter Comyn – a national
hero in the circumstances – contradict the vehemently anti-Comyn
sentiments against Walter elsewhere in *Gesta Annalia* and Walter
Bower. In fact the sentiments commending Walter Comyn's states-
manlike and leadership qualities, used in support of the Scottish
monarchy, are much more in keeping with the contemporary nationalist view of the *Melrose Chronicle* – that the Comyns (including Walter
Comyn) were pillars of the Scottish monarchy. Do the *Gesta Annalia*
and Walter Bower extracts reflect more concern about illustrating their
main themes, especially the importance of kingship to a country's
integrity and independence (and the threat to it of a too powerful
nobility), than a consistent analysis of the leading political figures
(except for the 'heroes' of both narratives – William Wallace and
Robert Bruce)? Was it simply a case of *Gesta Annalia* (followed by
Walter Bower) adding (without editing) unknown contemporary
sources which are at variance with their generally anti-Comyn commentary? *Gesta*/Bower used the *Melrose Chronicle* though often without
the pro-Comyn bias, but may also have used a lost *St Andrews
Chronicle*, also favourable to the Comyns. Such contradictions also
appear in the *Gesta Annalia* II/Walter Bower compilation on John
Comyn III, Lord of Badenoch (see Chapter 4) – a complete section

covering the years 1298–1304 (and from a contemporary pro-Comyn source) highlights the achievements of John Comyn in these years but is contradicted by very anti-Comyn passages in the sections both before and after these years. Something similar seems to have occurred to Walter Comyn in *Gesta Annalia* / Walter Bower compilations for the years 1249–58.

The fact that the Durward-led government in 1249 could not ignore Walter Comyn's power at this time is shown by Walter's attendance as a leading witness to a number of the young Alexander III's charters. The Durwards had office but not power and Walter Comyn's leadership of the Scottish political community, as seen by the argument surrounding the young king's knighting, seems generally to have been accepted. It was the Durward government's lack of control in the country that led to the intervention of Henry III in Scottish affairs late in 1251. This was the result of a joint magnate/clergy deputation which went to Henry III asking for both aid and support. Walter Comyn had first-hand knowledge of the decisiveness of Henry III's intervention in 1244. He was also working closely with the clergy in asking for Henry III's intervention to right the disorder in Scottish politics. There were complaints to the young Alexander III that laymen were despoiling the priory of St Andrews and that the Durward government was affording it no protection. Complaints to the king were followed by complaints to the pope, Innocent IV[60] – excommunications had been revoked by royal command, cases about Church possessions and Church patronage had been summoned before secular courts and recourse to papal judges delegate had been forbidden. The charges seem to have been aimed chiefly at the Durward-led government.

Henry III proved very willing to accept the invitation by Comyns and clergy to intervene in Scottish affairs. From the standpoint of the Scottish monarchy, Henry III's intervention could be seen as a blow to the development of an independent Scottish kingdom. However, in the political crisis which the minority caused (and the instability which came with it), there seems to have been a common regard, by the magnates and the clergy, for the English king as an agent for stability. Even *Gesta Annalia*, with its main theme as the growth of an independent Scottish kingdom reflected this in his praise for Henry III 'for, nearly the whole time of his reign, he was looked upon by the kings of Scotland, father and son, as their most faithful neighbour and adviser'.[61] This also reflects the good social, economic and religious networks in existence between the two kingdoms. However, the Comyns, under the leadership of Walter Comyn, and the Church were not naive in regard to the political and ecclesiastical relationships between England and Scotland. Both the Comyns and the Church supported an independent Scotland – their status was, in fact, largely dependent on an independent Scotland:

> Their [the Church's] nationalism was both informed and self-interested, it stemmed from two centuries and more of intermittent claims, of various parts of the English Church to jurisdiction over them.[62]

The Comyns, in a similar way, had since the early thirteenth century been the pillars of Scottish monarchy and received due benefits from that – their self-interest also was in the maintenance of an independent monarchy. It is increasingly acknowledged that by the time of Alexander III's reign, there was already a distinct sense of national identity within Scotland and that the leading magnates and the Church had already played key roles in forging that independent identity:

> The achievement in forging a notion of the kingdom of Scotland was also [along with the MacMalcolm line of kings] that of their chief partners: a composite but close-knit aristocracy and the Scottish Church.[63]

The Comyns had established a good reputation with the Church, mainly through the munificence of William Comyn, Earl of Buchan, and his son Walter was careful to maintain this reputation. The *Melrose Chronicle* reflected strong Church support for Walter as defender of an independent Scotland. Walter Comyn's status as a 'patriot hero' should be judged on his defence of Scotland's independent status after Henry III's intervention.

At Christmas 1251, Henry III's intervention in Scottish affairs was sealed by the marriage, at York, of young King Alexander III (aged ten) to Henry III's young daughter, Margaret (aged eleven). The year 1251 had a major significance for Anglo-Scottish relations. It soon became clear that Henry III took his new role as father-figure for the young Scottish royal family seriously, not only in regard to the young couple's welfare but also the welfare of the Scottish kingdom. Henry's authority was firstly represented by his bestowal on the young

Alexander III of the belt of knighthood at York. Both Scottish and English chronicles agree that Henry III – in Alexander III's name – made changes in the Scottish king's government after investigating the complaints by the joint clergy/Comyn delegation. Thus the chief officers, the justiciar (Alan Durward), chancellor and chamberlain were deprived of the offices in York. The charges of treason against Durward – he had tried to get papal permission to legitimise the daughters born to his wife, illegitimate half-sister of the new king, which would make succession to the throne a possibility – were upheld and the Comyns were placed in power with Durward sent into exile. Scottish narrative sources dwell on this change of counsellors in Scotland but the contemporary English chronicler Matthew Paris dwells (as he had done in 1244) at length on the formal political relationship between the kings of England and Scotland, an issue not mentioned in any Scottish sources:

> the king of Scotland did homage to the king of the English, by reason of the possessions which he holds of the lord king of the English to wit in the kingdom of England: namely for Lothian and the other lands.[64]

but then reports on a more contentious aspect of the relationship:

> And when in addition to this the king of Scotland was required to do homage and fealty with allegiance to his lord the king of the English by reason of the kingdom of Scotland as his predecessors had done to the English kings, according as it is clearly written in the chronicles in many places, the king of Scotland replied that he had come thither in peace and for the honour of the king of England, and by his command, to wit to be allied to him by mediation of a matrimonial alliance, and not to reply to him about so difficult a question, for he had not held full deliberation or suitable counsel concerning this with his chief men, as so difficult a matter demanded.[65]

The king's reply recognised that the time was not appropriate to deal with the issue. He 'dissembled everything, passing it over for the time in silence'.

It is clear, however, that Henry III wanted to establish effective supervision of the young royal couple and the Scottish government in this minority period and that he thought, on his return to England with his wife, he had set up enough safeguards:

> the surest guardianship was assigned to the queen for instruction in every way, namely the knights sir Robert le Noreis the lord king's marshal of guests and sir Stephen Bauzan. And with them a certain noble dame endowed with all honour, Matilda, the widow of William the second de Cantelupe, and certain other prudent and courteous men. And the lord king of England promised to send to the king of Scotland a prudent and faithful counsellor, providently to examine with the nobles of his kingdom into the affairs pertaining to the interest both of the queen and the king.

Henry, indeed, appointed two experienced Anglo-Scottish barons, namely Robert de Ros, Lord of Wark, Helmsley and Sanquhar (and the king's cousin), and John de Balliol,[66] as guardians of the young king and queen – and no doubt his own interests – between 1251 and 1255. It appears too that Geoffrey de Langley was sent to Scotland as the queen's counsellor. In addition, Henry used other Anglo-Scottish barons such as Roger de Quincy and Malise, Earl of Strathearn, on frequent embassies between the two countries during the minority period. Henry III's attention to the details of Scottish government also revealed how much control he desired to exercise in Scotland. He ensured, for example, that the great seal, by which Alan Durward had tried to enlarge his own authority, was broken and replaced with a small seal.[67] Henry's policy – to regard the government as subject to his overriding authority – seems to be confirmed by the fact that his next intervention in Scottish affairs took place exactly on Alexander III's fourteenth birthday. The intervention was planned.

Walter Comyn's achievement as a 'patriot hero' should be judged by how successful he was in denying Henry III the real control of the Scottish political scene which he desired. In practice, between 1251 and 1255, the Scottish government led by Walter was very successful in denying Henry III this control. The Comyn 'party' supporting Walter Comyn in government in 1251[68] had the same basic nucleus as in 1244, with Walter as its head and Alexander Comyn, Earl of Buchan, William, Earl of Mar and John Comyn of Badenoch (Walter's nephew) as its inner core. Still in the group from 1244 were Nicholas de Soules, John Le Blund and Alexander Vinet (Uvieth). Influential men gained from Patrick, Earl of Dunbar's, following in 1244 were David de Graham and Thomas de Normanville, both members of important noble families. Other men supporting the 1251–5 Comyn government were Hugh and William Gourlay (William was a feudal tenant of William Comyn of Kilbride), Thomas, son of Ranulf (perhaps connected to the Bonekils), Aymer de Maxwell and Mary, his wife, David de Lochore and John de Dundemore. Particularly notable among supporters of Walter Comyn's government were the leading bishops of Scotland. They included William Bondington, Bishop of Glasgow, Clement, Bishop of Dunblane, Gamelin, Bishop-elect of St Andrews, and William Wishart, Archdeacon of St Andrews (he was a future bishop of St Andrews), along with his brother Richard.

With such broad-based support, Walter Comyn seemed to have the general support of the country behind him. It is perhaps surprising, given the political use made of that office by his rival Alan Durward that Walter Comyn himself did not take on the most important position in government, the justiciarship of Scotia, which his own father had held. Walter, perhaps, still had an official role in Galloway. Alexander Comyn, since 1244 Earl of Buchan, became justiciar of Scotia from at latest 1253 (succeeding his father William, Earl of Buchan, in the role); William, Earl of Mar, became chamberlain in 1252; Gamelin, under Comyn patronage and probably a relative of William Comyn, Earl of Buchan, by marriage, had custody of the small royal seal but was not mentioned as chancellor before February 1254; and Thomas de Normanville was justiciar of Lothian by c.1251.

Walter Comyn's government was skilful in denying Henry III real control over the Scottish political scene. In practice Henry III's two guardians of the young Scottish king and queen, John Balliol and Robert de Ros, had no special precedence and little involvement in Scottish government activities. Robert de Ros occupied a lowly position when he witnessed occasional Alexander III charters, reflecting his lack of status in Scottish affairs. Walter Comyn's dominance over John Balliol was illustrated in the election to the bishopric of Galloway. The Comyn candidate in Galloway was elected despite the opposition of John Balliol in the name of the lordship of Galloway. The election of Henry, Abbot of Holyrood, was upheld at York in 1255. Walter Comyn's influence in Galloway seems to have won the day. Walter's success at limiting the influence of Henry III's two guardians is reflected in Henry's anger at the failure of his guardians. Matthew Paris commented:

And during the same times [1255] Robert de Ross and John de Balliol were seriously accused on the charge that they had unfaithfully and dishonourably controlled the kingdom of Scotland and the king and queen, whose tutelage had been entrusted to them . . .

For he was assured so he asserted, by frequent secret communications from his vassals, that they had treated both the king and queen and the kingdom of Scotland otherwise than as was fitting and expedient . . .

John Balliol . . . prudently made peace for himself by satisfying the king's needs with money . . .

The possessions of Robert de Ross were despoiled – cows, sheep, his utensils, everything which he had in the realm of England was mercilessly plundered, and sold on good terms at the will of the buyers . . . he followed the king, soliciting and awaiting his favour; but he could not yet obtain it.[69]

Walter Comyn's success was in direct proportion to Henry III's anger. Walter Comyn was also behind the scheme to remove Geoffrey de Langley, the queen's counsellor, from Scotland, again with common consent:

The same Geoffrey, by command of the king of England [was made] one of the guardians of the queen of Scots. But the magnates of Scotland refused long to endure his oppressions and removed him.[70]

As well as reducing the influence of the English king in Scotland, Walter Comyn was able to strengthen Comyn influence over the Church by pushing successive claims of two Comyn supporters, Abel of Gullane in 1253 and Gamelin in 1255 to the see of St Andrews. This was doubly important as control over the premier see in Scotland was vital and Durward influence in the cathedral chapter there could be effectively quashed.

Walter Comyn's effective thwarting of English interference in a difficult minority period was, strangely, not highlighted as a triumph by Scottish nationalist writers of the fourteenth and fifteenth centuries. Instead the fourteenth-century *Gesta Annalia* and the fifteenth-century Walter Bower, rather surprisingly, praised Henry III for bringing stability to Scotland and new officials – from Walter Comyn's party – into government in 1251 but then immediately condemned them:

But these councillors were so many kings. For he who saw the poor crushed down in those days, the nobles ousted from their inheritance the drudgery forced upon citizens, the violence done to churches, might with good reason say 'Woe unto the kingdom where the kingdom is a boy!'[71]

Gesta Annalia

Such accusations were repeated by Walter Bower who then developed his reflections on the need for good counsellors:

In exercising government nothing is more advantageous for a king than to have good counsellors ... [evil counsellors] are particularly dangerous in any community because, just as the honour, well-being and success of a king and of the state of which the king is a head depend most of all on good councillors; so confusion and the overthrow of the state arise especially from the presence of evil counsellors.[72]

Gesta Annalia, in summing up Walter Comyn's government between 1251 and 1255, noted 'judgement and righteousness in the kingdom of Scotland were slumbering' and that, as a result, 'Walter Comyn, Earl of Menteith, and his accomplices were more than once summoned before the king and his councillors, upon many grave charges'.[73]

Gesta Annalia, and especially Walter Bower, were clearly vilifying Walter Comyn and his government associates and justifying the overthrow of this government with the support of the English king. Bower commended the motives of those who successfully led this 'coup' in September 1255:

At that time Patrick earl of Dunbar and Alan Durward, fired by zeal for the realm, and their supporters, wishing to move against Walter Comyn and other magnates who were then members of the king's council so as to separate them from the lord king.[74]

The charges levelled by *Gesta Annalia* and Walter Bower against Walter Comyn's government are riddled with inaccuracies. The Comyn government were certainly guilty of hounding the recalcitrant Robert of Kenleith, chancellor of the previous government, out of office, but the Comyns, because of their vast influence throughout Scotland, had probably less need to pursue factional interest than their rival, Alan

Durward, did from 1255 to 1257. The description of Comyn excesses against the Church should also be set against the consistent Church support for Walter Comyn at key times during Alexander III's minority, i.e. 1249, 1251 and again in 1255.

The successful counter-coup of Alan Durward in 1255 proved that the continued confidence of the king of England was a necessity for any governing group in Scotland during the minority period. Alan Durward ingratiated himself into the English king's favour by serving in the English king's army in Gascony. By 1255, he was regarded as one of Henry III's 'beloved friends'. Henry III had his own reasons for supporting a counter-coup by Alan Durward – he had underestimated the Comyns and Walter Comyn's ability to make Henry III's guardians in Scotland so ineffective. The desire of Henry III to make firmer, more formal arrangements than in 1251 – a named council of fifteen to serve for seven years (the remaining years of minority)[75] – was a sure sign that Walter Comyn had exercised more political influence from 1251 to 1255 than Henry had intended.

The *Melrose Chronicle*, contemporary and nationalistic, gives a very different opinion of the 1255 coup than that contained in *Gesta Annalia* and Walter Bower. The *Melrose Chronicle* depicted the motives of Alan Durward as the treasonable motives of an outsider against the majority in Scotland:

There assembled at Edinburgh, to meet our lord the king, on the one side all the nobility of Scotland, and on the other side Alan the Doorward and his followers who were mightily increased in number and pretended that they wished to have a conference about the settlement of peace, but their real object was to capture the king . . . they [Alan Durward and his followers] seized their lord the king, and garrisoned the castle [Edinburgh] with their own troops . . . When the king's counsellors and guardians had heard that he was taken prisoner *they were exceedingly distressed and astonished at such a treasonable act* . . . He [Henry III] took it ill that the bishop of Glasgow and the [bishop] elect of St Andrews and W.[alter] Comyn, styled earl of Menteith, and others of the nobility of the land, refused to affix their seals to a certain most wicked writing which the said conspirators had framed and confirmed by their seals, and in which were contained *many matters which would have worked for the dishonour of the king and the kingdom.*[76]

After 1255 Walter Comyn and his party still had important backing from the clergy and it is noticeable that only two bishops, those of Aberdeen and Dunkeld, were members of the new 1255 council and only four abbots supported the Comyns' removal. Alan Durward's ambitions to increase his power and status now that he was, once more, justiciar of Scotia was also thwarted with the help of the Church. He tried to discredit the Comyns for their actions in government and also revived his family's claim to the earldom of Mar by challenging the legitimacy of the earl of Mar's father and grandfather. Durward, however, was unable to gain the earldom of Mar after a papal enquiry. Church support was also present for the Comyn candidate for the major Scottish see, the bishopric of St Andrews. Durward was unable to prevent the consecration of Gamelin, the Comyn government's chancellor. The *Chronicle of Melrose* narrates the struggles of Gamelin:

> In the same year [1256] bishop Gamelin was outlawed by the king's counsellors, partly because he would not acquiesce in their wicked designs, partly because he scorned to give a certain sum of money as if for the purchase of his bishopric . . .
>
> In this year [1257] ambassadors sent by the king of Scotland's guardians came to the lord pope, accusing the bishop of St Andrews on behalf of the king. After hearing and trying the cases of both sides, [the pope] pronounced with his own mouth that the bishop was guiltless of all the charges that had unjustly been brought against him; and that he was most worthy of the bishopric. And he excommunicated [Gamelin's] accusers, and the consumers and invaders of the bishopric.[77]

It is interesting in view of his generally vehement denunciation of Walter Comyn and his government officials and supporters, that Walter Bower later in his narrative includes a section (another one contradictory to his anti-Comyn bias) which casts Bishop Gamelin as a model bishop in relation to royal authority:

> From that time the lord king held Bishop Gamelin in great reverence and [devotion and] love, knowing him to be a just and holy man.[78]

This, perhaps, reflects Walter Bower's access to a contemporary St Andrews source. He uses it as a reflection on the importance of support for royal authority (his major theme) but is apparently oblivious to the fact that earlier he had 'used' the Comyns and their supporters as examples of opponents of royal authority. Gamelin (probably related to the Comyns) was a key member of the Comyn government between 1251 and 1255.

It soon became apparent that the new Durward government in Scotland could not control the Comyn 'party'. Comyn reaction to Durward's strong-arm tactics against their supporters, including Gamelin, was once more to seek Henry III's intervention as he had done in 1249. No doubt encouraged by Gamelin's consecration, Walter Comyn and his party put pressure on the council and in 1257 forced it to pass on to Henry III a draft document which no doubt advocated the reintroduction of Comyn members to the Scottish government.[79] Henry sent the prominent Anglo-Scottish baron, Roger de Quincy, Earl of Winchester, to mediate but apparently with instructions not to change the rigid structure set up in 1255.[80] Henry III regarded himself as the principal counsellor of the Scottish king and felt he had a better chance of controlling Scottish affairs by using a number of Anglo-Scottish barons and northern officials such as the archbishop of York, the bishop of Durham and the sheriffs of York and Northumberland to help restore order in Scotland.[81] By 1257 it was clear that Walter's tactics of trying to regain power through the English king – trying to persuade him that his party had majority support and Church support in Scotland – was failing. The year 1257 marked a significant change in Comyn tactics and one which has, unfortunately, resulted in them being forever labelled as irresponsible aggressors in Scottish history and tradition. The Comyn kidnapping of the young King Alexander at Kinross in 1257 has long been seen as characterising their contribution to Scottish history:

As they durst not await their trial [upon many grave charges] according to the statutes of the kingdom, they took counsel together, and, with one accord, seized the king, by night, while he was asleep in bed at Kinross, and, before dawn, carried him off with them to Stirling . . . They also took away by force the great seal . . . The ringleaders in this kidnapping were Walter Comyn, Earl of Menteith, Alexander Comyn, Earl of Buchan, William Earl of Mar, a man of great shrewdness in evil deeds, John Comyn, a man prone to robbery and rashness . . . and a great many other hangers-on of these disaffected men who did all as they pleased

and naught as was lawful, and reigned over the people, right or
wrong . . .[82]

Gesta Annalia

Walter Bower, while still critical of the Comyns, does at least point out
the apparent contradiction between Earl Walter's actions in 1257 and
1249–51:

> In his case this [the kidnapping] is much to be wondered at, for he
> was so loyal to the king at the time of the coronation and ensured
> that his first counsellors should be removed because they were
> guiding the king and the kingdom badly.[83]

This balanced approach was, however, only temporary as he specu-
lated that avarice soon led the Comyns to stray:

> But no doubt the possessions and revenues of the king which came
> into the hands of his counsellors and of those who did not think
> that they would have to render an account for them caused them
> to stray from the path of truth and equity.

He repeated *Gesta Annalia's* criticisims and strongly concluded that
the Comyns under Walter Comyn's leadership deserved their eventual
fate as opponents of royal authority:

> As I said earlier these Comyns were in the lead among those who
> rose against the king: as a consequence their name is now, so to
> speak, obliterated in the land.[84]

It is clear that Water Comyn and the Comyn 'party' are being used by
Bower to reflect bitter criticism of the king's counsellors during the
minority of James II in his own time. The *Liber Pluscardensis*, also in
the fifteenth century, went even further:

> they upset all the good government of the past counsellors and
> governors . . . in a word perpetrated every misdeed, ravaged the
> whole kingdom and plundered the inhabitants in such a way as
> had never been known in the kingdom of Scotland for a long
> time . . .[85]

and on Walter Comyn's death in 1258 – according to Pluscarden, by poison administered by his wife:

> he deserved it, for he was ringleader of those who brought the king captive to Stirling, and that the word of God spoken by the prophet might be fulfilled, who says, The ungodly shall perish from the earth, and workers of iniquity shall be taken from it . . . But this curse fell upon them through the vengeance of God, for they laid hands upon the lord king, in spite of the oath of allegiance and fealty.[86]

Yet inconsistences (and distortions of history) abound especially with these fifteenth-century accounts. In September 1255, for instance, the young king had been taken in a surprise counter-coup at Edinburgh Castle by Patrick, Earl of Dunbar, and Alan Durward who, far from being criticised by Walter Bower, were commended for their 'zeal for the realm'.[87] Thus the abduction of the young king in 1255 is seen very differently from that of 1257. As has been noted, the *contemporary* nationalist account of the *Melrose Chronicle* saw the 1255 capture of the king as 'treasonable' and this source should also be given more historical credit in its account of the 1257 Comyn coup.

Indeed, the fifteenth-century nationalist writings of Walter Bower, in particular, contain not only a very narrow agenda about 'evil counsellors' but a heavy bias against Walter Comyn and his 'party' in government. This bias is fitting for the pro-Bruce age in which it was written, but out of keeping with contemporary sentiments expressed in both Scottish and English narratives of the thirteenth century. In both the *Melrose Chronicle* and Matthew Paris, Walter Comyn appears as a formidable defender of native or patriot interests (the Church, as well as the king) and the accepted leader of the Scottish political community:

> When all the nobility of Scotland, of whom the leader was Walter Cumin styled earl of Menteith, perceived their king was the constant associate of men who had been excommunicated, and becoming apprehensive that the whole land would be placed under interdict, they made a rising, and taking him out of their hands at Kinross, they restored him to his kingdom. The masterbuilder of the whole mischief, Alan the Doorward, when he heard

of this, became apprehensive of the consequences of his treason in laying hands upon his sovereign, and fled to the king of England.[88]

Matthew Paris, a noted xenophobe, recognised the Scottish viewpoint, and was sympathetic to those Scottish nobles [i.e. Walter Comyn, Earl of Menteith, and his party] objecting to foreign intervention in their country. He, perhaps surprisingly, complained about the queen for causing English intervention in Scotland and justified the 1257 kidnapping:

> [1257] Alexander . . . misgoverned too unbecomingly, promoting and following foreigners and exalting and appointing them over his native subjects, the inhabitants and natives were indignant, and to prevent his breaking out in worse ways they placed the king himself and the queen under custody again . . . until . . . they should have removed to a distance all foreigners. And thenceforward the nobles of Scotland held the reigns of their kingdom with greater freedom and safety . . . They upbraided the queen, moreover in that she had incited and summoned her father to come upon them as an enemy with his army, and do lamentable destruction.[89]

It has been seen that Walter Comyn's leadership of the 'patriot' party was helped by Church support and by the pope's disapproval of the Durward government. It was an alliance of mutual interest (and self-interest) – an independent Scotland (and Scottish monarchy) and suspicion of English interference was their common cause. It was also clear that Walter Comyn was shrewd enough to strengthen his own position in Scotland with another anti-English alliance – an alliance with Llewelyn, Prince of Wales, and his supporters in 1258.[90] Walter Comyn's political pragmatism enabled him to realise that Henry III was in a difficult situation in 1257–8 – he was preoccupied with events in Sicily, baronial opposition in England (the baronial reform movement), the successful rebellions of the Welsh and the illness of the queen. These issues were probably taken into account when Earl Walter organised the 1257 coup and then in 1258 took positive action by allying with Llewelyn, Prince of Wales. Although it was the Welsh who seem to have taken the initiative in seeking such an alliance, it says much for the political initiative of Walter Comyn (and his 'patriot' credentials) that the two sides came together in an anti-English alliance.

The terms of the 1258 treaty with the Welsh show that Walter Comyn was not a threat to the Scottish monarchy. He was keenly aware of the king's position in Scotland – he symbolised an independent Scotland – and conscious to act with due reverence to royal authority. He had acted, with Church support, against the 'treachery' of Alan Durward in 1251 and 1257. Even in 1258 when he had *de facto* control, he showed himself unwilling to do anything without the young king's permission. The Comyn support in the 1258 treaty with the Welsh included seven members of the Comyn government of 1251–5 – Alexander Comyn, Earl of Buchan, William, Earl of Mar, John Comyn (named in 1258 as justiciar of Galloway), Aymer de Maxwell, John de Dundemore, David de Lochore and Hugh de Berkeley. The list, within the treaty, also included regular members of the Comyn following: Freskin de Moray, Hugh de Abernethy, two members of the Mowat family, Bernard and William, William de Airth and Reginald Cheyne. Also in the list were younger members of the Comyn family, William and Richard (brothers of John Comyn and William, Earl of Ross, a relative who had played little part in previous Comyn activities. The 1258 Comyn 'party' were still a powerful, close-knit group but they had less general support than in 1251 and little outside the Comyn affinity. The terms of the Welsh treaty show Walter Comyn unwilling to act without the backing of his king:

> If it should happen that we are compelled to enter into a peace or truce with the king of England or anyone else opposed to Llewelyn, *by command of our lord king of Scotland* we shall strive to see that this is done to Llewelyn's honour and advantage, nor shall we do anything contrary to the league unless it be by our lord the king's strictest compulsion, but rather *we shall do our best to bring the lord our king into this alliance.*[91]

These were not the words of an unprincipled leadership. The terms of the treaty give the strong impression that the Comyns did not 'control' Alexander III, were anxious to try to win the support of the young king, and were extremely hesitant to act without his backing. After all, the Comyns had been the real pillars of the Scottish monarchy from the 1230s.

The alliance with the Welsh had been an inspired attempt to broaden the anti-English alliance in 1258, but only three months after the treaty was made the Welsh agreed peace with Henry III. Compromise was in the air by the summer of 1258 with Alexander III becoming more actively involved on the political scene, and seeking a measure of reconciliation between the Comyn and Durward factions. That compromise was reached – and English interference much reduced – was due to Henry III's political weakness in the summer of 1258. Henry III was no longer in a position to insist that the arrangements he had made in Scotland in 1255 i.e. a seven-year council of fifteen governing Scotland, should be continued. On 2 May 1258, Henry promised reform to his English barons, and following the parliament of Oxford in June, the baronial reform movement began and Henry III was no longer in charge of English government. In September 1258, a reconciliation in Scotland was apparently agreed, a document of November 1258 issued by the English baronial council recording a compromise council of ten for Scotland with four key members of the Comyn party (Walter Comyn, Earl of Menteith, Alexander Comyn, Earl of Buchan, William, Earl of Mar, and Gamelin, Bishop of St Andrews) and four members of the Durward party (Alan Durward, Alexander Stewart, Robert Meyners (Menzies) and Gilbert de Hay). The naming of Queen Marie and her new husband, John of Acre, as the other two members may have been a sop to Henry III, giving the impression that Alexander III's minority still continued. In practice, Alexander III's minority had ended and the dangers of English interference, for the time being, averted. Walter Comyn's leadership of the political community during the minority of Alexander III has been very much underestimated, especially his great contribution to thwarting English 'control' over Scottish political affairs in the period 1251 to 1258. Such a conclusion can also be drawn for the period 1242–4.

It has been seen how limited and misleading is the image of Walter Comyn in Scottish tradition. The image of Walter Comyn as the leader of an unprincipled, overmighty baronial faction is, in truth, based largely on fourteenth and especially fifteenth-century Scottish narratives, *Gesta Annalia* (1380s) and Walter Bower (c.1440), with a narrow nationalistic agenda based on the dangers of evil counsellors to the Scottish monarchy in crisis during the later fourteenth and mid fifteenth centuries. Even then, it has been seen that *Gesta Annalia* and Walter Bower did include material contrary to their message, intended for a pro-Bruce, anti-Comyn age. However, a much more satisfactory account of Walter Comyn can be achieved using contemporary thirteenth-century Scottish narrative sources, especially the *Melrose Chronicle*, and contemporary English chronicles, especially that of Matthew Paris. When these sources are placed in the context of Walter Comyn's role as key royal trouble-shooter in areas difficult for Scottish kings to control – Moray, Caithness, Galloway and the Border region – an entirely different picture emerges of Walter Comyn. Walter Comyn emerges not as an enemy to the Scottish monarchy but as a key agent for royal authority and a patriot leader to the fore in the defence of Scottish independence against English interference in the 1240s and 1250s.

Walter Comyn, Earl of Menteith, must still have been the leading political figure in Scotland when he died in late October or early November 1258. The suddenness of his death and the reactions to it in both Scotland and England indicate the effect he had had on the political affairs of both countries in the 1240s and 1250s. Messengers came to Henry III at St Albans on 23 November especially to report that:

Walter Comyn, a most powerful earl in Scotland, had yielded to fate, having fallen from his horse, which had stumbled upon some obstacle.[92]

Matthew Paris

Scottish sources of the fourteenth and fifteenth centuries give a more sinister, bitter report of his death:

Walter Comyn, earl of Menteith, now an old man, died suddenly, poisoned by his wife, or so it is said. He had been the ringleader of those who had kidnapped the king.[93]

The *Book of Pluscarden* added that 'he deserved it'. In an age when worship of Robert Bruce as a patriot hero was already firmly accepted, it is unlikely that any member of the Comyn family would be recognised as a patriot hero.

Most later Scottish historians have followed the very partial fourteenth and fifteenth-century overview of Walter Comyn's contribution to Scottish history. Thus Buchanan highlighted his crimes rather than his achievements:

When the king took the government into his own hands, he pardoned the Cumins upon their humble submission, as if their crimes had been expiated by the death of [Earl] Walter.[94]

Lord Hailes described the 1257 kidnapping:

They flew to arms; strengthened with a hypocritical pretext, they seized the King and Queen at Kinross and detained them in separate confinement.[95]

However, some later writers have picked up aspects of the *Melrose Chronicle* rather than Walter Bower's. P. Hume Brown (1902) makes the assertion that the Comyns had popular support, a view followed by J. Fergusson (1937).[96] 'Popular' support reflects, perhaps, the fact that the *Melrose Chronicle* portrays Walter Comyn having majority support for his anti-English stance. William Fraser goes much further in support of Walter Comyn as a patriot hero:

He was the head of a large and powerful family, the chief of numerous vassals, possessed of high talents, and a strong love of his country, which enabled him to direct the great power thus lying in his hands for what he considered the interest of his country . . . the patriotism of the Earl of Menteith was devoted to the preservation of the liberties of his country.[97]

In fact, this is much closer to the truth of the matter than the often repeated narratives of Scottish nationalist writers of the fourteenth and fifteenth centuries. The moral lesson of Walter Bower at the end of the following passage:

He [Walter Comyn] had been the ringleader of those who kidnapped the king. As I said earlier these Comyns were in the lead among those who rose against the king: as a consequence their name is now, so to speak, obliterated in the land . . . *therefore knights and magnates ought to pay greater attention to the words of the apostle: 'Honour the king'.*[98]

was as appropriate for the time it was written (mid fifteenth century) as for the time it was here applied (mid thirteenth century) BUT the individual (and family) targeted as 'evil' counsellors could not be more *inappropriately* cast in this light. The pro-Bruce (and therefore anti-Comyn) bias of fourteenth and fifteenth-century writers has not only hidden the achievements of Walter Comyn as the foremost king's counsellor from c.1229 to 1258 but completely distorted it. Contradictions within these narratives have occasionally allowed a more positive view of Walter Comyn to emerge – both *Gesta Annalia* and Walter Bower praise Walter Comyn for rescuing the Scottish monarchy from the self-centred scheming of Alan Durward between 1249 and 1251 – before the diatribe against Walter Comyn and the Comyn family in general is resumed. This should cause extreme suspicion of their overall analysis of the Comyns in the 1240s and 1250s, a black picture so long etched into Scottish tradition. Sometimes *Gesta Annalia* and Walter Bower may have included in their narratives, almost accidentally, material from earlier chronicles with a pro-Comyn bias (the *Melrose Chronicle* or the lost *St Andrews Chronicle*). Sometimes, their strong message about the dangers of evil counsellors has caused them *not* to see the distortions and contradictions in the characters they have used to illustrate this theme. Fortunately, for the period c.1239 to 1258, there are contemporary nationalistic narratives in Scotland and England, principally the *Melrose Chronicle* and Matthew Paris, which have a powerful message of their own. In their day, Walter Comyn was seen as a vigorous trouble-shooter for the Scottish royal cause in those regions lacking in royal authority (Moray, Caithness and Galloway) or those areas (Galloway and the Borders) deemed to pose a threat to English interests. The *Melrose Chronicle* and Matthew Paris, from their different angles, are in agreement that Walter Comyn was a consistent opponent of English interference in Scottish affairs during the 1240s and 1250s. Walter Comyn is a worthy 'Patriot Hero' for a period in which Scottish royal authority was being defined and was in need of protection.

The Comyn following 1244–1258

The Comyn following in 1244 (*Cal. Docs Scot. I, Nos.* 2671–2)

41 names in the earl of Menteith's following

Earl Walter	Nicholas de Sules
Gilbert de la Hay	David Comin
Richard de Munfichet	William de Erht
Malcolm, son of the earl	Duncan Sibald
Randulf de Bonekil	Rolf Piuntona (?)
Henry de Graham	Roger Lohereng
Hugh de Flameng	William de Valoniis
Alexander de Stirling	William de la Hay
Walter de Bonekil	Richard Cuners
Thomas Crok	Philip le Futur
Alexander Quiot	Robert de Mayneres
John Comin	William de Veteri Ponte
Gilbert de Sewalistone	Ivo de Veteri Ponte
Thomas de Conigburt	William de Bosco
William de la Hay	Richard de Crag
Robert Cumin	John le Blund
Robert de Brokismu	Robert le Born
Johachim [*sic*]	Aimer de Anisley
Randulf de Halwtone	Henry de Wyntone
William de Hawdene	John de Fentone
Henry de Haliburtone	

The Comyn following in 1255 (Cal. Docs Scot. I, No. 2013)

26 names excluded from government in 1255

W. Bishop of Glasgow	C. Bishop of Dunblane
Gamelin, Elect of St Andrews	Walter Comyn, Earl of Menteith
Alexander Comyn, Earl of Menteith	William, Earl of Mar
John de Balliol	Robert de Ros
Aymer de Maxwell	Maria, his wife
John Comyn	Nicholas de Sules
Thomas de Normanville	Alexander Vinet (Uviet)
John de Dundemor	David de Graham
John le Blund	Thomas, son of Ranulf
Hugh Gourlay	William, his brother
William Wishard, Archdeacon of St Andrews	Brother Richard, Almoner of the Templars
David de Louchor	John Wischard
William de Cadyhou	William the chaplain

The inner core of Walter Comyn's following

Comyn supporters holding high office c.1251x1255

N.B. Walter Comyn did not hold any office.

Alexander Comyn, Earl of Buchan – Justiciar of Scotland c.1253–1255

(this office was held jointly by Philip de Fedarg and Michael de Mowat? 1253)

William, Earl of Mar – Chamberlain in 1252

Gamelin – Chancellor c.1254

Thomas de Normanville – Justiciar of Lothian c.1251–c.1253

Accomplices of Earl Walter in the 1257 Coup d'Etat
(Chron. Bower (Watt) V, p. 321)

Alexander Comyn, Earl of Buchan
William, Earl of Mar
John Comyn
Hugh de Abernethy
David de Lochor
Hugh de Berkley

The Comyn following in 1258 (Cal. Docs Scot. I, No. 2155)

Comyn supporters who made Treaty with the Welsh, 18 March 1258

Walter Comyn, Earl of Menteith	Alexander Comyn, Earl of Buchan, Justiciar of Scotland
William, Earl of Mar	William, Earl of Ross
John Comyn, Justiciar of Galloway	Aimer de Maxwell, Chamberlain of Scotland
Freskin de Moravia	Hugh de Abernethy
William de Mohaut	William Comyn and Richard Comyn, brothers of John Comyn
Hugh and Walter de Berkeley, brothers	Bernard de Mohaue
Reginald Chen	David Lochor
John Dundemor	William de Erth
Ector de Karrick	

3

Real Patriot 2

ALEXANDER COMYN, EARL OF BUCHAN (d. 1289)

A political career of almost fifty years is remarkable in modern politics; for the thirteenth century it is extra-ordinary. Yet the career of Alexander Comyn, which can be traced from c.1240 to 1289, has slipped underneath the radar of those who have looked for the 'great men' of Scotland's medieval past. The fact that Alexander's career covered *two* defining political crises in Scottish history – the minority of Alexander III (1249–1258) and the aftermath of Alexander III's sudden death without an adult heir in 1286 – makes Alexander Comyn as significant a figure for Scottish national identify as William Wallace or Robert Bruce. Alexander Comyn was the most senior political figure to live through (and learn from) the minority of Alexander III when the king's youth and the dangers of English political interference presented a real threat to Scotland's political integrity and independence. He was well-placed, therefore, to lead the political community in 1286 when Scotland again was without an adult king and Scotland's political integrity was under similar threat. These circumstances helped to define the Scottish 'cause' in the years before the Wars of Independence began in 1296 – Alexander Comyn was a major contributor to the Scottish cause. As well as bridging the gap between two formative political crises, he was also the principal contributor to the so-called 'Golden Age' of Alexander III's maturity c.1258–1286. As justiciar of Scotia c.1251–1255 and 1258–1289, Alexander Comyn occupied the senior Scottish royal government post and following the death of his half-brother, Walter Comyn, Earl of Menteith, in 1258, became the leader of the most dominant political group in Scotland, the Comyns and their affinity. Alexander Comyn came to mark the apogee of co-operation between noble families in government and the Scottish monarchy in the second half of the thirteenth century. Such co-operation contributed greatly to the political and geographical definition of the kingdom and the mature establishment of Scotland's independent identity in relationship to England.

From Poacher to Gamekeeper

Scottish tradition has painted Alexander Comyn above all as an aggressive, overmighty subject (and therefore as a threat to the king and kingdom) because of his involvement in two infamous episodes of Scottish history in the 1240s and 1250s – the harrying of the Bissets (1242–4) and the kidnapping of the young king, Alexander III, in 1257. Walter Bower (c.1440) described how two young members of the Comyn family took revenge for the suspected murder of their relative Patrick of Atholl:

> [Alexander] the heir of Buchan and John the Red his nephew, who was a keen fighter and a most outstanding participant in all knightly encounters . . . plundered and pillaged all the oxen, sheep and cattle and everything else that belonged to anyone of [Walter] Bisset's party.[1]

When in government (1251–5) during Alexander III's minority, Alexander Comyn, alongside the Comyn party leader, Walter Comyn, Earl of Menteith, was described by *Gesta Annalia* as 'councillors [who] were so many kings'.[2] After being removed from power in 1255, Alexander Comyn was cited in 1257 by both *Gesta Annalia* and Walter Bower as one of the 'ringleaders' in the kidnapping of Alexander III and one of the 'disaffected men, who did all as they pleased and naught that was lawful, and reigned over the people, right or wrong'.[3] Walter Bower was slightly less damning in his assessment (though he still described Alexander Comyn as one of the 'evil men' involved): 'no doubt the possessions and revenues of the king which came into the hands of his counsellors and of those who did not think that they would have to render an account to him caused them to stray from the path of truth and equity'[4]. It has been seen in the previous chapter how Walter Bower, in particular, sought to deliver a sharp homily on the dangers, to the king and kingdom, of evil counsellors for his own time, the mid fifteenth century:

> These [evil counsellors] are particularly dangerous in any community because, just as the honour, well-being and success of a king and of the state of which the king is a head depend most of all on good counsellors, so confusion and the overthrow of the state arise especially from the presence of evil counsellors.[5]

Such a message, and especially the use of the Comyns as a mid thirteenth-century example of 'evil counsellors' has been shown to be misleading and contradictory with regard to Walter Comyn. It is a complete anomaly when applied to Alexander Comyn who spent the entire period of Alexander III's maturity, i.e. 1258–86, as the Scottish king's *chief* counsellor. Clearly Alexander III did not regard Alexander Comyn as an evil counsellor even after his 'kidnapping'! In fact, if it had not been so necessary to conform to the propaganda of the pro-Bruce age in which Walter Bower was writing, Alexander Comyn would probably have been held up as the epitome of Bower's definition of a good counsellor:

> In exercising government nothing is more advantageous for a king than to have good counsellors . . . For Cicero in his *De Senectute* says that a counsellor in the state is like a helmsman in a ship. In a ship some bale out the water, others pull on the ropes, while yet others climb the mast. But the helmsman sits quietly in the stern, and yet does far more than the others.[6]

As 'the helmsman' of Alexander III's kingship, Alexander Comyn continued his family's hereditary role as Crown trouble-shooters in the south-west and north, defining further Scottish royal authority in these areas, and playing an active military role against Norwegian forces in the battle for the Western Isles. He was also to play a major role in the definition of his kingdom's relationship with England when, firstly, Alexander III's marriage and then later succession problems posed threats to Scotland's independence and political integrity. The period 1258 to 1286 proved that the Scottish cause was already well-defined before war with England broke out in 1296. Alexander Comyn was a major contributor to the forging of the Scottish cause in Alexander III's reign.

The compromise council (agreed in September 1258), in which supporters from rival political factions during Alexander III's minority, the Comyn and Durward groups, were apparently willing to work together, is normally taken as a sign that the unsettled minority period was drawing to a close and that the young king Alexander III was now starting to exert more royal authority over his nobility.[7] However, yet again the monarcho-centric views of *Gesta Annalia* and Walter Bower have been allowed to supply a misleading framework for what really happened during Alexander III's maturity. It has been pointed out, for instance, that details of the so-called compromise council of 1258 are only known from an English source: 'It is certainly possible that the text of the document of 6th November 1258 which gave recognition to a council of ten *represents more what the English thought should happen in Scotland* rather than what the Scots felt bound to put into effect – and this applies not only to the people mentioned, but also to the tone of the text in that it implies the perpetuation, for some unspecified period, of a system of minority government under English supervision.'[8] As far as the Comyns are concerned, it has been accepted, until recently, that either they were in decline and no longer able to dominate the political scene as they had done in the 1240s and 1250s[9] or that they were 'willing to co-operate with their seventeen year old king in letting him run his own show'[10]. However, analysis of royal charters, offices held, and royal missions accomplished present a very different picture. There is little evidence of any balance imposed by Alexander III on the Comyn and Durward groups, only of the Comyn party's continued dominance of Scottish politics. Far from being eclipsed, the Comyns dominated political and public offices, royal missions and witness lists to royal charters.[11] By contrast, Alan Durward, though recognised as one of the leading nobles in Scotland in the late 1250s and early 1260s[12] witnessed relatively few royal charters (compared to Alexander Comyn) and was at the royal court infrequently in the 1270s.

It is striking that the same members of the Comyn party so roundly condemned in 1257 and 1258 (at least by the fourteenth and fifteenth-century Scottish narratives of *Gesta Annalia* and Walter Bower) retained the offices which they then held. This has obvious implications for Alexander Comyn's influence as leader of the Comyn 'party' after the death of his half-brother, Walter Comyn, Earl of Menteith, in 1258. The premier political office, the justiciarship of Scotia, which assumed so much more political weight during the minority period, continued to be held by Alexander Comyn, Earl of Buchan, from 1258 until his death in 1289. Alexander Comyn control over this key office is further reflected in the choice of deputies for this office. In 1260, Freskin de Moray, David de Lochore and John Cameron (the latter two both afterwards sheriffs of Perth) performed the office of justiciar in Earl Alexander's place.[13] David de Lochore was prominent in Comyn 'party' activities in 1251 and 1258 and remained a member of the Comyn following in the 1260s and 1270s. Freskin de Moray was also in the Comyn 'party' in 1258, the family were linked to the Comyns through marriage and were quite frequently in the Comyn circle. It seems clear that two of the three deputies for the justiciar of Scotia were selected from Alexander Comyn's close associates.

Further to Comyn domination of key offices of state after 1258, John Comyn, chief of the Badenoch branch of the family after his uncle Walter Comyn's death in 1258, held the justiciarship of Galloway in 1258, for a time in the 1260s and again in 1275. Other members of the Comyn following[14] who held the justiciarships were Thomas de Normanville, justiciar of Lothian c.1259–60, Hugh de Berkeley, justiciar of Lothian c.1262–79, William de Soules (son of Nicholas de Soules), justiciar of Lothian c.1279–92, and Aymer de Maxwell, justiciar of Galloway in 1264. With regard to other important offices, William Wishart retained the post of chancellor between 1258 and 1273. A succession of prominent Comyn supporters held the office of chamberlain between 1251 and 1290 – William, Earl of Mar (1251–5), Aymer de Maxwell (1258–66), Reginald Cheyne (1266–78) and Thomas Randolf II. Known Comyn supporters, Gamelin (a probable Comyn relative) and William Wishart, held the office of chancellor from c.1254 (with a break from 1255–7) until c.1273.

The office of sheriff, the right hand of the king in the localities and a crucial part of royal attempts to define and control the country, embraced military, financial, judicial and administrative duties.[15] Comyn dominance of offices of state was very apparent when the office-holders of Scottish sheriffdoms (often hereditary) are analysed.[16] Comyn men held the sheriffdoms of Fife (through the Lascelles family), Roxburgh, Dumfries, Dingwall, Forfar (through the Mowat family), Peebles, Perth, Kincardine (or Mearns), Elgin (through the Munfort family), Lanark, Berwick, Cromarty, Dumbarton, Wigtown and Ayr for much of Alexander III's reign. Some key Comyn men held a multiplicity of offices. Alexander Comyn, as well as being justiciar of Scotia, was sheriff of Wigtown c.1263–6, sheriff of Dingwall c.1264–6 and from c.1275 he was constable of Scotland. Aymer de Maxwell was chamberlain c.1259–60, justiciar of Galloway c.1264, sheriff of Roxburgh c.1249, sheriff of Peebles c.1262 and sheriff of Dumfries 1264–6; Thomas Randolph was chamberlain c.1269–77, sheriff of Roxburgh in 1266 and sheriff of Berwick c.1264–6 and was a frequent witness to the king's charters; William de Soules, son of Nicholas de Soules (related to Alexander Comyn through marriage), was justiciar of Lothian 1279–92/3, sheriff of Roxburgh by 1289 and before

1289–91 sheriff of Inverness, while John de Soules was sheriff of Berwick by 1289; David de Graham, who had been deputy justiciar of Lothian in 1248, was sheriff of Berwick c.1264, while his son Patrick was very prominent in royal witness lists of the 1270s and 1280s and was to be sheriff of Stirling by 1289. Both Patrick de Graham and John de Soules took part in Alexander III's search for a second bride in 1284.

Another prominent Comyn supporter was William, Earl of Mar, who married a sister of Alexander Comyn, Earl of Buchan. William was, for a time, chamberlain c.1252–5 but was also sheriff of Dumbarton c.1264–6 and a prominent witness of Alexander III's charters. Regular Comyn followers, the Mowats, featured in office through William, sheriff of Cromarty c.1266, Robert, sheriff of Forfar c.1250–64 and Michael who had been justiciar of Scotia c.1251–3, while Bernard Mowat was one of the nobles who escorted Margaret, daughter of Alexander III, to Norway and was a regular witness to Alexander III's charters. Two members of the Lochore family David and William were respectively sheriff of Fife c.1264–75 and sheriff of Perth 1255–62; William de St Clair (or Sinclair) was sheriff of Edinburgh, Linlithgow and Haddington c.1264 and a frequent witness to royal charters in the 1270s, while perhaps a son was sheriff of Dumfries by 1290; Reginald Cheyne was chamberlain c.1267–c.1269, and sheriff of Kincardine c.1264–6 – either this man or his son was sheriff of Kincardine by 1290 and both appeared regularly in royal witness lists. Hugh de Abernethy, from another family regularly in the Comyn following, was sheriff of Roxburgh c.1264 and was seen frequently in royal witness lists in the 1260s and 1270s.

It is interesting to find similar Comyn domination of ecclesiastical offices between 1260 and 1286.[17] Familiar names recur: Gamelin (a Comyn relative) was bishop of St Andrews 1255–71; Henry Cheyne was bishop of Aberdeen 1282–1328; William Comyn of Kilconquhar was bishop of Brechin 1275–7; William Wishart (from a family prominent in the 1251–5 Comyn government list of supporters) was Bishop of Glasgow 1270–71 and Bishop of St Andrews 1271–9, while Robert Wishart (more noted as a prominent supporter of Robert Bruce's kingship in 1306) was bishop of Glasgow 1271–1316.

Analysis of offices held and presence in the royal circle indicate a clear dominating influence of Alexander Comyn, Earl of Buchan, and the noble families who accepted his political leadership during

Alexander III's maturity. Alexander Comyn, Earl of Buchan, was the most regular of all witnesses to Alexander III's charters.[18] The Badenoch branch of the Comyn family, represented by John Comyn, father and son, was also present in the royal circle and the Comyns of Kilbride were well represented in the royal charter witness lists by William Comyn of Kilbride. Comyn dominance in government hardly suggests a delicate balancing act between rival 'factions'. Alexander Comyn's role as Alexander III's premier counsellor – he was the most regular of all witnesses to Alexander III's charters – fits in very well with Walter Bower's appraisal of Alexander III's government and the role of the justiciar in it:

> And so that he might put down all civil discord and insubordina-tion everywhere within his realm, he had this habit of travelling all over his kingdom almost every year with a strong company of picked knights and nobles, and of staying in a quarter of its districts for a fixed proportion of the year. He had his justiciar with him to administer justice to anyone at all, so that all the circumstances might be taken into account and justice promptly meted out to everyone. Also wherever it happened that the king approached on horseback from afar, it was customary for the sheriff of that shire, when warned of the king's approach, to go to meet him at the boundary of his sheriffdom with all the chosen knights of the shire.[19]

Alexander Comyn's itinerary with the king's court during Alexander III's maturity was certainly extensive[20] – Edinburgh, Stirling, Forfar, Scone, Arbroath, Roxburgh, Balmerino, Perth, Haddington, Linlithgow, Berwick, Selkirk, Holyrood, Lindores, Tyningham, Kinross, Kintore, Kelly (in his own earldom of Buchan) and Inverness. Journeys on the king's business, of course, caused Alexander Comyn to travel more widely within Scotland, for example for enquiries (justi-ciar's business) in Ayrshire and Kincardineshire, and his own land-holding in England as well as the Scottish king's business ensured that he was a regular visitor to England. It seems incongruous that he has been tarred by Walter Bower with the role of unprincipled aggressor, a threat to Scottish kingship itself on the basis of specific episodes in 1242–4 and 1257. However, Bower largely ignores his major role in government during Alexander III's maturity. It seems that the monar-cho-centric Walter Bower could not acknowledge the leading role of

Alexander Comyn in Alexander III's government, even if Alexander III, by his actions, certainly did. Perhaps he did not have the courage in a pro-Bruce environment to name Alexander Comyn as the epitome of a good king's counsellor!

The role of Alexander Comyn and his followers in Alexander III's government is contrasted with the roles of the four members of the so-called 1258 'compromise' council, men regarded by the English source as balancing the 'overmighty' Comyn presence – Alan Durward, Robert de Meyers (Menzies), Alexander Stewart and Gilbert de Hay. Of these men, only Gilbert de Hay is known to have held office, as sheriff of Perth (1262–3). Gilbert had been in the Comyn following in 1244 but was named in the non-Comyn council of fifteen in 1255. He was married to a sister of Alexander Comyn and it seems possible that he became reconciled to the Comyns after 1258. Robert de Menzies, who had also been in the Comyn following in 1244, appeared only occasionally in the royal circle in the 1260s. Alan Durward and Alexander Stewart appeared slightly more frequently at the royal court in the 1260s and 1270s, though without holding any office other than that indicated by their surnames: Durward – Doorward; Stewart – Steward.

When the other eleven names associated with the 1255 non-Comyn council are looked at, the dominance of Alexander Comyn's leadership of the political establishment becomes more apparent. Only Patrick, Earl of Dunbar, perhaps the leading baron of the 1255 non-Comyn council, appeared frequently in the royal circle in the 1260s and 1270s. In fact, only Alexander Comyn, Earl of Buchan, was a more frequent witness to Alexander III's charters in this period. Earl Patrick, however, remained without any political office or apparent government responsibility. Of the other three earls, associated with the non-Comyn council of seven years – Malise, Earl of Strathearn, Nigel, Earl of Carrick, and Malcolm, Earl of Fife – Earls Malise and Malcolm continued, albeit infrequently, to witness royal charters, and the successors to Earls Nigel and Malcolm appeared infrequently too. Of the other men named in the 1255 non-Comyn council – Robert Bruce, Walter de Moray, David de Lindsay, William de Brechin and Hugh Giffard – Walter de Moray appeared occasionally at the royal court in the 1260s, Robert de Bruce rather infrequently, and another member of the Lindsay family, Walter, appeared occasionally.

Marriage alliances extended the range of families under the influence of the Comyns and their leader, Alexander Comyn, and included families such as the earls of Dunbar, Strathearn and Fife as well as William de Brechin who had not previously been in the Comyn affinity. Alexander Comyn's sisters made good 'political' marriages – Elizabeth married William, Earl of Mar, prominent in Comyn support in the 1250s and a continuing influence through the 1260s; his half-sister Jean, married William, Earl of Ross; Idonea married Gilbert de Hay; and Agnes married Philip de Meldrum. This trend continued with five of Alexander Comyn's daughters marrying major Scottish barons: Patrick, Earl of Dunbar, Malise, Earl of Strathearn, Gilbert de Umphraville, Earl of Angus, William de Brechin and Nicholas de Soules. Further, Alexander's son and heir John married Isabella, daughter of Colban, Earl of Fife. The marriages of the Badenoch branch of the Comyn family further strengthened this network of influence for Alexander Comyn. John Comyn I, Lord of Badenoch (d. 1277), had a large family – five sons and four daughters. His son and heir, John II, Lord of Badenoch (d. c.1302), married Mary or Marjorie sister of John Balliol (the future king), probably in the 1270s; according to Andrew Wyntoun who was very knowledgeable about the Comyns (perhaps through access to a pro-Comyn *St Andrews Chronicle*), John Comyn I's four daughters married Richard Siward, Geoffrey de Mowbray, Alexander MacDougall, Lord of Argyll, and Alexander Moray. These marriages helped to consolidate Alexander Comyn's leadership of the Scottish aristocratic governing community, both socially and politically, after 1258.

The reality of the Scottish political establishment in Alexander III's reign was Comyn dominance, but other families grew in prominence in the period too. Members of the Moray family gathered political strength in the period 1258–86. Alexander de Moray was sheriff of Inverness after 1264 and sheriff of Ayr by 1288. Malcolm de Moray was sheriff of Perth 1255X89 and other members of the family, Walter and William, were witnesses to several royal charters. They seem to have been associated with the Comyns. Freskin de Moray was linked to the Comyns by marriage and was certainly in the Comyn following in 1258 when a treaty was made with the Welsh. Other members of the family (Walter and Malcolm) appeared as witnesses to charters of Alexander Comyn in the 1260s. A daughter of John Comyn I, Lord of Badenoch, married Alexander de Moray. Thus it seems that the rise of the Morays was principally due to their association with the Comyns. This did not, however, apply to the Stewarts. With their hereditary position as steward of Scotland and their vast estates derived from the first royal grants to the family in the twelfth century, the power of the Stewarts was already established by the middle of the thirteenth century, with access to the royal council.[21] They were prominent in the non-Comyn political groupings in 1255 and 1258 and stepped more firmly to the forefront of the political stage after 1260. Walter Stewart, a younger member of the family, became Earl of Menteith in controversial circumstances c.1261, was sheriff of Ayr by 1264, sheriff of Dumbarton between 1271 and 1288 and was also prominent in royal witness lists in the 1280s. Alexander Stewart and his son James were regularly in the royal circle from the 1250s to the 1280s and James was sheriff of Ayr late in 1288 and sheriff of Dumbarton in 1289. From a less prominent background and with no known affiliation at first (though they were linked with the Comyns by the 1290s) were the Frasers, especially in the person of Simon Fraser, sheriff of Peebles, in the 1260s and a very regular witness to royal charters in the 1260s and 1270s. Richard Fraser and William Fraser, chancellor (and later Bishop of St Andrews), also appeared in the royal circle and the family had emerged to a position of some importance.

Comyns, Stewarts and Morays seem to have been the principal beneficiaries of an alliance of mutual benefit between Crown and aristocracy. They had sufficient territorial influence for their authority in the regions, wielded on behalf of the king, to be accepted in the north and the south-west, or, in the case of the Comyns, in both areas. The Crown was dependent on its magnates for wielding royal power successfully in the provinces. Interdependence was the logical outcome of a situation where the Scottish king had enough material wealth to reward nobles but not enough to overawe them. The nobility did not (unlike their counterparts in England) have to suffer the consequences of an aggressive and expensive foreign policy with its heavy taxes (aides, scutages and tallages). It does, however, help to explain why the aristocratic leadership in Scotland was prepared to fight for the preservation of Scotland's independence. The nobles who were the Scottish king's aristocratic governing community had a real interest in preserving the integrity of the Scottish kingdom and extending (as well as defending) the authority of a king who could give them and their followers rich rewards. The long-believed notion that there was, in Scotland, an 'inveterate hostility of great houses to the Crown and to each other'[22] could hardly be further from the reality of politics between 1260 and 1286. It is also appropriate to note that the names which dominated the politics of the 1290s – Bruce and Balliol – featured very little in the politics of 1260–86. Members of the Balliol family made only occasional appearances in the Scottish king's circle. The name Bruce made very little impact at the Scottish court in the 1260s, though after gaining the earldom of Carrick in 1272 Robert Bruce (the father of the future king) began to make some impact in the later 1270s. Neither Balliols or Bruces, however, held political office or looked like disturbing the Comyn grip on the aristocratic governing elite. It is hardly surprising that the Bruce family had to resort to violent measures to break into this elite after Alexander III's sudden death in 1286.

The Patriot Lessons from Alexander III's Minority

What is clear is that the Scottish political community under the leadership of Alexander Comyn, Earl of Buchan, after 1258 had 'patriot' credentials from their experience of the 1250s and were very keen to curtail Henry III's further involvement in Scottish affairs. In 1255, the Scots – though the Comyn party led by Walter Comyn and including Alexander Comyn, Earl of Buchan, and William, Earl of Mar, had refused to put their names to the document setting up the new council which excluded them – had agreed to the continuation of the minority until 1262. This implied Henry III would still have some supervisory role until that date. Those Scottish lords (including Alexander Comyn) supervising the young Alexander III in 1258 (the king was still only seventeen at the time) were keen to counter, with force, any English interference in that year as the contemporary Scottish chronicle, the *Melrose Chronicle* demonstrated:

> About the Nativity of blessed Mary [8 September], the king of Scotland came, with his army, against the aforesaid traitors [Durward and his supporters]; he had heard that they had arrived with forces, *and certain magnates, from the king of England* . . . the earl of Hereford, and the earl of Aumale, and John Balliol came to him [at Melrose] as if with a view to tranquillise the people . . . but in reality (as rumour declared) on purpose to take the king again, and carry him off with them to the king of England. But this was no means concealed from the king of Scotland . . .
>
> And after the completion of three weeks [at a conference at Jedburgh], the aforesaid envoys perceiving that the army of Scotland had now assembled [at Melrose] and was ready to fall upon them, if they delayed; and also that they had not sufficient

strength to resist, concluded peace between the aforesaid traitors and their opponents.[23]

The contemporary nationalistic narratives from Scotland (*Melrose Chronicle*) and England (Matthew Paris) again prove to give a more detailed picture of Anglo-Scottish relations (and patriot activities) in this period than either *Gesta Annalia* and Walter Bower. In 1259, Master William de Horton came to Scotland on behalf of Henry III to discuss with the Scottish king matters concerning the minority and the king of England's part in it. He asked that the young king and queen should come to England to discuss the matter with Henry. Matthew Paris reflects the nationalist suspicions of the Scottish king's counsellors:

> And after [the Scots] had put in the way much opposition and obstruction of difficulties he at last, after various disputes, by persisting in diligent petition persuaded them prudently to this, so that he obtained their consent according to his desire. For they wrote to him their letters patent, sealed in common both with the king's seal and that of all the magnates of Scotland, to the king of England and the whole community, and gladly agreed to do their will *provided only that the king of England and his magnates would assure them of the document* which had been faithfully promised to them.[24]

The document referred to must surely have been the agreement (1255) to continue the minority (under the supervision of the anti-Comyn council and, by implication, Henry III). The matter required further discussion by the most influential members of the Scottish government, probably under the leadership of Alexander Comyn:

> and immediately after his [William de Horton's] return, [the Scottish king and magnates] sent to England their messengers of state, to wit the earl of Buchan [Alexander], master William [Wishart] the chancellor and sir Alan Durward, to treat more fully with the king of England and his council concerning the affair aforesaid. And when they had come and spoken with the said William, who had preceded them, they returned, leaving no testimony in public concerning the success of their affair with the king and the community of the realm.[25]

The episode revealed how the new compromise government in Scotland was working in practice (rather than the theory of the 'English' document of November 1258) – it showed that Comyn dominance continued under Alexander Comyn, the Scottish king's justiciar and chief counsellor. The Scottish 'attitude' to English interference was firmly articulated in 1259, no doubt taking advantage of Henry III's political difficulties in England after 1258. Neither Scottish or English king was in full control of their governments in the period 1258–60.[26]

Alexander Comyn and his supporters, on behalf of their young king, were fully prepared to take advantage of Henry III's political discomfiture in Scottish interests as revealed by *Flores Historiarum* in 1260:[27]

> the king of Scotland came to London, led by various causes: namely to visit the king of England and the queen, and to exercise lordship and dominion over his earldom of Huntingdon. Moreover, he declared the more especial cause of his arrival, and asked from the king four thousand marks to be given to him, as he said had been previously promised him by the same king in the espousal of his wife; also the whole land between Tyne and Tweed, which he asserted had been formerly given to his predecessors; also aid of men from the king and the magnates of the land against his enemies, even as he had formerly promised them and the nobles of Scotland by his signed document, taken charge of and sent by brother William de Horton.

Henry III's preoccupations and the pressures applied by the Comyn-led Scottish council were already evident in a letter of 14 May 1259 from the English king to the king of Scotland:

> [Henry] acknowledges the messages delivered by his envoy John de Dundemor [in the Comyn following and witness to the Treaty with the Welsh princes on 18 March 1258] regarding the money which the writer owes. On account of the peace between himself and the King of France, his expedition against his rebels in Wales, and the affairs of Sicily, he is involved in great expenses, and is unable to pay at present. But by Michaelmas next he hopes to do so in whole or part. Regarding a writing made between them, which the King of Scotland wishes restored, the King can do nothing in the absence of his nobles and councillors present at its execution. As to Alexander's request by his said envoy that the

king would not object to his coronation, the King thinks the present an unsuitable time for it, but when a better season arrives, will act as befits his honour.[28]

It is clear that the Comyn-led Scottish council, acting on behalf of the Scottish king, was pressing for 'patriot' rights and that Alexander Comyn was continuing the policy of Walter Comyn in protecting Scottish rights and guarding against Henry's interference. Alexander was now pushing for more rights which would increase the status of both king and kingdom, for example Henry's consent to Alexander's coronation.

The arrangements for a visit to the English royal court by the young Scottish king and queen in the late summer of 1260 further illustrates the 'patriot' credentials of Alexander Comyn and his Scottish council. It seems as if the king's council may not have been in favour of the visit but they were certainly aware of the political and constitutional dangers for Scotland's integrity and independence:

> [30 Sept 1260] Neither he [Alexander] nor his attendants are to be required to treat of state affairs during their visit.

and:

> The King made an oath on his soul, by his knight William le Latimer, that should his daughter the Queen of Scotland become pregnant in England, he should neither detain her, nor her child, if born there, and should the King its father die, it should be delivered to the magnates of Scotland.[29]

An English source claimed that the Scots were ignorant of the young queen's pregnancy before she came to England:

> [February 1261] ... the Scots took it very ill that their queen should have been delivered outside of her own realm; for they had been altogether ignorant when she departed that she was so near to her confinement. For she had carefully hidden this from them and from the king.[30]

The response to the pregnancy on 16 November 1260 showed extremely shrewd counsel and political pressure from the Scottish king's advisers. Lessons had been learnt from 1249 by Alexander Comyn and other experienced councillors as no formal plans had apparently been made before Alexander II's sudden death. The dangers of a minority were certainly grasped by those magnates like Alexander Comyn who were involved in the power struggles between 1249 and 1258. These dangers were implicit in their terms and conditions which tried to counter any possibility of Scottish government disintegrating:

> Alexander King of Scotland having granted that his spouse should remain with her mother in England till her lying-in, the King her father promises to deliver his daughter and her offspring, after her purification, viz. forty days after the birth, or at least at Easter 1261, to her husband or his envoys sent for them. Should the mother die, he promises to restore her child; and if the latter die, to allow the mother to return freely. Should the King, its father die meanwhile, or other unforeseen event occur to him, the King promises that the Bishops of St. Andrews, Aberdeen, Dunblane and Whithorn; and the Earls of Fife, Buchan, Strathearn, Dunbar and Mar; and John Comyn, Alexander the Steward of Scotland, Alan Durward and Hugh de Abernethy, barons, or four or three of them, shall receive and take the child to Scotland; the state of neither kingdom being taken into account.[31]

The blueprint for a future minority government was laid – if the Scottish king should die, a body of thirteen men (in effect, a regency council of four bishops, five earls and four barons) or three or four of them would take his heir to Scotland and have responsibility for government. It is significant that the council of regency was carefully thought out. The formal arrangements were probably based on the informal alliance worked out in September 1258. It was an arrangement which also formalised Comyn dominance – Comyn members of the group were Alexander Comyn, Earl of Buchan, and John Comyn I of Badenoch with their associates William, Earl of Mar, and Hugh de Abernethy. Malise, Earl of Strathearn, may also have been in the Comyn 'party' – he had married a daughter of Alexander Comyn. Comyn influence was dominant amongst the bishops. Such formal and mature constitutional procedures were a sign of a responsible, aristocratic governing community in which the Comyns played a key part and Alexander, Earl of Buchan, a leading part.

The early years of Alexander III's kingship had shown consistent Church support for Comyn leadership of the Scottish political community and the 'patriot' cause which they shared (see pages 48–9, 53–6). Church support had sanctioned the Comyn kidnapping of young Alexander III in 1257 and condemned the taking of the king by Alan Durward in 1255 as 'treason'. The Church had held a long-term policy of resistance to claims of the English Church to jurisdiction over them. Papal taxation also posed a threat to the 'freedom' of the Scottish Church despite the position of the Scottish Church, since the 1192 papal bull '*Cum Universi*', as the 'special daughter' of the papacy which promised protection from external interference. The issue of papal taxation for crusades caused a complication for Scotland's relationship with England and threatened Scotland's special protection. In 1250, the papacy had ordered the bishops of St Andrews and Aberdeen to collect offerings in Scotland for the Holy Land but added that anything left over from Scottish crusaders was to go to Henry III when he set out on crusade. The Scottish Church fiercely resisted 'crusade money' being diverted for English use, but the issue was a constant one in Alexander III's reign[32] and engendered heightened 'nationalist' feelings. Henry III tried to exploit the ambiguity in the papal position. For example, when Henry III (after agreeing to lead a crusade in 1251) asked for clerical taxation granted in his lands to be extended to Scotland, Pope Innocent IV rejected this as 'unheard of in another's kingdom' but in 1254 reversed this decision. Henry III's need for money had increased in 1254 as he sought a Mediterranean kingdom for his son and agreed with the pope that Edmund would gain the Hohenstaufen kingdom of Sicily on payment of £90,000 to the papacy *and* finance a Mediterranean war. Pressure on Scotland to contribute clerical taxation mounted after this. The Scottish Church tended to reject taxation to pay the English king's schemes but agreed a general crusading tax in 1274.

The Scottish Church's sense of national identity and independence was given focus by the increased interest in national religious icons. Queen Margaret, the ancestor of the Scottish royal house of Canmore, was canonised in c.1250 and the 'placing of her remains in a jewel-covered shrine and their removal to a newly-built reliquary chapel behind the high altar [Dunfermline] was an event of supreme national religious and political significance'.[33] Margaret was not the only Scottish saint given special attention as the Scottish Church sought to demonstrate a distinct sense of its own national identity in

Alexander III's reign. The early years of Alexander's reign saw the completion of a new Gothic shrine of St Kentigern in Glasgow while the same period saw the remains of St Duthac of Tain translated from Ireland to his birthplace. Above all, however, was the growth of the cult of St Andrew as a focus for both the national identity of the Scottish Church and the kingdom itself. The authority of the bishopric of St Andrews increased along with the cult of St Andrew. The accession of William Fraser to the bishopric of St Andrews in 1279 saw the seal of the bishopric bearing the image of St Andrews crucified. The seal, altogether more elaborate and self-important than previous representations, has, on one side, the bishop in pontificals with the legend 'Seal of William Fraser, Bishop of the Scots,' with, on the other side, St Andrew tied onto his cross of martyrdom with the bishop kneeling below the legend 'Seal of William Fraser, Bishop of St Andrews'.[34] As noted by Marinell Ash, the final phase in the development of the St Andrews legend made clear that St Andrew ruled over all the people of Scotland 'the Picts, Scots, Danes and Norwegians'. That St Andrew had come to represent not only the Scottish Church but Scotland itself is shown in the Seal of Guardianship after Alexander III's sudden death in 1286 – on one side a shield of the royal arms, on the other side the figure of St Andrew on his cross with the inscription 'Andrew be leader of the compatriot Scots'.

Both the Scottish Church and the Scottish monarchy sought, and to a large extent, gained increasing definition of their rights, integrity and independence as the thirteenth century progressed. Whilst this is increasingly acknowledged, the role of the aristocratic governing community in this development has been obscured by the anti-nobility writings of nationalist narratives of the fourteenth and fifteenth centuries. The Comyns, as the dominant aristocratic family of thirteenth-century Scottish government, contributed significantly to the defence of royal and ecclesiastical rights. In the second half of the thirteenth century, bishops were either royal servants or from families linked to noble families such as the Comyns (or, indeed, both): 'the favour of Alexander III and the tentacles of Comyn patronage extended far into the benefice structure of the late thirteenth-century secular Church'.[35] The Comyns were integral to the developments of an independent Scottish kingdom and an 'ecclesia Scoticana' maturing together in Alexander III's reign. It is, therefore, to be wondered why they have not been given greater credit for these key aspects of Scottish national identity in the thirteenth century. Perhaps more credence should be given to the main contemporary Scottish narrative of the thirteenth century, the *Melrose Chronicle*, and its consistently pro-Comyn line. Evidence from the now lost *St Andrews Chronicle* would surely have confirmed and strengthened this pro-Comyn version of key thirteenth-century developments. Comyn domination of Scottish politics in the second of the thirteenth century had been supported by a line of pro-Comyn bishops of St Andrews. Gamelin (1255–71) was probably a member of the Comyn family; William Wishart (from a family prominent in the 1251–5 list of Comyn supporters) was bishop of St Andrews 1271–9, while William Fraser (from a family of Comyn supporters)[36] was bishop of St Andrews 1279–97. As has been seen, Comyn domination of ecclesiastical offices was apparent in other bishoprics and Church support for the Comyns was clear throughout Alexander III's minority.

Definition of the Kingdom in the West

Just as the nobility in Scotland, especially those actively involved in government, had a real interest in preserving the independence and integrity of both the Scottish Church and the Scottish kingdom, they also had a real incentive in extending the authority of its king. Alexander Comyn's role as justiciar was invaluable to the king politically, administratively, judicially and financially, but it was also very important militarily. Alexander Comyn played a leading part along with Alexander Stewart in the defence of the country against a Norwegian threat in the 1260s and also in the extension of royal authority in the Western Isles. He can thus be seen as continuing the family's role as royal trouble-shooters in thirteenth-century Scotland – his father, William Comyn, Earl of Buchan, had brought a degree of royal control to northern Scotland in 1211–12 and 1229. During the 1240s Alexander II had turned his royal focus on the Western Isles and the attempt to annexe the Isles from Norway, but died unexpectedly during an expedition against Argyll in 1249. Not long after the end of the minority of Alexander III (in the early 1260s) Alexander III sought to resume his father's policy. Hakon IV, King of Norway, continued to maintain his lordship over the Western Isles from Man to Lewis. Henry III's own political problems after 1258 gave Alexander III the opportunity to pursue his father's policy. In the 1250s, Henry had enjoyed good relationships with Hakon and c.1255–6 a marriage alliance was being planned between Hakon's eldest son Magnus, and

Henry III's daughter Beatrice. This alliance was intended to help Henry with his wider European schemes but also to exercise some strategic control in the isles and the western coast of Scotland and also improve his position in northern Ireland.[37]

Alexander III, in conjunction with his chief lords in the west, was able to exploit Henry III's diminishing capacity to exert influence there after 1258. Alexander initially sought to buy Hakon's rights in the Western Isles in 1261, but this pressure, along with the plundering of the Isle of Skye by the earl of Ross, produced a hostile reaction. In 1263, Alexander and his lords with lands and interests neighbouring the Western Isles had to prepare the country for defence. The Comyns – all three branches, Buchan, Badenoch and Kilbride – Alexander Stewart and his brother Walter, Earl of Menteith, as well as the earls of Ross and Strathearn (both earls were related to the Comyns by marriage) were involved. Alexander Comyn's role was a very prominent one in the Scottish counter to the Norwegian threat.

In 1263, King Hakon of Norway 'with a large number of ships, came over the western sea to attack the king of Scotland' according to the contemporary *Melrose Chronicle*. The later *Gesta Annalia* account elaborated (and exaggerated): 'Hako, king of Norway, came to the new castle of Ayr, with eight score warships, having on board 20,000 fighting men: for he said that all the Scottish islands lying between Ireland and Scotland were his by right of inheritance. So he took the castles of Bute and Man, and sacked the churches along the seaboard.'[38] It is not certain whether the Norwegian action was planned as an invasion or merely a show of strength. There was no large pitched battle. A storm arose, many Norwegian ships were blown aground near Largs and after fighting ensued, the Norwegians were defeated. Though the defeat of the Norwegians could be put down largely to the unfriendliness of the elements, Alexander Comyn's supervisory role in the Scottish defence is obvious from the records.

Initially, Alexander Comyn and Alan Durward had joint responsibilities in the defence against the Norwegians.[39] In 1264 Alexander III had sent a fleet to Man to force King Magnus, son-in-law of the Norwegian king, into submission – Magnus was forced to do homage to the Scottish king at Dumfries. After this business was settled:

Alexander Comyn, earl of Buchan, William earl of Mar, and Alan the Hostiary [Durward], took with them, with due haste, by the king's instructions, no mean band of knights and natives, and

went to the Western Isles of Scotland, where they slew those traitors who had, the year before, encouraged the king of Norway to
bring up in Scotland. Some of these they put to flight, and having
hanged some of the chiefs, they brought with them thence exceed-
ing great plunder.[40]

Gesta Annalia

This shows that, while defence against Norwegian forces was one
priority, the establishment of firmer royal control in the region against
dissident Scots was also a major concern. In addition to strategic
command, Alexander Comyn, as shown by the Exchequer Roll
accounts between 1264 and 1266, was also given added tactical
responsibility for coastal defence as both sheriff and baillie.[41] Baillies
were administrators of portions of Crown lands or sometimes of lands
temporarily in Crown occupation for strategic reasons (as in 1263–4).
In his account as baillie of Inverie (probably Inverie in Knoydart) there
is direct evidence of Alexander Comyn's involvement in the prepara-
tions against the Norwegian threat. Besides outlay on repairs for the
royal castle and drawbridge at Inverie, he dispersed 104 shillings on
the food for eight soldiers garrisoning Inverie Castle for six months. In
1265, in his account as sheriff of Wigtown, he referred to 40 marks
attorned to master Peter the mason in order that he might repair the
houses inside the castle of Wigtown. In his account as sheriff of
Wigtown in 1266, there is reference to Alexander's payment of envoys
between the kings of Scotland and Man. He must have been sheriff of
Wigtown by c.1263–4 and he was also baillie of Dingwall by 1264–6
– this was another key area for coastal defence against possible
invasion.

By the Treaty of Perth of 2 July 1266, the Western Isles and the Isle
of Man were ceded to Scotland in return for payment of 4,000 marks
and an annual rent of 100 marks.[42] In the definition of the kingdom of
Scotland and royal authority within it, the Treaty of Perth was an
important treaty and it is a reflection of Alexander Comyn's importance in this process that he was the first layman to append his seal to
this significant document. In his various roles as justiciar of Scotia,
sheriff of Wigtown, sheriff of Dingwall and baillie of Inverie, Alexander
Comyn played a major role, not only in the defence of Scotland but in
the reorganisation of royal authority in the south-west and north of
the kingdom. The erection of sheriffdoms at Wigtown and Dingwall
c.1263 was an important extension of the general pattern of

sheriffdoms made in the 1260s. That both sheriffdoms were placed under Alexander Comyn's control, apparently as hereditary offices, showed a continuing royal confidence in the Comyn family as royal agents for settling areas of ill-defined authority. Alexander Comyn's personal interest in the remote isles did not end in the 1260s. In 1282 he was sent on urgent royal business to the 'remote' isles.[43] In a letter to excuse his absence from conflicting responsibilities in England – he had been summoned as an English tenant-in-chief to serve Edward I in a campaign against the Welsh – Alexander III made it clear to the English king that Earl Alexander's activities in the Isles were indispensable to both the Scottish king and kingdom. Alexander Comyn himself wrote to Edward I that 'we cannot leave this road [to the Isles] by our honour'.

Other families such as the Stewarts played a leading role in defining royal authority in the west with Walter Stewart, Earl of Menteith c.1261, becoming sheriff of Ayr by 1264 and sheriff of Dumbarton between 1271 and 1288 and Alexander Stewart's son James had become sheriff of Ayr by 1288 and sheriff of Dumbarton by 1289. However, as well as Alexander Comyn's personal role in the west there was his leadership role of the Comyn party and their associates which greatly extended Comyn influence in the west. John Comyn of Badenoch (d. c.1277) had important landed influence in Dumfriesshire and held the important post of justiciar of Galloway in 1258, probably 1262X1272 and again in 1275. In 1275 John Comyn was one of the leaders of a royal military expedition against a revolt in Man:

> the king of Scotland heard that the people of Man had conspired with Godfrey, and that [Godfrey] ruled in the land as king . . . and caused more than ninety ships to be collected, with a great army, from Galloway and the islands. And the leaders of the army were John de Vescy, a great baron of England; John Comyn, justiciar of Galloway; Alan Fitz Count; Alexander Fitz John, of Argyle; and Alan Fitz Rother.[44]
>
> *Annals of Furness*

Comyn presence in the south-west was further emphasised by the involvement of William Comyn of Kilbride as sheriff of Ayr c.1265. The importance attached to William Comyn's contribution to the development of royal authority in the west is perhaps gauged by the regular appearances in the royal circle especially in the 1270s. The contribution of all three branches of the Comyn family – under the co-ordination of their leader Alexander Comyn – to the extension of royal authority in the west is further highlighted when the role of Comyn associates is taken into consideration. Thus William, Earl of Mar (married to Alexander's sister Elizabeth), was sheriff of Dumbarton c.1264–6, Aymer de Maxwell was sheriff of Dumfries c.1264–5, while in the north the sheriffdom of Cromarty was founded c.1266 as another hereditary office for the Mowat family. The marriage of a daughter of John I, Lord of Badenoch, to Alexander MacDougall of Argyll was an important strategic strengthening of Comyn influence (and therefore royal influence) in an important area for Scottish royal authority. Similarly, Alexander Comyn's half-sister Jean, married William, Earl of Ross, giving him another key area of influence in northern Scotland. It can easily be seen how much Alexander III relied on Alexander Comyn and his wide-ranging web of influence in the west and north.

The Heart of Alexander Comyn's Power

The personal and political power of Scotland's noble elite depended to a large extent on their territorial influence. Alexander Comyn's principal landholding came to him through the earldom of Buchan[45] which he inherited c.1244. The Comyn earls of Buchan held considerable lands elsewhere. South of the Tay, his father and mother (the heiress of Buchan) held substantial lands in Fife including Kennoway, Kilrenny, Fithkil (now Leslie) and Balmullo (Leuchars) which had probably come to the Celtic earls of Buchan through Earl Colban. Alexander Comyn also inherited landed interests in Strathisla (Banffshire) and Dumbennan, just west of Huntly in Strathbogie, land near Coull in Mar, and Fordoun in the Mearns. Evidence from Alexander Comyn's charters and the witnesses to these charters indicate that the most significant part of his possessions was in Buchan supplemented by the earldom lands in Fife. The majority of Alexander Comyn's charters dealt with land in Buchan while their witness lists have a distinct north of Scotland bias. The Buchan families of Mowat of (probably) Balquholly, Meldrum (Fedarg) of Meldrum, and Cheyne of Inverugie were prominent as well as being firm political supporters. Other north-easterners such as William of Slains, John of Kindroucht, Andrew of Garioch, and Walter and Maurice de Moray, can also be found in the earl of Buchan's following. The ecclesiastical witnesses to Earl

Alexander's charters were almost all connected with the north-east: they include Bishop Richard de Pottun of Aberdeen, Roger of Derby, canon (1259) and precentor (1264–5) of Aberdeen, Roger 'Paternoster', later chancellor of Aberdeen (1321), Roger of Scartheburg, 'official' of Aberdeen and Robert of Leslie, rector of Slains. The witness lists of Alexander Comyn included a number of men from Fife, such as William of Abernethy, David of Lochore, Richard of Bickerton, Michael of Arnot, Duncan of Crombie and John of Kinnear. Members of the Lascelles family, who held 'Balmonethe' in Fife of the earls of Buchan, were especially prominent in these witness lists, appeared in Alexander Comyn's entourage and continued to be seen as Comyn supporters in 1292 and 1296.

Alexander Comyn's territorial wealth in Scotland was greatly increased in 1264 on the death of Roger de Quincy, one of the greatest magnates of the thirteenth century.[46] Alexander had married Elizabeth, one of the three daughters and co-heiresses of Roger de Quincy, who thus inherited vast estates in 1264. Through his wife, Alexander acquired large estates in Fife, Galloway, Dumfriesshire and Lothian. It is in keeping with Alexander's status within the royal circle that the custody of Roger de Quincy's lands went to him (one of the interested parties) and not to royal clerks. Alexander was keeper of two-thirds of Roger's Galloway lands and also held two parts of Carrick at farm. Earl Alexander established himself even more closely with the king by acquiring another office, the office of constable, c.1275, again as a result of the de Quincy inheritance. The office of constable brought with it lands in Perth, Clackmannan, Inverness and Cowie near Stonehaven. The combination of de Quincy and Buchan lands made Alexander Comyn one of the greatest magnates in Scotland. The Buchan branch's new interests in the south-west, through royal office (the sheriffdom of Wigtown) and inheritance added to those of the Badenoch branch of the Comyn family in the region. John Comyn of Badenoch had important estates in Dumfriesshire and well as being justiciar of Galloway from c.1258.

It is clear, however, that Alexander Comyn was not diverted southwards by the de Quincy inheritance. In fact, he surrendered part of the inheritance in order to build up his north-east possessions. Significantly, Alexander Comyn exchanged territory in Tranent (East Lothian) for Mortlach and its important castle of Balvenie, in Highland Banffshire – a charter of 1285 shows this transaction had taken place a generation earlier.[47] Balvenie was a most valuable strategic site, making a bridge between Buchan and the lordship of Badenoch (and Lochaber) the two real seats of power for the Comyns in thirteenth-century Scotland. Alexander also gained the thanage of Conveth on the western border of the earldom at an annual ferme (rent) of 80 marks.[48] Though Alexander's territorial gains in the south-west via the de Quincy inheritance were strategically important for the Comyn family and their role as a royal agent in the region, the value and status of these lands were probably much less than that of the earldom of Buchan. The value of Roger de Quincy's Scottish lands has been estimated at around £400 per annum and Alexander Comyn's income from his wife's Scottish lands can hardly have been much more than £150 per year, considerably less than that from the earldom of Buchan.[49] In 1293, Alexander's son and successor John was asked for a relief of 1,417 marks to succeed to his overall Buchan inheritance in Scotland.[50]

Alexander's charters, witness lists and castles all show where his true power lay. The sparseness of documentary and architectural/archaeological evidence for Comyn castles in Buchan makes it difficult to date Alexander Comyn's architectural patronage precisely, but several clues suggest that most development took place from c.1260 in the more settled political conditions after Alexander III's minority had ended. Evidence from his better recorded ecclesiastical patronage gives some clues. Alexander Comyn founded two almshouses in Buchan in 1261 and 1272 – one was founded in the south-east of the earldom at Newburgh, probably the earldom's main burgh in 1261; the second almshouse, rather larger, was founded at Turriff to the west of the earldom in 1272. It is probable that visible signs of secular lordship complemented these foundations. The acquisition of Balvenie after 1264 (and before c.1285) could also have been part of a concentrated programme of castle building and strengthening by Alexander Comyn after 1260. It is not certain how much building was actually undertaken by Alexander after his acquisition of Balvenie, strategically situated only 20 miles from Badenoch's eastern boundary and therefore an invaluable link between the castles of the lordship of Badenoch and those of the earldom of Buchan. Perched on a high promontory above the River Fiddich, Balvenie Castle commanded the mouths of Glen Rinnes and Glenfiddich, the passes to Huntly, Keith and Cullen and the route to Elgin.[51] The earliest plan of the castle – a large quadrangular court (158 feet by 130 feet) enclosed by high walls (over 25 feet in places and 7 feet thick) with towers (now gone) at the west and north corners with another tower probably at the east where there is now a large sixteenth-century round tower – has been dated to the close of the thirteenth century. This suggests that most of the work was done after Alexander Comyn acquired the site. One of the most noteworthy features of Balvenie Castle is the wide (averaging 40 feet) peat-bottomed ditch, 12 feet deep in places, which enclosed the castle on three sides. The greater outer ditch, together with the wall walk which claimed the thirteenth-century enceinte, formed the chief defence of the castle.[52]

There are few visible remains of the thirteenth-century Comyn castles in Buchan due to the destruction of these symbols of Comyn power by Robert Bruce in the infamous 'herschip' (harrying) of Buchan in 1308. The coastal castles of Buchan – Dundarg, Cairnbulg, Rattray and Slains – form an impressive well-sited grouping. On the north coast was Dundarg (New Aberdour) positioned on a rock of red sandstone looking northwards over the Moray Firth. It seems probable that there was a castle here in the thirteenth century though archaeological evidence is inconclusive. East of Dundarg, in the corner of Buchan, is Cairnbulg (originally known as Philorth). Cairnbulg's impressive tower house rises over a mid thirteenth-century basement. Further down the coast at Rattray, there is another probable motte site, which commanded the chief port of thirteenth-century Buchan. Recent excavation of two-thirds of the castle mound has revealed the foundations of the main thirteenth-century phase, with perimeter walls including two mural buildings and harbour side entrance and a multi-storeyed building free-standing on the mound centre. Further south is Slains standing on a rocky peninsula where documentary evidence has shown there was a castle in 1261. There is little archaeological or architectural evidence to show the structure of that thirteenth-century castle. At Slains there is a stone tower of the fourteenth century; the outer ward, on the slopes of the mainland, enclosed a wall and was defended by earthen ramparts which may be older than the stone castle. Inland, there was a prominent Comyn of Buchan stronghold at Kingedward whose constable was referred to in 1272. Situated prominently on a bold precipitous rock protected by the Kingedward Burn on the south and on the north-east angle by a deep ditch which severed the neck of the peninsula, Kingedward appears to have been a motte and the ground plan indicates a castle belonging exclusively to the thirteenth century. Its enclosing walls had no angle towers. Like other Comyn castles in Buchan, Kingedward suffered in Bruce's 'herschip' and was subsequently rebuilt.

Other important inland centres of Alexander Comyn's earldom of Buchan were Kelly (now Haddo) and Ellon, though there is no direct evidence that there were castles at these sites. We know that at least two of Earl Alexander's charters were issued at Kelly in 1261 and 1272, the latter witnessed by King Alexander III himself as well as the leading nobles of the land. That Kelly was where the king and his court were entertained indicates its significance – it appears probable that there was a medieval manor house there rather than a castle. The use of fourteenth-century documentary evidence to supplement the sparse thirteenth-century evidence[53] has helped to establish Ellon as the legal centre of the earldom. Ellon was the caput (head) of the earldom in the pre-Comyn and in the early modern period, but there is no evidence of thirteenth-century building and there was much rebuilding later in the Middle Ages. Fourteenth-century evidence after the fall of the Comyns has shown that the castles at Kingedward, Rattray, Slains, Dundarg and Cairnbulg all acted as administrative centres for running five local subdivisions within the earldom of Buchan. With Kelly as the domestic centre, Ellon the legal centre, and Deer Abbey the religious centre, the key centres at the heart of Alexander Comyn's power base can be revealed though the lack of architectural/archaeological evidence makes it difficult to be precise about his architectural patronage.

Alexander Comyn inherited another important castle site in Galloway through the de Quincy inheritance of his wife Elizabeth. Cruggleton Castle, inherited after 1264, and originally a stronghold of the lords of Galloway, was well situated on a cliff top. Although in the twelfth century it had a motte, excavation has revealed that this was replaced in the middle of the thirteenth century by a substantial stone castle of enclosure with a keep located on the summit of the motte. It is not clear whether the first stone castle (thought to be of the 1260s) was the responsibility of Roger de Quincy or Alexander Comyn, Earl of Buchan, but a further phase of strengthening did occur in the 1280s. In 1292, John, Alexander's son and successor, received permission to export lead from the Isle of Man to cover eight towers at Cruggleton.

The evidence for Alexander Comyn engaging in a concentrated programme of castle building and strengthening in the period c.1260–1280s is unfortunately limited by the 'herschip' of Buchan in 1308. However, the circumstantial evidence for such a programme – especially evidence from the acquisition and strengthening of Balvenie c.1264–85 – is supported by the more plentiful documentary and

Plans of Comyn Castles
(Inverlochy, Lochindorb and Balvenie)

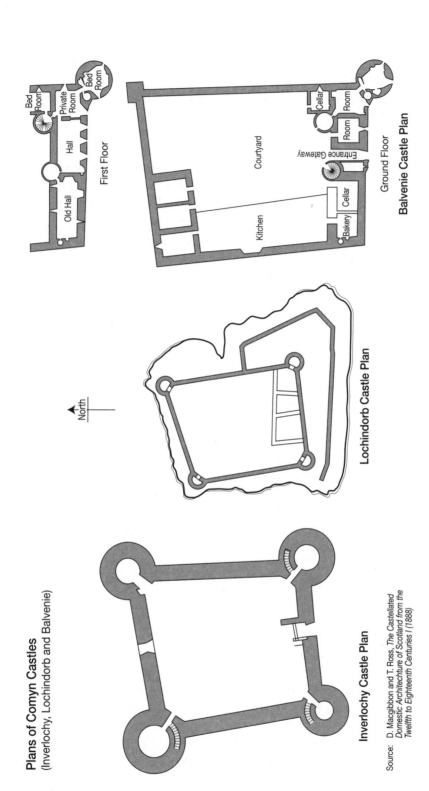

North

Inverlochy Castle Plan

Lochindorb Castle Plan

First Floor

Bed Room

Bed Room

Private Room

Hall

Old Hall

Cellar

Room

Courtyard

Entrance Gateway

Kitchen

Bakery

Cellar

Cellar

Room

Ground Floor

Balvenie Castle Plan

Source: D. Macgibbon and T. Ross, *The Castellated Domestic Architecture of Scotland from the Twelfth to Eighteenth Centuries I* (1888)

architectural evidence for a parallel strategic castle building and strengthening programme by the Comyns of Badenoch. John Comyn I, Lord of Badenoch, was behind the building of Blair Atholl c.1269 and in 1267 was fortifying Tarset in Tynedale, Northumberland. The Comyns of Badenoch were active at Lochindorb, Inverlochy and Ruthven at some time before that date. Lochindorb had more substantial remains and documentary evidence suggests that the castle was in existence by 1279 at the latest, while architectural evidence points to buildings of the second half of the thirteenth century. Towers to the north-east and south-west have long fish-tailed slits heavily plunged downwards (which suggests a date in the second half of the thirteenth century). Inverlochy, the chief castle of the Comyns in Lochaber, has been dated on archaeological grounds to c.1270–80 which again confirms documentary evidence. Inverlochy Castle is a rare example of the quadrangular castle in Scotland (90 feet by 101 feet) with high curtain walls, fortified with round towers (a type not uncommon in England and Wales where comparisons can be made with Kidwelly (1275) Flint (1277) and Harlech (1283)). The Comyns of Badenoch also had castles further south by the end of the thirteenth century – Dalswinton in Nithsdale, Kirkintilloch (caput of the lordship of Lenzie, Dumbartonshire), Machan (the Clyde Valley), Bedrule and Scraesburgh (Roxburghshire). Few details remain about their building phases though at Bedrule there is evidence of a motte superseded by a castle of enceinte. Although the enclosure is not complete, the discernible features and layout suggest a late-thirteenth-century date, suggesting further evidence of a Comyn castle building programme after c.1260. To the castles of the Comyns of Buchan and Badenoch is to be added the castle of Kilbride, the main residence of the Comyn lords of East Kilbride.

During Alexander Comyn's leadership of the Comyn party, the Comyns had control of a network of major castles, and therefore main lines of communication across Scotland. Their power in northern Scotland was virtually vice-regal, from Inverlochy in the west to Slains in the east – their castles controlled the western passes through the Mounth as well as the east–west passage across northern Scotland via the Spey and Spean valleys. With Inverlochy, the Comyns controlled the southern end of the Great Glen, the other main east–west route. The Comyns' role as pillars of the Scottish monarchy was bolstered by castle-holding and this was further emphasised in the period after 1260 under Alexander Comyn's leadership through their appointment as sheriffs and keepers (see pages 73, 88–90). As has been seen, Alexander Comyn's role as sheriff of Dingwall and Wigtown and baillie of Inverie (Knoydart), complemented by his family's castles in the north and west, helped to defend Scotland from the Norwegian military threat but also contributed to a further definition of royal authority in those areas. Castles of the Comyn family and their allies (for example, the MacDougalls of Argyll added Dunstaffnage to Comyn strength in the north) gave Alexander Comyn's political power added military and administrative strength in both the north, west and south-west. This was especially significant in the north – without control over the north, no authority could be secure in Scotland. When this strength was allied to the interests of the Scottish king and kingdom, it can be seen how much a contribution Alexander Comyn, Earl of Buchan and justiciar of Scotia, could make to the development of an independent Scottish kingdom.

Dual Loyalties?

It has been seen how Alexander Comyn, Earl of Buchan's, already considerable territorial power in Scotland was increased after 1264 through his wife's de Quincy inheritance. However, this inheritance also made Alexander Comyn into one of the greatest cross-border barons almost on a par with Roger de Quincy, or the Balliols, Huntingdons and Bruces. Although the three-way division of the de Quincy estates was a long and complex affair lasting from c.1264 to c.1279, it resulted in Alexander Comyn gaining widespread properties in northern England (in Cumberland, Yorkshire, Lincolnshire and Derbyshire), in the central Midlands (especially in Leicestershire, Warwickshire, Northamptonshire and Huntingdonshire), to the south-east (in Cambridgeshire, Bedfordshire, Buckinghamshire, Hertfordshire and Essex), and in the south-west (stretching through Oxfordshire, Berkshire, Gloucestershire and Wiltshire as far as Dorset on the south coast). Though Alexander Comyn was heavily involved in Scottish government, after 1258, as Alexander III's chief counsellor, he showed himself to be anxious to secure the full rights of his wife in England as the break-up of the de Quincy estates proved to be a protracted affair. During the period 1264–79, frequent safe-conducts were issued for Alexander and his wife and envoys to come to England. He was constantly asking and receiving permission to appoint attorneys in his place. He could not be travelling continually from Buchan to England so generally appointed attorneys to see to his English affairs.[54] Some of these attorneys were English, but many were northern Scottish, such as Ralph and William Lascelles (Fife), Thomas and Gilbert of Kinross, Robert of Leslie, Nicholas of Slains, Maurice de Murray and John of Buchan who were all working for him in England between 1266 and 1282. As for Alexander Comyn himself, he was slow to come to the king's court in person to do homage for Elizabeth's inherited share, a sign perhaps of the distance involved or his responsibilities in Scottish government, but it would be unfair to call him an absentee landlord. He did appear in person at Shepshed, one of his administrative centres in the Midlands, to receive the homage of William of Brideport in 1281.[55] Alexander preferred to involve his sons in his family's English interests. The 'post mortem' inquisition on his death reveals that by then he held no lands in chief of the English Crown, for more than seven years previously he had enfeoffed (granted land in return for specific feudal service) to John his son and heir, in the manor of Whitwick (worth £100 a year) and all his other lands in Leicestershire and Warwickshire[56]. Also, he gave his second son Roger the manor of East Farndon in Northamptonshire;[57] and wrote to Edward I asking that, if Roger's right to that property were questioned, then the king's agents should come to Elizabeth in Scotland to obtain her recognisance and testimony in the matter, and that Elizabeth should not have to go to England.[58] This is one of several examples which show that Alexander Comyn's interest remained essentially Scottish.

Cross-border nobles were not a coherent group in Scottish society. They exhibited varying degrees of attachment to the kingdoms in which their lands lay, though they all accepted the commitments which went with land ownership on both sides of the border. Historians, over the centuries, have relied too much on hindsight to emphasise the political problems (especially the problems of loyalty) liable to arise (after 1290) from nobles in Alexander III's reign holding land on both sides of the border. Thus cross-border land ownership was linked to lack of patriotism amongst the Scottish nobility, one of the most enduring myths of Scottish tradition: 'the truth is, and it must be confessed with shame and sorrow, that the Scottish nobility as a body were not true to Scotland'.[59] The truth is more prosaic. Access to the larger resources of the Angevin monarchy and the greater wealth of the kingdom of England were attractive considerations for all Scottish nobles holding land in England. The realities of peace rather than the potentialities of war governed baronical attitudes. Certainly nobles such as

Alexander Comyn showed the importance of English landholding by acknowledging the commitments, both military and financial, which were owed to the English king as a result of these English lands. In 1276, Alexander was among 178 tenants-in-chief summoned to meet Edward I at Worcester in order to fight the Welsh, and although he did not serve personally, he paid the 'scutage' of 50 marks (one-third of two knights' fees). Similarly, in 1282, his recognition of his duty to serve the English king was clearly shown in his letter to Edward I which expressed his regret at being unable to serve personally against the Welsh – on this occasion his son Roger served in his stead. This episode showed how dual allegiance worked in practice. It is clear from the correspondence of both Alexander III and Alexander Comyn that Earl Alexander's duty – Alexander Comyn had been dispatched on important royal business to the remote parts of the Scottish islands – was to the Scottish king and kingdom first. This sense of political and national duty – 'we cannot leave this road [to the Isles] by our honour'[60] – came before personal feudal duty to the English king. Alexander Comyn's patriotism was of a very practical, pragmatic kind.

Edward I failed to appreciate the political and constitutional maturity of the Scottish kingdom in its development since the minority of Alexander III. The English king failed to appreciate that the Scottish nobility in government, chiefly the Comyns and their supporters, now represented the political community of the realm and this duty came before other responsibilities such as English landownership. Simply, the actions of Alexander Comyn and the Scottish nobles in Alexander III's government do not support Joseph Stevenson's view (and that of many other writers of the nineteenth century) that 'their [the Scottish nobles] ardour was cooled and their efforts paralysed by the knowledge that their possessions in that kingdom [England] would be forfeited to the Crown on the first moment they exhibited any active sympathy with their countrymen in arms against Edward'.[61] This would become very apparent between 1294 and 1296 when the aristocratic governing community's sense of national duty was tested by Edward I's increasing tendency to redefine his overlordship not only over cross-border landowners but over the Scottish kingdom itself.

The question of English overlordship over Scotland was an important background issue in 1244, 1251 and 1255. Alexander Comyn had lived through and learned from these years. As leader and chief officer of Alexander III's government in maturity, he was to the fore in establishing formal constitutional plans for an emergency council in 1260–1 when the Scottish queen travelled to England to stay with her mother during her confinement prior to the birth of the heiress to the Scottish throne. The perpetuation of kingship and kingdom was to remain the key issue to the Scottish political community despite the good social relationships between the royal families of Scotland and England between 1260 and 1286.

The issue of English claims to suzerainty over Scotland was raised in 1251 (at Alexander III's wedding in York to Henry III's daughter) and rejected, but it was raised again in 1278 when Alexander III came to the English court to pay homage to Edward I. By this period, there was clear awareness of the rights of the Scottish king and his kingdom.[62] Alexander III's status was reflected by the fact that he had, no doubt at his request, been granted by Edward I a prestigious escort of the archbishop of Canterbury and York, and the earls of Gloucester, Lincoln and Warenne. Alexander's envoys also asked that 'the coming of the Scottish king to England should not hereafter injure him or his heir' and extracted the promise from the English king that 'the safe conduct granted to Alexander King of Scotland to come to England should not tend to the future prejudice of that King or his heirs'. It is also noticeable that after 1275, there was an increased number of complaints by the Scots about border matters and especially about English administration in the north (particularly when it interfered in the Scottish liberty of Tynedale[63]). This awareness of Scottish rights is fully reflected in the circumstances surrounding Alexander III's homage to Edward I. After Alexander had done homage for his English lands, William of Middleton, Bishop of Norwich, a lawyer, and one of Edward's counsellors said: 'and let it be reserved to the king of England, if he should have right to your homage for the kingdom'. Alexander's answer was clear, firm and instant:

> The king answered him publicly at once, saying that 'nobody but God himself has the right to the homage for my realm of Scotland, and I hold it of nobody but God himself ... Then the king of Scotland added, according to the form of the homage which he had done alone, 'for the lands that I hold of you in the realm of England'. And the king of Scotland agreed to perform the proper and customary services to the kingdom of England for the lands for which he had done homage to him, *reserving the rights of his kingdom.*[64]

The fact that Alexander III, even in his maturity, relied on his magnates to help him preserve the integrity of his kingdom is clear in a letter between Alexander III and Edward I in 1275:

> He has received his letter as to collecting the aid for him within his liberty at Tyndale, but cannot reply thereto plainly without first consulting his magnates.[65]

Family circumstances in the 1270s and 1280s meant that Alexander III needed Alexander Comyn and his chief magnates to ensure the perpetuation of Scottish kingship. Alexander Comyn took a leading part in the negotiations for the marriage of Alexander III's eldest daughter Margaret to the king of Norway in 1281.[66] The succession was threatened by the deaths of Alexander III's son David in 1281, his daughter Margaret in 1283 and his eldest son, the Prince Alexander, in 1284. In February 1284, in a parliament at Scone, the most important magnates in Scotland (thirteen earls and twenty-five barons) bound themselves to maintain the succession of Margaret, 'Maid of Norway', the child of the marriage of Alexander III's daughter and the king of Norway.[67] Such formal and mature constitutional procedures in the period c.1260–86 were borne out of Alexander III's minority and the active co-operation between Alexander III and the aristocratic governing community under the leadership of Alexander Comyn. They point to a very clear sense of nationality in Scotland.

The essence of the governing aristocratic establishment is effectively captured in the list of barons who swore to uphold the principle of primogeniture in 1284 and uphold the succession of young Margaret, Maid of Norway, to the Scottish throne. It is noteworthy that Alexander Comyn, styled justiciar and constable of Scotland, headed the list of Scotland's major magnates who swore to maintain the succession. No doubt his position as the king's chief counsellor, his political experience and familiarity with crisis periods merited this pre-eminent position. The Comyns' domination of Scottish government was well reflected in the 1284 document – two members of the family, John Comyn of Badenoch and Alexander Comyn, and familiar names connected to the family by marriage, political association, or both – Patrick, Earl of Dunbar, Malise, Earl of Strathearn, Gilbert, Earl of Angus, Alexander MacDougall, Lord of Lorn, Balliol, Brechin, Soules, Hay, Graham, Maxwell and Cheyne.

Guardian in a Crisis

Alexander III married again in October 1285, his second wife being Yolande de Dreux. However, disaster followed when, on 18 March 1286, Alexander III was killed in a tragic accident when he was on his way from Edinburgh to Kingholm to see his new wife. Another period of turmoil in Scotland seemed imminent. Discussion of the consequences of Alexander III's death had long been dominated by the powerful, emotional accounts of the fourteenth and fifteenth-century commentators, *Gesta Annalia* (formally attributed to John of Fordun), Walter Bower and Andrew of Wyntoun:

> How worthy of tears, and how hurtful his death was to the kingdom of Scotland, is plainly shown forth by the evils of after times ... O Scotland, truly unhappy when bereft of so great a leader and pilot; while – greater unhappiness still! he left no lawful offspring to succeed him ...
>
> *Gesta Annalia*[68]

> your lyre changed to playing a lament and your pipes became the voice of the mourners when you learnt of the sudden death of your dearly beloved king, as bitter as it was unwelcome. But if you too had recognised how many evils were bullying you on all sides, your heart, foreseeing the news to come, would have trembled violently from fear.
>
> Walter Bower[69]

> > Our gold was changyd in to lede
> > Chryst, borne in to Vyrgynte
> > Succoure Scotland and remede
> > That stad [is in] perplexyte
> >
> > Andrew of Wyntoun[70]

Such dramatic language has lived long in Scottish tradition, cementing our view of the years 1286–96 and contributing substantially to the myth of the 'Golden Age' of Alexander III, an idealised kingship destroyed by baronial faction and 'overmighty' subject after 1286 before finally being restored by the hero of the fourteenth and fifteenth-century narratives, Robert Bruce, in 1306. Contemporary narratives and record evidence for the period 1249–86 do not support 'traditional' account of self-seeking noble factions causing difficulties for the Scottish monarchy during the minority, being 'tamed' during Alexander III's maturity, and lapsing once more into destructive faction-fighting after his death in 1286. Analysis of Alexander III's reign, divorced from the framework (and agenda) of fourteenth and fifteenth-century Scottish narratives, reveals that Alexander III himself should not be given all the credit for the 'Golden Age' 1258–86. The achievements of his reign were, in practice, the result of an effective, mutually beneficial alliance between the Crown and his great magnates such as the Comyns, Stewarts, Morays and Frasers. In particular, Alexander Comyn's leadership of the Scottish political community between 1258 and 1286 and his role as chief counsellor to Alexander III made him integral to the definition and growth of the Scottish kingdom, also the defence of its independence and integrity. It is more appropriate that the 'Golden Age' of the period is seen as the age of the 'Two Alexanders'.

Similarly, the retrospective view (from the fourteenth and fifteenth centuries) of the period after 1286 was not reflected by contemporary record. It is in keeping with contemporary evidence that Scotland in 1286 was more centralised and more stable than it had been in 1249, that the actions of the leaders of the Scottish political community in 1286 reflect maturity and lack of panic. The speedy implementation of a formal, rational plan for a provisional government of six Guardians can be seen to be the mature development from the unplanned informal regency of 1249 and the consequent provision of an emergency council of regency set up for the delicate political and constitutional circumstances of 1260–1. Alexander Comyn had experienced the instability of Alexander III's minority, had no doubt contributed to the planning of 1260–1 emergency council, and was present on Alexander III's death to impart his experience and pragmatic political sense to the unfortunate circumstances of 1286. In 1286, at an assembly (parliament) at Scone around 28 April 1286, the formality of the occasion was shown as the nobility first swore fealty to the heir, and took a solemn oath both to guard the land of Scotland on the heir's behalf, and keep the peace there.[71] In circumstances very different from those in 1249, a provisional government was swiftly set up to implement these promises – the realm would be governed by six wardens or 'Guardians' comprising two earls (Alexander Comyn, Earl of Buchan, and Duncan, Earl of Fife), two bishops (William Fraser of St Andrews and Robert Wishart of Glasgow) and two barons (John Comyn of Badenoch and James Stewart).[72]

Contemporary English sources such as the *Lanercost Chronicle* reflect the political reality of 1286 better than the agenda-ridden commentaries of fourteenth and fifteenth-century nationalist writings according to which Alexander III's 'idealised' kingship was destroyed by baronial faction-fighting after 1286 before being restored by the hero of these later narratives, Robert Bruce, in 1306:

> the greatest men of the land of Scotland provided for themselves salutary counsel and chose for the community guardians of peace, both from among the nobles and the bishops; until it should be decided by discussion who should be put in a position of so great authority.[73]

This reflects the wisdom and relative sophistication of the decisions taken in 1286 – prudent reflection rather than panic! The contemporary descriptions of the Guardians, their role and constitutional position, are interesting. The *Lanercost Chronicle* referred to them as 'guardians of peace'. The Guardians described themselves as 'appointed by common counsel' or 'elected by the community of the realm'.[74] The idea of the 'community of the realm' became openly expressed in 1286, symbolising the political maturity and constitutional formality which had developed in the second half of the thirteenth century. In practice, the Scottish political community had been evolving throughout the thirteenth century under the 'aegis' of a very settled aristocratic governing community led by the Comyns, Walter Comyn, Earl of Menteith (c.1244–58), and Alexander Comyn, Earl of Buchan (1258–89). This political community was based on consensus between Crown and aristocratic establishment in an alliance of mutual benefit. The seal of the Guardians, cut especially for their use, symbolically sums up their role, acting on behalf of the community of the realm while at the same time acting as delegates of the Crown. Professor Barrow eloquently described the relationship between Crown and community of the realm: 'The king of Scots was one side, the community of the realm of Scotland the other side, of a single coin.'[75] This idea is emphasised in both the design of the Guardians' seal – on one side a shield of the royal arms, on the other side the figure of St Andrew on his cross – as well as its inscriptions: 'the seal of Scotland appointed for the government of the kingdom' and 'St Andrew be leader of the compatriot Scots'. The leadership of the community of the realm (under Alexander Comyn in 1286) should be acknowledged as much as the Crown and the Church as keystones of an independent Scottish kingdom in 1286.

The *Lanercost Chronicle's* description of the Guardians as 'guardians of peace' highlights perhaps the most important 'royal' role to be performed by Guardians: to maintain peace and stability within the kingdom and secure freedom from external interference. A brieve issued by the Guardians (probably late in 1286) refers to army service due to the 'royal dignity' after the death of a king.[76] One of the Guardians, James Stewart, justified by reference to the public peace the decision to override Melrose Abbey tenants' exemption from musters and military aid in Kyle Stewart: 'because the peace and tranquillity of the realm were disturbed after King Alexander's death and the state was threatened by conflict'.[77] In 1287, 'the peace and tranquillity of the realm of Scotland' was again an issue when Malise, Earl of Strathearn, had to raise men in his earldom from among the tenants of Inchaffray Abbey. The Guardians were ready to act against any threat to national order, but most of their government business in the period between 1286 and 1290 was of a fairly routine sort, mainly writs to the chamberlain of Scotland requesting him to pay the fees of certain knights and government affairs, but also inquests on land rights.[78] Such routine business gives an impression of stability and conscientious, efficient government. However, two matters in which the Guardians expressed national concern reflected also an active government keenly aware of Scottish rights and the rights of Scottish men in England. On 11 November 1286, the Guardians complained to Edward, Earl of Cornwall, warden of England, that a certain Sir Andrew de Moray and his wife were aggrieved by Edward I's escheator.[79] The complaint referred to the escheator, Thomas de Normanville's harsh conduct north of the Trent towards Scots. In another letter of 13 May 1288, again to Edward, Earl of Cornwall, the Guardians asked for the security of the advowson of the church of Knaresdale for John Wishart. The complaint was against the bailiff of Tynedale for troubling John Wishart. Both complaints about the actions of the English officials reflect a continuation of a Scottish policy held consistently since c.1260 – a keen desire to protect Scottish rights, wherever held, and to resist any attempt at the imposition of English authority.

When Alexander III died in March 1286, there was uncertainty rather than a crisis over the succession. Yolande his queen was believed to be pregnant. Failing the birth of a living child as heir, the Maid of

Norway, Alexander III's granddaughter, acknowledged as rightful heir by the magnates of Scotland in February 1284, and less than three years of age when Alexander III died, would succeed to the Scottish throne. The contemporary English chronicle, the *Lanercost Chronicle*, relayed the story that Yolande tried to deceive the Guardians into believing that she was pregnant:

> she, resorting to feminine craft, was pretending to be pregnant, in order to cause patriots to postpone their decision [to decide on the succession], and that she might more readily attract popularity to herself . . . so she disquieted the land with her pretences from the day of the king's death till the feast of the Purification [2 February] . . . she contrived to have the son of a play-actor to be brought [to her] so that it might pass for hers.[80]

It is interesting that the *Lanercost Chronicle* gives credit for the detection of this ruse to 'William of Buchan' [surely Alexander Comyn]:

> her fraud was detected and revealed by the sagacity of William [sic] of Buchan, to the confusion of all present, and to all those willing to trust her who heard of it afterwards.[81]

This probably reflects the leadership qualities and experience of Alexander Comyn in a vital matter of Guardian responsibility, the succession.

It has been claimed that the six Guardians chosen in 1286 represented 'a nice compromise between rival factions' or 'were probably elected to provide a balance in the government between those supporting each of the two main factions in the country at that time, the Bruces and the Balliols'.[82] However, the composition of the Guardianship reflected the reality of Scottish politics in 1286, i.e. Comyn domination of Scottish government[83] rather than the 1291/1292 legal battle to come. If the committee had been set up to balance the aspirations of Balliols and Bruces as heirs presumptive, it failed. The Bruces in 1286 evidently felt that the Guardians would not effectively represent their interests (and aspirations) – they feared a long period of Guardianship under Comyn leadership and very soon resorted to strong-arm tactics. They launched attacks in south-west Scotland on the Balliol lordship at Buittle and also the royal castles of Wigtown and Dumfries. The attacks reveal more than an attack on the Balliols; they reveal an attack on the Comyn position in the south-west as the Comyns (under Alexander Comyn, Earl of Buchan) had become hereditary sheriffs of Wigtown since c.1264–64. The attacks show clear resistance to Comyn leadership of the political community of the realm. There were very few known members of the Bruce following in public office between 1286 and 1290. Even James Stewart, an ally of the Bruces, seemed to put his public duty as Guardian and concern for the 'peace and tranquillity of the realm' before personal support for the Bruces' dynastic claims – he overrode Melrose Abbey tenants' exemption from musters and military aid in Kyle Stewart because 'the state was threatened by conflict'.[84]

The extent of the threat posed by the Bruces between 1286 and 1288 is well revealed in the royal accounts of 1288–90. Actions were taken at the Guardians' command to secure the castles at Dumfries, Ayr and Stirling. The existence of war or the danger of war is made the grounds for claiming additional sums for the defence, custody and watching of the castles of Dumfries, Ayr, Wigtown and Jedburgh. The accounts of the sheriffdoms of Dumfries, Wigtown and Edinburgh refer to lands uncultivated for two years because of war or remission for tenants 'lest they leave the land and leave the king's land uncultivated'.[85] The accounts of the sheriffs of Ayr, Dumfries and Wigtown and also the account of the justiciar of Galloway revealed that most of the disruption occurred in the south-west. However, the impact of the war or the fear of war was felt outside of the south-west of Scotland. The accounts of the sheriffdom of Edinburgh refer to extra watches needed at the castle because of the danger of war and to the fear engendered in the king's tenants. The accounts of the sheriffdom of Stirling detail the building work undertaken at Stirling Castle. The account of John Comyn of Buchan as sheriff of Wigtown refers specifically to the Earl of Carrick, i.e. Robert Bruce (the future king's father), as the instigator of war after the death of the king.[86] It is ironic, in the light of this evidence, that Robert Bruce, the future king, was given credit by the pro-Bruce nationalist writings of the fourteenth and fifteenth centuries for rescuing Scotland in 1306 from twenty years of faction-fighting when *it was clearly the Bruce family who initiated destabilising strong-arm tactics against the Comyns and their leadership (i.e. Alexander Comyn's leadership) of the Scottish regency in 1286 and were proactive in opposition to this leadership for the next twenty years.* It was the start of a fierce rivalry that would involve physical violence (1299), a murder (1306) and continue until the Battle of Bannockburn (1314) tilted the balance in favour of the Bruces. However, in 1286 the Comyns were leaders of the political community of the realm, foremost defenders of the rights of the successors to Alexander III whether that successor was the Maid of Norway or the child of Queen Yolande. Although the Bruces had, with the rest of the major Scottish magnates, agreed in 1284 to support the succession of Margaret, their actions in 1286 suggest that they no longer recognised Margaret's claim to the throne but were intent on pursuing their own dynastic claim (and frightening off a potential rival, John Balliol). It is interesting to note that the partisan Bruce source, John Barbour, in his epic biography of the hero-king Robert Bruce omits all mention of the child-queen Margaret. This too could be taken to imply, in the pro-Bruce version of Scottish medieval history, that the Bruces did not recognise the legitimate Maid of Norway's claim.

The reaction of the Comyn-led regency government to the Bruce attacks on royal and Balliol castles and property, especially in the south-west, was to strengthen Comyn military power there. Alexander Comyn, through his wife's de Quincy inheritance, had acquired large areas of land in Galloway and Dumfriesshire and, since 1263–4, was sheriff of Wigtown. In 1288, Alexander's son and heir, John, the future Earl of Buchan, took extra responsibility in response to the Bruce threat. He became keeper of the king's castle and lands in Kirkcudbright as well as having responsibility for the sheriffdom of Wigtown[87] – perhaps his aged father was not now fit for such active roles. The Badenoch branch of the Comyn family also took extra responsibility because of the disturbances after 1286. John Comyn II, Lord of Badenoch, strengthened his family's presence in southern Scotland, especially Roxburghshire, by becoming baillie of Jedburgh in 1288, being responsible for the garrison of the castle and for the farm of the manor of Jedburgh.[88]

The Guardians as 'Guardians of Peace' had responsibility for main-taining peace in Scotland and this meant improving local defence and being prepared to ask for the host to be on twenty-four-hour alert, but the real threat of civil war (as seen in the royal accounts) and the need for the Maid of Norway to be formally inaugurated as queen meant that there was also need for outside help. It is hardly surprising that the council of 1286, the Guardians, were seeking advice, perhaps aid, from Edward I. The first embassy in May 1286 was led by William Fraser, Bishop of St Andrews, the second in August consisted of William

Comyn, Bishop of Brechin, Geoffrey de Mowbray, Lord of Dalmeny (and related to the Comyns by marriage) and the abbot of Jedburgh.[89] The composition of these embassies shows a distinctly Comyn-led government in Scotland. Their purpose is not clear though Bower reported that the second embassy was to 'appeal for his [Edward's] advice and patronage over the state of the kingdom of Scotland and of the lands of Penrith'. It is not known whether a possible marriage alliance involving the Maid of Norway and the English royal family was mooted as early as 1286 (at that time the question of Queen Yolande's pregnancy may have clouded the issue). Alexander Comyn, the most experienced Scottish counsellor in the Guardianship must have been well aware of the precedent of marriage treaty as a guarantee of help in a crisis. An agreement for a marriage between the young Alexander of Scotland (the future Alexander III) and Henry's daughter Margaret was discussed as early as 1244 (during another period of political unrest in Scotland) before being implemented in 1251. Alexander Comyn must have been very aware of the advantages (and disadvantages) of such an agreement to curb internal commotion – his half-brother had actively sought Henry III's assistance in 1249, 1251 and 1255.

Whether or not a marriage alliance was mooted in 1286 – it is interesting to note that correspondence between Alexander III and Edward I in 1284 already hinted at the desirability of a future marriage alliance involving the Maid: 'we [Alexander III] would recall, if we may, to your recollection, that in the providence of God much good may come to pass yet through your kinswoman, the daughter of your niece, the daughter, too, of our beloved, the late queen of Norway, of happy memory, who is now our heir-apparent'[90] – it certainly was on the agenda in 1289. A Scottish embassy led by the Guardian, William Fraser, Bishop of St Andrews, made its way to Edward I in Gascony (where his political priority had lain since 1286) early in 1289 – again its business is not known but there is direct evidence of Edward's involvement in negotiations concerning the Maid and a future marriage by 1 May 1289.[91]

Alexander Comyn, Earl of Buchan, the most experienced political leader in Scotland must have been behind the policy of securing political stability in Scotland through a marriage alliance but he was not alive to see it implemented. He died shortly after 10 July 1289,[92] after nearly fifty years at the heart of Scottish politics and over thirty years as Alexander III's chief counsellor and adviser. Alexander's experience would have taught him of the advantages of a marriage alliance with the English royal family but it would also have made him very aware of the dangers of a more powerful neighbour taking advantage of Scotland's internal difficulties. Certainly, the Comyns, under Walter Comyn's leadership, had to resist Henry III's attempts to control Scottish political affairs between 1251 and 1258 – Walter's success must have encouraged Alexander. The issue of England's overlordship of Scotland had been raised in 1251 and 1278 – it may have been raised in 1286! Alexander Comyn's leadership of the Scottish political community had been marked by his defence of Scotland's political independence and integrity and by co-operation with the Scottish king in all attempts to define and strengthen royal authority.

Alexander Comyn's Legacy

The Treaty of Birgham/Northampton, eventually signed in July 1290, was a marriage treaty uniting the heir of England with the heiress of Scotland, but the terms of the treaty are, above all, a fitting testimony to Alexander Comyn's role as *the* pillar of the Scottish monarchy between 1258 and 1289. The terms of the treaty represent an attempt by an experienced Scottish political community to define the conditions by which they agreed to the marriage. The experience deriving from the contingency plans of 1260–1 (for the confinement of the Scottish queen in England), the refusal to acknowledge English claims to overlordship of Scotland in 1251 and 1278, the determination to limit English interference in Scottish political affairs between 1251 and 1258 and the increasing tendency to resist the intrusion of English officials in Scotland's border lands after 1275 are all reflected in the terms of the Birgham treaty. The terms were basically that Scotland would retain its independence and would keep intact its own rights, laws, liberties and customs. No parliaments would be held outside Scotland to deal with matters concerning the kingdom. The words may have been supplied by senior churchmen amongst the remaining Guardians, William Fraser, Bishop of St Andrews, or Robert Wishart, Bishop of Glasgow, but they embody the practical politics of no one more than Alexander Comyn, Earl of Buchan:

> we authorise in the name and place our lord [Edward I] and his heirs *that the rights, laws, liberties and customs of the realm of Scotland in all matters and in all ways shall be wholly and*

inviolably preserved for all time throughout the whole of that realm and its borders . . .

. . . if the above-named Edward and Margaret, or either one of them, should die without leaving a living child, in any circumstances in which the aforesaid realm ought rightfully to revert to its nearest heirs, it shall revert and be restored to them whole, free, quit and without any subjection . . .

. . . the realm of Scotland shall remain separated and divided and free in itself, without subjection to the realm of England, by its rightful boundaries and marches, as it has been preserved down to the present . . .

No tenant-in-chief of the above-mentioned king of Scotland shall be forced to go furth of the realm [of Scotland] to do homage, swear fealty or make a payment for relief . . .

Parliaments shall not be held outside the realm of Scotland or its marches to deal with those matters which concern that realm or its marches, or to deal with the status of the inhabitants within that realm.

No tallages, aids, military service or maltolts [additional tax on exports/imports] shall be demanded from the aforesaid realm, unless it be to meet the common needs of the realm and in circumstances in which the kings of Scotland have been used to demand such things.[93]

These terms represent the most detailed and eloquent exposition of the 'Scottish cause' to this date. Described as 'the high-water mark of the common endeavour by Guardians and community',[94] the treaty is a testament to the Comyns as leaders of the patriot cause and protectors of the liberties of the kingdom. Though long overshadowed by the Declaration of Arbroath (1320) as an expression of Scottish nationalism, the terms of the Treaty of Birgham/Northampton show that the Scottish cause was fully and clearly articulated *before* the outbreak of the Wars of Independence. The wars were the result of well-defined commitment to Scottish independence as expressed at Birgham and the treaty, therefore, needs to be acknowledged as a key document in the early independence movement. Alexander Comyn, Earl of Buchan, as leader of the Scottish political community from 1258 to 1289, should also be acknowledged as the 'Patriot Hero' most responsible for helping to define the Scottish kingdom, its independence and political integrity in this period.

**1 Great Seal (1227) of Alexander II (1214–1249)
who died in Kerrera, Argyll, on 8 July 1249**

Walter Comyn was a key trouble-shooter for Alexander II in areas where royal authority needed to be reinforced. He also provoked Henry III's intervention at the Border by what was deemed anti-English activities.

a) Obverse. The king is depicted bare-headed, wearing a girdled tunic and seated on a throne. The throne is bench-shaped with ornament in front and a rectangular footboard. In his right hand the king holds a deeply grooved sword pointing upwards and in his left an orb surmounted by a long cross. (By permission of the Court of the Lord Lyon) (Photograph, David Wakeley)

b) Reverse. The king is depicted on horseback, in chain armour with a surcoat and a flat-topped helmet with aventail over his face. In his right hand, extended backwards, he holds a grooved sword. A shield bearing arms – a lion rampant – is suspended from his shoulders. (By permission of the Court of Lord Lyon) (Photograph, David Wakeley)

2 Deer Abbey (reconstruction)

Founded by William Comyn, Earl of Buchan, in 1219, the Cistercian abbey of Deer was always a small house with a simple cruciform plan for the church. Undoubtedly, this period would have been marked by visible signs of the Comyns' secular lordship in Buchan, but the 'herschip' of Buchan by Robert Bruce has destroyed much evidence of the Comyns' power base. (© Crown Copyright Historic Scotland, reproduced courtesy of Historic Scotland, www.historicscotlandimages.gov.uk)

3 Tarset Castle, Northumberland

alter Comyn had incurred the wrath of Henry III by arming and supplying this castle by 1244. The
glish chronicler Matthew Paris also accused Walter Comyn of aggressively building castles in Lothian
d Galloway at this time. (Copyright reserved Cambridge University Collection of Aerial Photography
AI-99)

4 Ruthven Castle

Ruthven Castle was probably first built for a clear political military and political purpose in the tin
of Walter Comyn, first lord of Badenoch, shortly after the creation of this lordship (c.1229). Ruthve
regarded as head of the Badenoch lordship, held a strategic position commanding the northern end
two passes over the Mounth, the Drumochter and Minigaig passes. (Copyright St Andrews Libra
Licensor: www.scran.ac.uk)

5 Inchmahome Priory

Walter Comyn became earl of Menteith in 1234 and, like his father William, Earl of Buchan, marked his elevation to an earldom by founding a monastery. Walter Comyn founded the Augustinian priory of Inchmahome in 1238 on the largest of the three islands in the Lake of Menteith.

**6 Second Great Seal of Alexander III (1249–1286),
killed by a fall near Kinghorn on 18 March 1286**

Alexander Comyn guarded Scotland from English interference during Alexander III's minority and was Alexander III's chief counsellor from 1258 to 1286.

(a) Obverse. The king is shown seated on a richly carved throne, the back raised and divided into three parts by four finials, ending in fleurs-de-lis and with a footboard on an arcaded corbel. The king is seen here with long curling hair and a beard and moustache. He wears a small crown with three fleurs-de-lis and a loose garment with sleeves to the elbow. (By permission of the Court of the Lord Lyon) (Photograph, David Wakeley)

(b) Reverse. The king is on horseback. He wears chainmail, a loose surcoat and a flat-topped helmet with grated front slits for vision and a fan plume. The king holds a grooved sword in his right hand and a shield bearing royal arms is suspended from his shoulders. The horse has a fan plume on its head and spikes on its shoes. (By permission of the Court of the Lord Lyon) (Photograph, David Wakeley)

7 Blair Atholl Castle

ohn Comyn I, Lord of Badenoch, nephew and heir of Walter Comyn, built the castle in 1269. The Blair Atholl site controlled the southern end of the Drumochter and Minigaig passes just as Ruthven controlled the northern end. The castle which, like that at Ruthven, is covered by later buildings, was part of a precise Comyn of Badenoch castle-building strategy in the second half of the thirteenth century. (Copyright James Gardiner, Licensor: www.scran.ac.uk)

8 Balvenie Castle

Alexander Comyn, Earl of Buchan, acquired Balvenie (Mortlach) in Highland Banffshire between 1264 and 1282. Located only 20 miles from Badenoch's eastern boundary, it formed a strategic bridge linking the Comyn castles of Buchan and Badenoch. The castle featured prominently in Edward I's invasion of Scotland in 1303. Balvenie relied for its strength on massive defensive walls (25 feet high and 7 feet thick) and a greater outer ditch which enclosed the castle on three sides. (© Crown Copyright Historic Scotland, reproduced courtesy of Historic Scotland, www.historicscotland images.gov.uk)

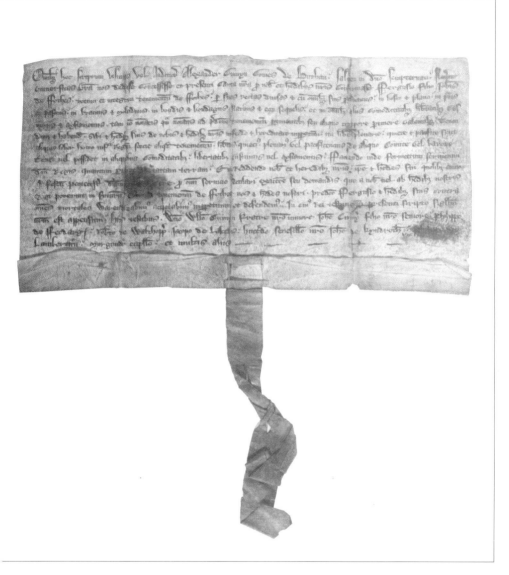

9 Charter of Alexander Comyn, Earl of Buchan, dated 1270

The charter, dated c.1270, was a grant by Alexander Comyn, Earl of Buchan, to Fergus, son of John de Fothes of the estate of Fothes (Fiddes, Newburgh). Newburgh was the urban foundation of the Comyns in Buchan. The strength of the Comyn 'party' is revealed in the witness list. First witness was Earl Alexander's younger brother William; second witness, Alexander's eldest son and heir John; third witness, Philip de Feodarg (Meldrum) who married Alexander's sister Agnes; fourth witness, Robert de Walchop, a regular witness to Earl Alexander's charters; and fifth witness, Jacob de Lascelles, from a family with feudal connections to the earl. (By permission of Lord and Lady Forbes, NRS GD55/388).

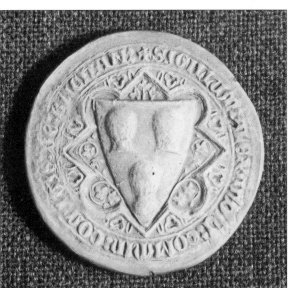

10 Seal of Alexander Comyn, Earl of Buchan (1244–1289)

Alexander Comyn, Earl of Buchan was the most experienced and influential counsellor of Alexander III's reign and contributed greatly to the political definition of an independent Scotland.

(a) Obverse. Depicts Alexander Comyn as a knight on horseback. He wears chain mail, a short surcoat and a conical-topped helmet with a fan crest. He holds a long sword in his right hand and the reins in his left. A shield bearing arms is suspended from his neck. The galloping horse has a fan crest and long caparisons with arms. (By permission of the Court of the Lord Lyon) (Photograph, David Wakeley).

(b) Reverse. Features a shield bearing arms – three garbs, two and one – within a finely curved, rounded and pointed quatrefoil panel with trefoils between annulets in the spandrils. The background has vine branches. The legend in capitals is SIGILLUM: ALEXANDRI: COMMIN: COMITIS: DE: BUCHAN (By permission of the Court of the Lord Lyon) (Photograph, David Wakeley).

11 The Guardians' Seal (1286–1292): Great Seal

The provisional government of six Guardians, formed shortly after the sudden and unexpected death of Alexander III in 1286, acted on behalf of the community of the realm while at the same time acting as delegates of the Crown. The seal of the Guardians, cut especially for their use, symbolically sums up this role. This side of the seal (reverse) bears the figure of Saint Andrew on his cross with the inscription 'St Andrew the leader of the compatriot Scots'. Saint Andrew by this date had become the symbol of the country and not just the Scottish Church. The obverse (not shown) of the seal bears a shield of the royal arms with the lion rampant and the inscription 'The seal of Scotland appointed for the government of the kingdom'. Both symbols reflect the role of the Comyns, dominant in the Guardianship (two of the six Guardians were Alexander Comyn, Earl of Buchan, and John Comyn II, Lord of Badenoch) and pillars of monarchy in thirteenth-century Scotland. (By permission of the National Records of Scotland)

12 Lochindorb Castle

Documentary evidence suggests that the castle was in existence by 1279, while architectural evidence points to buildings of the second half of the thirteenth century. The strategic importance of this castle, which fully occupied an island, 1 acre in area, on a loch, 2 miles long and 3 miles wide, in the heart of Moray, was shown by the way Edward I targeted Lochindorb after the English defeat at Roslin by John Comyn III of Badenoch. Edward I used Lochindorb as a base to accept the formal admission of the Scots in the north in 1304 (Copyright The Rourke Collection, Licensor: www.scran.ac.uk)

13 Seal of John Comyn II, Lord of Badenoch, the Competitor (d. c.1302)

The seal is 1 inch in diameter. It depicts a knight on horseback. The knight wears a hauberk of mail, a short surcoat, and a flat-topped helmet. He has a sword in his right hand and a shield bearing arms is suspended from his neck. John Comyn II, Lord of Badenoch, was one of the Competitors for the Scottish throne during the 'Great Cause' (1291–2), his claim being based on the descent from Donald Ban, King of Scots, after the death of his brother, Malcolm III, in 1093. John did not press his claim as he did not want to prejudice the stronger claim of John Balliol, his brother-in-law – he married Balliol's sister Eleanor in the 1270s. (By permission of the Court of the Lord Lyon) (Photograph David Wakeley)

14 King John (Balliol) swears homage and fealty to Edward I

n 1292, Edward I took homage and fealty from John Balliol but then sought to exploit his overlordship
o the full. The Comyns were foremost among those defending the principles of Scottish independence
s established in the Treaty of Birgham/Northampton (1290); they took over executive power from
King John in 1295 and led Scotland into war with England, on the Scottish king's behalf, in 1296.
© The British Library Board: MSS. No Roy.20 CVII Folio 28)

15 Great Seal of John Balliol (1292–1313), forced to abdicate in 1296, died in France 1313

(a) Obverse. The king is shown with curling hair and a large crown with three fleurs-de-lis and seated on a throne. He wears a loose girdled robe and cloak, the cords of which he holds with his left hand. In his right hand he holds a sceptre with a large foliated top. The throne has an openwork back with two high and two low crocketed finials and a footboard mounted on a corbel. At each side of the throne is a shield bearing arms. (By permission of the Court of the Lord Lyon) (Photograph, David Wakeley)

(b) Reverse. The king is shown on horseback and wearing chainmail, a loose-flowing sleeveless tunic and crowned helmet with grated front and slits for sight. He carries a sword in his right hand, and a large shield bearing arms – a lion rampant with a royal tressure – is suspended from his shoulders. The horse has similar arms on its caparisons. The Comyns were the power behind John Balliol's kingship and took Scotland to war with England on his behalf in 1296. John Comyn III, Lord of Badenoch was the most consistent defender of the Balliol kingship, and therefore Scottish independence, from 1296. It seems that his loyalty to the legitimate Balliol kingship caused his murder by Robert Bruce in 1306. (By permission of the Court of the Lord Lyon) (Photograph, David Wakeley)

16 Inverlochy Castle (reconstruction)

Inverlochy Castle was the chief castle of the Comyns in Lochaber. It commanded the entrance to the Great Glen, securing its southern sea outlet, and the scarcely less important overland route to the Spey. Its strategic significance for the Scottish cause was shown in the 1297 revolt of Comyn allies, the MacDougalls, against Edward I's agents in the area. Inverlochy Castle played a key role for the Comyn lords of Badenoch (and Lochaber) in dominating northern Scotland. (© Crown Copyright Historic Scotland, reproduced courtesy of Historic Scotland, www.historicscotlandimages.gov.uk)

17 (*Right*) Edward I

The Edward I whom John Comyn III, Lord of Badenoch, and Robert Bruce sought to take advantage of was elderly and not the youthful king pictured here. (© The British Library Board: MSS No. Roy.2AXII 219v)

18 (*Below*) Dumfries Mural of the Murder of John Comyn

The large mural by artist Josephine McSkimming, painted in Friars Vennel, Dumfries, vividly captures the enormity of this sacrilegious murder. It is not clear in this depiction if John Comyn was carrying arms.

4

Real Patriot 3

JOHN COMYN III, LORD OF BADENOCH (D. 1306)

Murders Most Foul?

How could the victim of a sacrilegious murder in front of the altar at the Greyfriars Church, Dumfries, on 10 February 1306 – John Comyn III, Lord of Badenoch – become vilified as a traitor to the Scottish 'cause' from the fourteenth century to the present day while the perpetrator of this heinous crime – Robert Bruce – rose to be a 'patriot' hero of epic stature? After all, a very different scenario emerged after the most notorious sacrilegious murder in English history – the murder of Thomas Becket, Archbishop of Canterbury, in the cathedral church at Canterbury on 29 December 1170. The consequences of this murder were the sanctification of Thomas Becket in record time and the elevation of his tomb to be the most popular pilgrim site in Britain. Becket became generally accepted as the kingdom's patron saint which further perpetuated the cult of St Thomas. Henry II was seen as responsible for Becket's death and forced to accept a humiliating punishment:

> Henry II set out with penitent heart to the tomb of St Thomas at Canterbury . . . (he) walked barefoot and clad in a woollen smock all the way to the martyr's tomb. There he lay prostrate for a good while in devout humility, and of his own free will, was scourged by all the bishops and abbots there present and each individual monk of the church of Canterbury.[1]
> The penance of Henry II at Canterbury, 13 July 1174, as described by Gervase of Canterbury

Henry's crime was neither to commit the deed himself nor even to order the murder directly but merely to cry out in exasperation at the difficulties he faced as king dealing with Thomas Becket's personality and policies: 'Will no-one rid me of this turbulent priest?' The plea was taken quite literally by four of Henry's knights who sought out Becket and murdered him in the cathedral church at Canterbury.

The contrast with the circumstances surrounding the murder of John Comyn III by Robert Bruce on 10 February 1306 at the Greyfriars Church at Dumfries is very striking. Sources (even pro-Bruce) acknowledge that Robert Bruce himself delivered the first blow on John Comyn in the church. Moreover, most sources also agree that John Comyn was killed in two stages – and that Robert Bruce not only dealt the first blow but authorised the final killing of the stricken Comyn. The consequences to perpetrator and victim contrast vividly with the aftermath to the Becket murder.

In 1306, Robert Bruce, showing no remorse for the murder, pushed ahead with (indeed brought forward) his attempt to seize the Scottish throne. Despite the highest ecclesiastical court in Christendom, the papal court, excommunicating him for the sacrilegious murder, the most prominent churchmen in Scotland, William Lamberton, Bishop of St Andrews, and Robert Wishart, Bishop of Glasgow, actually supported Bruce's coup and his illegal inauguration at Scone only six weeks after the murder. Robert Wishart even went so far as to forgive Bruce's heinous crime and later encouraged support for Bruce's campaign against Edward I by designating it as a crusade. By contrast, the victim in 1306 – John Comyn III, Lord of Badenoch – was pressed firmly by Scottish sources into the role of traitor as the long-standing and bitter rivalry between the Bruces and the erstwhile Comyn-led Scottish government broke out into another, more violent stage – bloody civil war. This civil war – in practice settled in Bruce's favour by the Battle of Bannockburn in 1314 – was accompanied after 1306 by a successful propaganda campaign by the new but illegal Bruce government which neither had majority support in Scotland nor international recognition for a number of years after the coup. Bannockburn made it easier for Robert Bruce's dubious and violent seizure of power to be pushed into the background and the battle itself then became the focus for the hero worship of Robert Bruce in the fourteenth and fifteenth-century Scottish writings of the *Gesta Annalia* (formerly attributed to John of Fordun), John Barbour, Walter Bower and Andrew Wyntoun. This meant, of course, that Bruce's murder of John Comyn in 1306 had to be justified by these writers and a suitable storyline invented to damn the murder victim as traitor to Robert Bruce and therefore to the Scottish independence movement itself.

John Comyn not only lost his life but also his reputation (and that of his whole family). The contrast between perpetrators and victims in the Becket murder of 1170 and the John Comyn murder of 1306 could not be more stark and should arouse deep suspicion of the Scottish sources at the heart of Scottish tradition. In the story surrounding the 1306 murder, Scottish tradition has stood Scottish history on its head!

As seen in Chapters 2 and 3, the political careers of Walter Comyn, Earl of Menteith (d. 1258), and Alexander Comyn, Earl of Buchan (d. 1289), have shown that the Comyns were far from the self-seeking faction painted by the post-Bannockburn Scottish sources. In the case of Walter Comyn and Alexander Comyn, it has been possible to set the contemporary pro- Comyn *Melrose Chronicle* (the principal contemporary Scottish narrative source from 1171 to 1263) against the overwhelmingly negative image of the family in post-Bannockburn narrative sources to achieve a more balanced and truer image of the family in the thirteenth century. The family has emerged as pillars of an increasingly independent-minded national monarchy rather than a consistently disruptive and damaging influence on that monarchy's development. The contribution of John Comyn (known as 'the Younger' before his father's death c.1302) to Scottish history must be seen in the context of his family role, central to Scottish royal government since the 1230s. It must also be assessed in the context of the time he lived rather than through the false prism of fourteenth and fifteenth-century Scottish writers who wanted to fashion the past to influence their audiences living in the difficult political climates of the later fourteenth and fifteenth centuries. Of course, the story of John Comyn's contribution to the early Scottish independence movement in the period 1286 to 1306 is made more difficult by the fact that he occupied the same chronological and historical ground as the heroes of Scottish tradition – William Wallace and Robert Bruce – and both had difficult relationships with John Comyn (and he with them!). However, the fact that Wallace and Bruce also had fundamental differences – Wallace being the most fervent of fighters for the Balliol kingship, and Bruce, like his father and especially his grandfather, being in constant opposition to Balliol since 1286 and more often in the camp of Edward I than the Scottish camp – has been glossed over in the post-Bannockburn writings. Indeed, a totally artificial, literary device has had to be employed (as illustrated in Chapter 1) to make it appear that Robert Bruce was the natural successor to William Wallace as champion of the Scottish independence movement. As will be seen, the Wars of

Independence were not all about William Wallace and Robert Bruce – nor was the national cause.

Despite all the problems in the way of an untainted picture emerging of John Comyn's contribution to the Scottish cause, it is still possible to rebalance the post Bruce writings. Recent discoveries, for instance, of contemporary narrative sources (some pro-Comyn) hidden away within predominantly pro-Bruce writings of the later fourteenth and fifteenth centuries shed valuable light on the key years between 1298 and 1304 if only for this short period (see Chapter 1). Contemporary (or near-contemporary) English sources too (especially northern English ones) give more valuable detail for the military campaigns of the wars than generally contained in the major Scottish sources of the fourteenth and fifteenth centuries and add to our understanding of Scottish leadership in the campaigns before 1306. When John Comyn is finally freed from the yoke of seemingly pervasive pro-Wallace and pro-Bruce writings, a strong Scottish patriot hero emerges.

John Comyn's story, in brief, is one of a young Scottish knight who was involved in the first military actions for the Scottish army when the Wars of Independence broke out in 1296 and therefore must have struck some of the first blows for the Scottish cause – Robert Bruce and his family were on the English side at the outbreak of war! John Comyn was then captured at Dunbar Castle and taken as prisoner to England to be held in the Tower of London but gained release by agreeing to fight for the English army against the French in Flanders in 1297. This was a subterfuge as John Comyn escaped and fled to France where he sought help for the Scottish cause from the king of France. On return to Scotland in 1298, he was soon accepted as political and military leader of the Scottish war effort following William Wallace's defeat at the Battle of Falkirk. He showed great leadership qualities between 1298 and 1304. He won a great victory (a much underestimated one) against a strong English force at the Battle of Roslin in 1303. His stout defence of the principles of the Scottish cause (so well expressed in the Treaty of Birgham/Northampton in 1290) and the legitimate Balliol dynasty came to the fore when he had to negotiate (as head of the Scottish political community) with the English in 1300–1 and 1304. It was his refusal to compromise with these principles and sanction the illegal overthrow of the legitimate dynasty by Robert Bruce which led to his murder – a truly heroic figure in the Scottish independence movement (had it not been for pro-Bruce propaganda!). It is a story worth telling in full and is sufficient reason, in itself, for placing his murder under further scrutiny.

John Comyn's Political Inheritance: The Spirit of Birgham

The Treaty of Birgham/Northampton (1290) in practice contained a summary of Scotland's rights as an independent nation. John Comyn inherited the spirit of Birgham and, when he entered onto the political stage, acted upon it, following the example of his family in government. The political world he entered was not the one painted by Scottish writers of the fourteenth and fifteenth centuries who deliberately exaggerated the amount of political chaos in Scotland between Alexander III's death in 1286 and 1306 when Scotland was ' rescued' by Robert Bruce's assumption of kingship (no matter how this was achieved, apparently). Their view did not allow for the story of a resilient Comyn-led Scottish government with continuity in personnel and policy after 1286 and insistent on the integrity and independence of their kingdom being upheld. Comyn dominance of the Scottish political community continued after the death of Alexander Comyn, Earl of Buchan, in 1289 with John Comyn the Younger's father, John Comyn II, Lord of Badenoch (d. 1302), and John Comyn, Earl of Buchan (d. 1308), always prominent. John Comyn II, Lord of Badenoch, had been Guardian of Scotland since 1286 and remained in that role until 1292 – he was prominent in negotiations with the English king's representatives concerning the return of the Scottish heiress Margaret, 'the Maid of Norway', to Scotland and was among the prelates and barons who confirmed the resulting Treaty of Birgham/Northampton which sought to safeguard Scotland from the possible loss of national identity through a union of Scotland and England following the prospective marriage between the child queen Margaret and the son of Edward I. John Comyn, Earl of Buchan, (aged over thirty in 1289) also played a prominent role in government during the interregnum as keeper of key castles such as Aberdeen, Banff, Kirkcudbright and Wigtown and would prove to be a stout ally to both John Comyns of Badenoch, father and son, in the 1290s when the spirit of Birgham needed to be defended against Edward I's increasingly interventionist approach.

At Birgham, Edward's representatives had apparently demanded that the Scots should surrender certain castles, presumably as an act of good faith for their co-operation. The reaction of one prominent

Scottish government representative Robert Wishart (like John Comyn II, Lord of Badenoch, a Guardian since 1286) and his colleagues was to refuse to concede such a demand and to delay discussion of the issue until the Scottish heiress should arrive from Norway. Immediately after Birgham, Edward I asked the Guardians to recognise Anthony Bek, Bishop of Durham, as his lieutenant in Scotland, but made it clear that his interests were not purely paternal – Bek was not only to act for the young couple but to establish peace in Scotland by carrying out reform of the Scottish realm. This was clearly going against the safeguards the Scottish government had written into the Treaty of Birgham/ Northampton.

The political crisis in Scotland deepened and the interventionist tendencies of Edward I intensified in September 1290 when the young Scottish heiress, on her way from Norway, was taken ill and died in Orkney. The threat of civil war, always near the surface – the Bruces showed that they were ready to use force after 1286 to advance their dynastic claims – led to a key member of the Scottish government and Guardian, William Fraser, Bishop of St Andrews, appealing for help from Edward I to prevent civil war. The fact that Robert Bruce (the future king's grandfather) also appealed for Edward's help against the Comyn-led government whom he accused of acting outside their authority and also to put forward the Bruce dynastic claim must have given Edward I real belief that both of the political forces in Scotland actually welcomed his direct intervention – an ideal time for him to insist on his recognition as lord superior of Scotland. He made this clear at an assembly held at Norham in June 1291 to discuss the issue, when he declared the reason for his coming: 'by virtue of the overlordship which belongs to him, he may do justice to everyone, and after all the disturbances have been quelled, may restore settled peace to the kingdom of Scotland'.[2]

However, this assumption was contrary to Edward's commitment less than a year earlier to recognise Scotland as an independent country and the Scottish representatives at Norham therefore asked for time to consider this sudden claim to overlordship 'of any such right or demand made or used by yourself or your ancestors they knew nothing . . . they have no power to reply in the absence of the lord (i.e. the king of Scots) to whom such a demand should be addressed and who could reply to it . . . meanwhile they can only refer to the oath they took after the death of the king (Alexander III) saving your faith and theirs and (? to the Treaty of Birgham) confirmed in your presence at Northampton'.[3]

Edward I rejected this response and outmanoeuvred the leaders of the Scottish political community by asking the claimants to the Scottish throne – one of whom must be king and have the right to reply – to reply. Thus the thirteen competitors – among whom were the two favourites, John Balliol and Robert Bruce (grandfather of the future king), but also John Comyn II, Lord of Badenoch, the Guardian – agreed that Edward should have possession of the kingdom and the royal castles. By this clever legal ploy, the acting Scottish government – the Guardians – had been outflanked and had compromised their clear stance on Scottish independence, but it is clear that they were still prepared to fight for Scotland's integrity in these difficult political circumstances. Robert Wishart, for instance, spoke out against Edward's claims to suzerainty and some of the castle commanders refused at first to hand over their castles. Edward was forced into some concessions by agreeing that he would maintain the customary laws and liberties of the kingdom until a decision about the rightful king was made. The spirit of Birgham was still alive and recent research has argued convincingly that the Guardians had, in fact, only conceded partial overlordship, i.e. only for the time when Scotland was without a king.[4] A rare contemporary Scottish source, 'The Scottish Poem' in *Liber Extravagans* appended to *Scotichronicon* by Walter Bower, shows how the Scots were still clinging to the rights they thought they had secured at Birgham:

> A great part of the Scots agreed to this under compulsion, provided that their laws and liberties were preserved. The king promised on oath that he would preserve these so nothing new would be introduced without the taking of common counsel.[5]

However, Edward I wanted more – full overlordship! After the final judgement of the 'Great Cause' was made (on 17 November 1292) in favour of John Balliol (the candidate of the Comyn party, and brother in-law of John Comyn II, Lord of Badenoch), the spirit of Birgham would have to be exercised again in defence of the new Scottish king.

The Kingship of John Balliol (1292–1296) and the Emergence of John Comyn the Younger of Badenoch

The fifteenth-century writings of Walter Bower encapsulate two great myths at the heart of Scottish tradition today – that John Balliol was a 'puppet' of Edward I and that Scotland was in chaos before being rescued by Robert Bruce in 1306:

> King John intruded through the guile and power of the king of England, was king for less than four years, in very great servitude and bondage to the king of England; before this the kingdom was so to speak headless for seven years after the death of the peace-making King Alexander III, and abnormal in the time of this disastrous King John.[6]

Focusing narrowly on Edward I and John Balliol has also distracted attention from the policies which John Balliol's Comyn-led government pursued in defence of Scottish independence and the principles of Birgham. Far from being 'abnormal', the reality of 1292–6 was an experienced government team backing the new king (and more especially defending the principles of Birgham). Dominance of the Comyn family and their allies in Scottish government continued much as it had done in Alexander III's reign and through the Guardianship period from 1286 to 1292. This was natural as John Balliol was the candidate of the dominant Comyn governing elite. The inner core of advisers under the new Scottish kingship were John Comyn II, Lord of Badenoch (John Balliol's brother-in-law), John Comyn, Earl of Buchan (the new king's cousin), Geoffrey de Mowbray (related to the Comyns through marriage), Patrick Graham (from a family consistently in support of the Comyns), Alexander de Balliol (a member of the Balliol family but one who had held the post of chamberlain in Scottish government since 1286 and continued in that role under Balliol) and Thomas Randulf. Also prominent in the royal circle were William Fraser, Bishop of St Andrews, and Robert Wishart, Bishop of Glasgow, and members of the Umphraville, Soules and Sinclair families. This experienced team had to face three major political problems:

1. the new king was inexperienced in government and not conversant with the Scottish political community's increasingly self-conscious attitude to its rights, liberties and independence
2. Edward I's determination to establish full overlordship over the Scottish king and kingdom
3. the resentment of the Bruce family to their exclusion from power in Scotland since 1286 and the failure of their dynastic claim in the 'Great Cause'.

John Comyn the Younger of Badenoch, heir of John Comyn II, Lord of Badenoch, would have to face all three problems directly as he took his first steps on the Scottish political stage. Naturally, the Comyn family, as relatives of the new king as well as the mainstays of Scottish government, at first benefited further from royal patronage. King John gave John Comyn, Earl of Buchan, his cousin, all the lands of his than-ages of Formartine and 'Dereley' (probably Belhelvie) except the burgh and castle of Fyvie. These thanages were together worth over 250 marks per year. In return, Earl John surrendered his claims on the lord-ship of Galloway. The Balliol/Comyn government in Scotland was strengthened by bolstering Comyn power in the north and Balliol power in the south-west. John Comyn II, Lord of Badenoch, and his son, John Comyn the Younger, also benefited with land from the royal patronage of their brother-in-law and uncle. It was probably early in John Balliol's reign that John Comyn the Younger of Badenoch was knighted by his uncle, the king.

Edward I was extremely conscious of the families who wielded power in 1290s Scotland and tried to influence them through gifts and marriage alliances with either members of the English royal family or noble English families close to the royal family. John Balliol already had such a connection by 1281 through his marriage to Isabel daughter of John de Warenne, Earl of Surrey. It is interesting that John Comyn the Younger of Badenoch, was picked out for a marriage alliance with the English royal family early in John Balliol's reign when he married Joan de Valence, daughter of William, Earl of Pembroke, and cousin of Edward I himself. Edward was clearly aware of the political power of the Comyns in Scotland and their control over key castles and communications and wished to exercise as much influence and control over them as he could. During the period Edward ruled Scotland directly between June 1291 and November 1292, he had seen how much Scottish government relied on the family and its associates for its stability. Edward I felt that he had the means – through largesse and a deliberate show of financial authority – to control the individuals who mattered in Scotland, the new king and his main political advisers. The Comyns of Badenoch, like other families of Scottish government, certainly received favour from Edward – Edward allocated £200 to John Comyn II, Lord of Badenoch, from the fines of Cumberland and Northumberland; in 1292–3 this John Comyn and his son, John Comyn the Younger of Badenoch, were acquitted from the common summons in justice eyres in Tynedale. John Comyn the

Younger must also have been made aware of the privileges that came through marriage into the powerful family of the earl of Pembroke. William de Valence, Earl of Pembroke, asked permission from Edward I for his son-in-law to send attorneys in all pleas before justices in eyre in Tynedale.

If gifts were the 'velvet glove' of Edward I's policy to achieve control over key political figures in Scottish government, the 'iron fist' was never far away. Edward I was keen to show his capacity to exert financial control over them too. He made, for example, maximum use of his overlordship and direct rule of Scotland from June 1291 to December 1292 to assert financial lordship over John Balliol and the Comyns of Badenoch and Buchan. It is slightly sinister that on 28 November 1292, two days before John Balliol's enthronement, Edward I ordered the barons of the exchequer to produce a report on the debts of John Balliol, King of Scotland. As for John Comyn II, Lord of Badenoch, he was found to have arrears of £1563 14s 6d which were presumably owed for the 'fermes' from his baillies of Jedburgh, Dull, Kilbride and Barburgh (Bridburgh).

Confident in his powers of control, Edward I pushed on at the very beginning of John Balliol's kingship to establish his full overlordship of the Scottish king and kingdom. In fact, as soon as judgement was made in favour of John Balliol's claim to the Scottish throne, there was, apparently, a warning that if he did not rule justly Edward I would have to intervene. However, Edward I was to learn that there was more to establishing full overlordship over the Scottish kingdom than by controlling individuals. The Scottish kingdom was more mature and sophisticated in the 1290s than it had been fifty years earlier and experienced Scottish leaders in those fifty years (chiefly the Comyns and the bishops) had begun to devise, if not a formal constitution, a formula for what the rights and liberties of an independent Scottish kingdom should be. The fullest expression of this formula was contained in the Treaty of Birgham/Northampton (1290). It is not surprising therefore that there was a clear response to Edward I's early attempt to establish his right to hear appeals outside Scotland. Only one week after John Balliol's enthronement on 7 December, Roger Bartholomew, a Berwick burgess, complained to Edward about three adverse judgements of the Guardians. Edward's rapid response to this –compensation repayments were made by 6 January 1293 – shows the English king's eagerness to demonstrate his right to hear appeals. The Comyn-led leaders of Balliol's government – in this instance, John

Comyn, Earl of Buchan, Bishop William Fraser of St Andrews, Patrick Graham and Thomas Randulf – challenged this by lodging a petition on behalf of their king. It objected to Edward taking appeals outside Scotland and asked that the English king should keep the promises made in the Treaty of Birgham/Northampton. Unfortunately, Edward's unambiguous reply highlighted the legal weaknesses in the Scottish leaders' position after 1291 – they had abdicated their power as Guardians of the Scottish realm, to be reappointed by Edward, and recognised, through the Competitors, Edward's right to overlordship. Edward simply stated that he had a right to review their decisions as the Guardians after 1291 were responsible to him alone as their overlord; any promises made in the interregnum were for that time alone and were no longer binding.

Edward I followed this up on 2 January 1293 by forcing an important concession from King John who 'solemnly freed Edward from all obligations and promises which the English king might have entered into with the guardians and responsible men of the Scottish realm, declaring null and void any written evidence of such promises and explicitly annulling the Treaty of Birgham'.[7] There was some resistance to this from the Scottish political community as Edward had to make a partial concession on 4 January promising that if the king of Scotland left an undisputed heir to the Scottish throne in the future, he would demand no rights in Scotland except those of homage and overlordship. This episode made two issues clear – that the Treaty of Birgham/Northampton had become a manifesto for the beliefs of the Scottish political leadership and would remain so despite Edward's attempts to remove it from the record; and that John Balliol was too inexperienced a figurehead to carry out this policy in the face of pressure from Edward I. John Balliol unlike his Scottish advisers, was not imbued with the spirit of Birgham but was accustomed to give deference to Edward as his overlord in England.[8] Both Edward I and the Comyn leadership in Scotland were competing to impose their policies on John Balliol. English chroniclers complained that Comyn counsellors drove away all in Balliol's household who were of his kin and replaced them with choices of their own. To English chroniclers at this stage, the Comyn-led government was seen as the enemy, a 'patriot' party getting in the way of Edward's imposition of overlordship on John Balliol.

The next test in this battle over Scottish policy came when Balliol was pressed to appear in person at the Michaelmas parliament of 1293 to defend his government's judgement in the suit of Macduff of Fife – it is notable that appeals to Edward I came mainly from malcontents in Scotland with either political or economic grievances against the government. Undoubtedly Balliol was rehearsed by his more experienced Scottish counsellors: 'the king of Scotland says that he is king of the realm of Scotland and dare not make answer at the suit of Macduff without the advice of the "probi homines" [responsible men] of his realm'.[9] Balliol also added (or was advised to add) that that he would not accept an adjournment as this would be seen as recognition of English jurisdiction. His reply was very much in line with consistent Comyn-led government policy focused on the rights they thought Edward I had confirmed at Birgham. However, Edward I knew how to better the inexperienced Balliol by judging him as being in his mercy for contempt of court and threatening him with the forfeiture of his three main castles and towns. At this, Balliol abandoned all resistance and once more acknowledged Edward's overlordship in abject terms and also asked for an adjournment. One of the few contemporary Scottish sources, 'The Scottish Poem' in *Liber Extravagans* appended to *Scotichronicon* by Walter Bower, reports that Edward:

> forced the aforesaid king of Scots to seek a legal judgement in London, a place where he was unable to have anyone close to him to stand behind him, so that he might prove the rights of the kingdom which the Scots had always been accustomed to possess.[10]

The next stage in Edward I's assertion of overlordship on Scotland occurred in 1294 when, after war broke out between England and France, Edward summoned John Balliol along with ten Scottish earls and sixteen barons to perform personal service for him against the French. This particular test was postponed because the Welsh rose in revolt shortly afterwards, but English reports suggesting that Balliol had already indicated his willingness to give whatever aid Edward required must have alarmed Balliol's advisers. No Scottish king had taken part in an English army expedition since 1159! The Comyn-led government therefore started to look for external help to avoid such a breach in the principles of Birgham and preserve the independence of the Scottish kingdom. They sought to free the Scots 'from any oaths exacted from them under duress'[11] and gained this absolution from the pope before December 1294. Between March and May of 1295, an alliance with the French had been negotiated. The clear desire to strengthen the Balliol dynasty was seen when King John addressed letters to Philip IV of France appointing four persons to negotiate in France for a marriage alliance between Balliol's son and a relative of Philip.[12] The proposed marriage of Edward Balliol with Jeanne de Valois, daughter of King Philip IV's brother, Charles de Valois, would also give the Scottish political community active French interest in (and support for) the Balliol dynasty in the future. The treaty with France followed on 23 October 1295. At the same time as external help was being sought, it was decided to take government out of the hands of King John and give it to a Council of Twelve. According to the *Lanercost Chronicle*:

> the magnates, prelates and other nobles of the kingdom of Scotland, having assembled, a solemn parliament was held at Stirling, where by common assent it was agreed that their king could do no act by himself, and that he should have twelve peers, after the manner of the French, and these they then and there elected and constituted.[13]

This looked like (but was not) a political revolution. The Scottish government wanted to *strengthen* the Balliol dynasty and the institution of Scottish kingship but felt that the long-held policy of Scottish kingship and government – to preserve the integrity and independence of its monarchy – was being compromised by the inexperience and political naivety of John Balliol who was no match against Edward I's cunning and forcefulness. The Council of Twelve was, in practice, a return to the Guardianship of 1286, which was in turn a development of the special emergency council set up to safeguard the integrity of the Scottish kingdom when Queen Margaret came to England to give birth to her first child in 1260–1. The common factor in all three constitutional developments was the Comyn family who dominated the political community in 1260–1, 1286 and 1295. The Council of Twelve, comprising four bishops, four earls and four barons – following the same symmetry as the Guardianship of 1286 though doubling the number – again included two members of the Comyn family, John Comyn II, Lord of Badenoch, and John Comyn, Earl of Buchan, and was dominated by Comyn associates. Notably, there was no Bruce presence in the 1295 Council (as with the 1286 Guardianship).

Tension between the English and Scottish governments increased in the autumn of 1295. The Scottish government was able to act more decisively in the country's interest now that their king was not free to compromise the 'national cause' by submitting too readily to English pressure. When the postponed Macduff of Fife case was brought to a parliament at Bury St Edmunds, after Michaelmas 1295, this time the Scots leaders did not send the king in person but sent the abbot of Arbroath who excused his king and complained about the harsh English treatment of Scots. Already it seemed by October 1295, Edward was preparing for action against opposition in Scotland – on 16 October, Edward ordered English sheriffs to take all the lands and goods of King John and all those Scotsmen who 'remain in Scotland' into the English king's hands. He also demanded that the Border castles and towns of Berwick, Roxburgh and Jedburgh should be handed over until the end of the French war. In the same month he also committed to 'his liege' Robert Bruce, Lord of Annandale, who had done homage earlier in the year, the keeping of Carlisle castle. Robert Bruce the elder as well as Robert Bruce the younger (the future king) were among a number of nobles who testified on 25 March 1296 that they had done homage to Edward: 'we are, and always have been faithful to and subject to the will of the most noble prince and our beloved lord Edward . . . we will serve him well and loyally against all men'.[14] The appeals to Edward against judgements made by the Scottish government had revealed some of the opposition to the Comyn-led government in Scotland – the Macdonalds and Macduff of Fife – but there was no greater opponent to the Balliol/ Comyn government than the Bruce family. Like Angus Macdonald, the two elder Bruces (the grandfather and father of the future king) refused to do homage to King John Balliol. Robert Bruce, one of the Competitors for the throne in 1291–2, skilfully kept open the family's claim by resigning it to his son on 2 November 1292 when he realised his claim was going to be unsuccessful. On 9 November, this son in turn surrendered the earldom of Carrick to his son and heir, another Robert (aged eighteen, the future king). It seems unlikely that the youngest Robert Bruce would have been confirmed as earl of Carrick in August 1293 without doing homage for this earldom.

John Comyn the Younger of Badenoch, the Early Stages of the Wars of Independence and the Shadow of William Wallace

What is clear, in the build-up to the first action of the Wars of Independence, and the first action of John Comyn the Younger of

Badenoch in these wars, was that the Bruce family still retained its claim to the throne, thought that alliance with the English king was probably the best way to achieve this, and was in opposition to a Comyn-led Scottish government prepared to fight for the principles of independence they had helped to encapsulate in the Treaty of Birgham/ Northampton. As a result of the Bruces' commitment to Edward I, according to the *Lanercost Chronicle*, the Scottish magnates:

> pronounced forfeiture of his paternal heritage upon Robert Bruce the younger, who had fled to England, because he would not do homage to them. Also they forfeited his son [the future king] in the earldom of Carrick, wherein he had been infeft, because he adhered to his father.[15]

War was imminent. Edward had summoned the feudal host to meet at Newcastle on 1 March, but the focus for the first action was on the Border between south-west Scotland and north-west England. It already appeared as if Edward was trying to govern south-west Scotland directly when on 6 March he sent letters to 'the good men and the whole community of Galloway' at the request of Thomas of Galloway in order to grant them all their liberties and customs. On 26 March 1296, John Comyn, Earl of Buchan – his powerful landholding in the south-west enhanced by the resources of the forfeited earldom of Carrick – led an attack on behalf of the Scottish cause on the Bruce-controlled Carlisle Castle. In the Scottish army were six other Scottish earls (Menteith, Strathearn, Lennox, Ross and Atholl) and John Comyn the Younger of Badenoch, the former Guardian's son. A few days afterwards, on 6 April, John Balliol formally renounced his homage to Edward I in a defiant letter which reflected the strength of feeling of the Comyn-led government better than his own:

> You yourself and others of your realm ... have caused harm beyond measure to the liberties of ourselves and of our king- dom ... for instance by summoning us outside our realm at the mere beck and call of anybody, as your whim dictated, and by harassing us unjustifiably ... now you have come to the frontiers of our realm in warlike array, with a vast concourse of soldiers ... to disinherit us and the inhabitants of our realm ... we desire to assert ourselves against you, for our own defence and that of our realm, to whose defence and safekeeping we are constrained by

the bond of an oath; and so by the present letter we renounce the
fealty and homage which we have done to you . . ."[16]

The words and deeds of defiance on 26 March and 5 April 1296 sum
up the Comyn leadership of the 'national cause' at this time. The
Comyns led Scotland into the Wars of Independence after many years
leading a Scottish government either without a king (since 1286) or
with a king (since 1292) unable to translate the government policy into
practice. That policy was clearly set out in the Treaty of Birgham/
Northampton in 1290. It was a cause worth fighting for in 1296. The
Comyn cause was the 'national cause' as war broke out – it would be
a long time before the Bruce cause was the national one!

John Comyn the Younger of Badenoch was in the vanguard of
Scottish forces when the Scots took the initiative in the wars by attacking Carlisle. With his cousin, John Comyn, Earl of Buchan, he was to
be at the forefront of the Scottish war effort for the first ten years of
the Wars of Independence. His father, John Comyn II, Lord of
Badenoch, was not involved in the fighting in 1296. He had been one
of John Balliol's chief advisers since 1292 and remained his close aide
in 1296, but it is apparent that he was struggling with illness before
1296. Although he lived until c.1302, in practice his son, John Comyn
the Younger of Badenoch, seems to have taken over the active leadership of the Badenoch branch of the family both militarily and politically after 1296. No doubt, the full resources of the Badenoch branch
of the family – based on almost vice-regal authority over vast areas of
northern Scotland and control of key communication routes in both ·
northern and southern Scotland through castles at Lochindorb,
Inverlochy, Ruthven and Blair Atholl (in the north) and Dalswinton,
Kirkintilloch, Scraesburgh and Bedrule (further south) – were placed at
his disposal in the war effort. John the Younger's authority was also
boosted by the family's alliance with two very powerful families in the
north – the MacDougalls and the Morays – both of whom were related
by marriage to the Badenoch branch of the Comyn family.

In the early 1290s the Comyns of Badenoch had exercised control
over the important castle of Jedburgh and this was the base from which
the next major move of the Scottish army took place. Responding to
the English army's storming of Berwick, a Scottish army under the
leadership of the earls of Ross, Mar and Menteith, made a reprisal raid
on Redesdale, Coquetdale and Tynedale in Northumberland. It is
probable that John Comyn the Younger of Badenoch was with this

Scottish force. On their way back, this army took Dunbar with the help of the Comyn countess of Dunbar – Patrick, Earl of Dunbar, married Marjorie, a daughter of Alexander Comyn, Earl of Buchan – who, unlike her husband, remained loyal to the Scottish government. Dunbar came under siege by the English army and on 27 April 1296, in the first major battle of the war, the Scottish army trying to relieve the siege was routed and those within the castle surrendered. John Comyn the Younger was among those captured at Dunbar with the earls of Ross, Atholl and Menteith and other key Scots such as Andrew de Moray (the justiciar of Scotia), John de Inchmartin, David son of Patrick de Graham (Patrick had been the only major fatality of the battle on the Scottish side), John son of Geoffrey de Mowbray, Alexander de Menzies and Nicholas Randulf, son of Thomas Randulf – the prominence of these men is shown by the fact that they were all sent to the Tower of London for imprisonment.[17]

Other members of the Comyn family taken in Dunbar Castle were Robert Comyn (uncle of John Comyn the Younger, later John Comyn III, Lord of Badenoch, and murdered with him in the Greyfriars Church at Dumfries on 10 February 1306), who was sent to Northampton Castle; Alexander Comyn of Badenoch (another brother of John Comyn II, Lord of Badenoch), who was sent to Bristol Castle and Edmund Comyn of Kilbride, who was sent to Northampton Castle. But these were not the only members of the Comyn family to suffer imprisonment in England. John Comyn II, Lord of Badenoch, and John Comyn, Earl of Buchan, had initially escaped north with their king after the Battle of Dunbar – it seems unlikely that they actually fought at Dunbar. After reaching Aberdeen, the Comyns decided to adopt a more pragmatic approach and hope surrender would achieve more favourable terms and avoid the destruction of their lands and castles! On 8 and 10 July at Montrose they submitted at the same time as John Balliol and were ordered to stay south of the Trent, albeit in greater luxury than other members of their family. John Comyn II, Lord of Badenoch, stayed with his family at the manor of Geddington, Northamptonshire, where he was given the privilege of taking twelve deer in the forest as well as permission to hunt fox, hare and cat in the same forest. The imprisonment of his son and heir John Comyn the Younger of Badenoch in the Tower was, of course, intended to guarantee the good behaviour of this senior Scottish figure. Alexander Comyn of Buchan, Earl John's brother, and John Comyn of Kilbride (Edmund's brother) were also sent to prison in England to join those members of the family captured at Dunbar Castle. There were in total, therefore, eight members of the Comyn family in prison in England for their belief in the Scottish cause of independence – it was a mass imprisonment of Scotland's dominant political family, an imprisonment which has received little acknowledgement in the Scottish independence movement and from Scottish tradition. The English king clearly thought it was necessary and the contemporary English chroniclers, rightly, saw the Comyns as the real controllers of the Scottish cause rather than John Balliol. The *Lanercost Chronicle*, for instance, commented on how the Scots, i.e. the Comyn leadership, controlled the initial movements and actions of John Balliol after the Battle of Dunbar:

> it had been *laid down by the Scots to their king John* that he was neither to offer battle nor accept peace but that he should keep in hiding by constant flight.[18]

It was not only the Comyns who suffered from imprisonment in England. Edward wanted all those families who had contributed to Scottish government and the defence of the Scottish cause to feel his anger for their declaration of war on England. Families supporting the Comyn leadership and captured at Dunbar were also committed to prisons in England. The Earl of Ross, who had taken a leading role in the 1296 campaign, was sent to the Tower, as were Andrew de Moray, who had held the key post of justiciar of Scotia in the Balliol government; John de Mowbray, son of Geoffrey de Mowbray who had been justiciar of Lothian – both Mowbray and Moray families were connected to the Comyns through marriage; David de Graham, son of Patrick, again a stalwart of the Balliol/Comyn government, the most senior political casualty of the Battle of Dunbar; Nicholas Randolph, son of Thomas Randolph; and Richard Siward who had been castellan of royal castles in Scotland in the 1290s – he was castellan of Dunbar in 1296 and also related to the Comyns by marriage. Other English prisons held members of the Sinclair family who had been justiciars of Galloway and sheriffs of Dumfries, Edinburgh and Linlithgow; members of the Lochore family who had been sheriffs of Fife in the 1290s; members of the Cheyne family who had been sheriffs of Elgin and Kincardine; members of the Ros family who had been sheriffs of Lanark; a member of the de la Hay family who had been sheriffs of Perth; a member of the Sinton family who had been sheriff of Selkirk;

Robert Lovel who had been sheriff of Inverness in King John's reign; and Hugh de Airth, who had been bailiff for John Comyn II, Lord of Badenoch, in Dull. Other families associated with the Comyns and Scottish government, Mowat and Scot, were also among the prisoners from Dunbar.

It is a great pity that those captured and imprisoned at Dunbar – the battle and the siege – have not been given their due credit as stalwarts of the Scottish cause. Documentary evidence varies slightly over numbers, but around three to four earls, seven barons, twenty-five to thirty knights, and ninety squires were captured at Dunbar Castle alone before being imprisoned in England. Rather more attention has been given to the symbolism of 1296 – the public humiliation of John Balliol having his royal arms stripped from his tabard on surrendering to Edward I at Montrose on 8 July; and more especially the removal of the Stone of Destiny, the most precious symbol of Scottish monarchy, from Scone to Westminster, (along with the seizure of other Scottish muniments and government records). Both were forceful assertions of control over Scottish government and their removal was a direct contravention of the rights of the Scots agreed in the Treaty of Birgham/ Northampton: 'the relics, charters, privileges and other muniments which concern the royal dignity and realm of Scotland shall be deposited in a secure place within the kingdom of Scotland'.[19] A greater contravention, however, was the removal of the king himself and especially the pillars of the Balliol monarchy, the Comyns and their associates. Yet this was probably more important at the time as reflected in the contemporary Scottish source, 'The Scottish Poem' in *Liber Extravagans* appended to *Scotichronicon* by Walter Bower:

> But the king did not (only) despoil the kingdom of its treasures
>   in this way
> but what is worse, he shamefully led off its magnates
> along with its king. But he did this without the sanction of law;
> for the Scots kept the agreement they had made,
> which King Edward was first to break[20]

The Comyns and their associates represented the Scottish cause and the active resistance movement to Edward's imperial ambitions in Scotland.

Scottish tradition, as reflected in *Gesta Annalia* II, has seriously underestimated the maturity and consistency of the Scottish

government's response to Edward I's interventionist policy from 1292
and their willingness to fight for the cause in 1296 – and to keep fighting for it afterwards. As a result, it has appeared as if William Wallace
alone responded to the crisis by leading a new resistance movement in
1297. *Gesta Annalia* II, covering the period after 1285, gives the
impression that William Wallace was not only the chief resistance
leader from the beginning of the 1297 revolt to his defeat at the Battle
of Falkirk but the *only* one:

> [Wallace] brought all the magnates of Scotland under his sway
> whether they would or not. Such of the magnates, moreover, as
> did not thankfully obey his commands, he took and browbeat,
> and handed over to custody, until they should utterly submit to
> his good pleasure.[21]

This emphasis by the main Scottish writers of the fourteenth and
fifteenth centuries – *Gesta Annalia* II (formerly attributed to John of
Fordun) plus Walter Bower and Andrew Wyntoun – on Wallace's
'leadership' in 1297 has distorted the history of the early independence
movement in a number of important ways. The necessity for them to
tie Wallace to their main theme, i.e. the need for strong leadership in
Scotland, has exaggerated the leadership role of Wallace in 1297 as
well as underplayed and even ignored the contributions of a number of
other 'patriot' leaders who were prepared to fight for the Scottish
cause.

Northern English chroniclers – they were both more contemporary
to the action in 1297 and more detailed in their coverage – give a more
realistic impression of William Wallace's role in the revolt.[22] They see
him in a subordinate role until after the death of Andrew Moray, a few
months after the victory at Stirling Bridge (July 1297). To these chroniclers, Wallace was an agent of surviving members of the Comyn-led
Scottish government, James Stewart and Robert Wishart, Bishop of
Glasgow, both former Guardians and active participants in John
Balliol's government who had escaped imprisonment in 1296, in
Stewart's case by an early surrender. Wallace too was aided in the
fighting in the south by William de Douglas, who probably outranked
him. The *Chronicle of Walter of Guisborough* also seems to have
considered William Wallace as a junior partner to Andrew Moray at
the time of the Battle of Stirling Bridge and shortly after. Andrew
Moray was from a distinguished family in Scottish government – his

father, also called Andrew, held the important office of justiciar of Scotia in the Balliol government. Guisborough notably gave the younger Andrew Moray priority over William Wallace when describing two letters concerning their invasions of northern England after Stirling Bridge – one letter only gives the name of Andrew Moray.

The northern chroniclers, Walter of Guisborough and the *Lanercost Chronicle* chiefly, hint that behind the southern-based revolt of 1297, often seen in tradition only as William Wallace's revolt, was an official Scottish government response by those few members of the Scottish government free and willing (albeit in a largely cautious, secretive manner) to stand up for the cause to which they had contributed in government. Certainly when James Stewart and Robert Wishart did come out into the open briefly to lead a force before surrendering ignominiously at Irvine in early July 1297, they clearly regarded themselves as leaders and official representatives of the 'whole community of the realm in Scotland'. Interestingly, they were joined, after the revolt started, by the young Robert Bruce, the future king, seeming to take advantage of family friendship with Stewart and Wishart as well as the absence of the Comyns to join the Scottish political community from which his family had been excluded.

This hint at an official Scottish government response in the south to Edward I's invasion and government take-over in 1296 is confirmed when revolts in northern Scotland in 1297 are taken into account. These were not reported by English chroniclers and this has, consequently, added to the widely-held belief that the 1297 revolt was based in the south as well as being led by William Wallace. Revolts in the north were also primarily a reaction from families – especially the Morays and the MacDougalls – who had played a key part in John Balliol's government and were resistant to Edward I's new agents of government. Revolt in the north also happened despite the fact that senior members of the Moray and MacDougall families were held in English prisons seemingly as guarantors of their families' good behaviour! Revolt in the north also showed that the support of the Comyn family for renewed Scottish resistance was still, in fact, present despite the imprisonment of all key members of that family.

The revolt of the MacDougalls early in 1297 (arguably earlier than those in the south) was led by Duncan son of Alexander MacDougall, a prisoner in Berwick Castle, against Edward I's agent in the north-west of Scotland, Alexander MacDonald, who had been appointed in April 1296 as baillie of Kintyre, formerly under James Stewart's authority, and baillie in the sheriffdoms of Lorn, Ross and the Isles, formerly under the authority of Duncan's father, Alexander. Duncan had never sworn homage to Edward I. The MacDougalls were closely related to the Comyns by marriage – a sister of John Comyn II, Lord of Badenoch, had married Alexander MacDougall. In this regard it is very notable that the strategic Comyn of Badenoch castle of Inverlochy and the two galleys outside were used in Duncan MacDougall's resistance to Alexander MacDonald.[23] More significant resistance in the north against Edward I's administration came from another of Scotland's government families, the Morays. A successful revolt was led by Andrew de Moray, son of Andrew de Moray of Petty who had been justiciar of Scotia (the government's chief political and administrative officer) during the Balliol kingship up to 1296 – his status was well attested by his imprisonment in the Tower with other senior figures of Scotland's government. The younger Andrew, one of Scotland's most unsung patriot heroes, along with John Comyn the Younger of Badenoch, escaped from his own imprisonment in Chester Castle and between May and July 1297 recaptured English-held castles in the north including Inverness, Urquhart, Banff, Elgin and Aberdeen. It is known that there were English garrisons under Sir Henry Lathum at Aberdeen and William fitz Warin at Urquhart Castle, a key strategic site guarding the north of the Great Glen. Again the connection with the Comyns is significant – Andrew's father had married another sister of John Comyn II, Lord of Badenoch. Given the areas covered by Moray's successful military ventures – all areas very much under Comyn influence – it seems certain that Moray's success was facilitated by tacit support from the Comyns. It is unlikely that Andrew Moray could have gathered such a large infantry force in the north without Comyn approval. The MacDougalls and Morays were part of a large Comyn patronage system.

It should be borne in mind that the famous Scottish victory of Stirling Bridge (11 September 1297) was the responsibility of William Wallace *and* Andrew Moray, with Andrew Moray as the more probable senior partner. Only critical injury at that battle and subsequent death later in that same year has robbed Andrew Moray of the mantle of political and military leader of the Scottish resistance movement at this point. As for the tradition that William Wallace uniquely brought with him the popular element into the revolt against Edward I's administration in Scotland, that also needs qualification. It was hardly surprising that there was a popular element in the 1297 revolt – there was a real fear that Edward I would seize 'all the middle people of Scotland to send them beyond the Scottish sea in his army' and Edward's demand for a wool tax affected many levels of society.[24] Both Andrew Moray in the north and William Wallace in the south had popular support, which no doubt increased further with their military success.[25]

Participation in the 1297 revolt by families such as Stewart, Moray and MacDougall, all leading contributors to the Comyn-led government, as well as by Robert Wishart, Bishop of Glasgow, a forceful advocate for an independent Scotland since the 1290s, would indicate that the defence of the ideas encapsulated in the Treaty of Birgham/ Northampton was ongoing. It would be surprising if the Comyns, leaders of the government that led Scotland to war, would acquiesce meekly. The active roles of Andrew Moray and Duncan MacDougall in the north seem to indicate, contrary to tradition, that the Comyn contribution to the war had *not* come to an end. The Comyns, in fact, were successful in fooling Edward I, until late 1297, into thinking that imprisonment had made them compliant. Edward had persuaded himself that he had established sufficient military control in Scotland and that their political leaders were now obedient, duly chastened by their imprisonment. He now wanted to give greater priority to a military campaign in Flanders against the French. The Scots in prison in England were promised freedom if they served Edward I on his Flanders campaign (the English king was having great resistance to this campaign from the English nobility). In early June 1297, Edward released from prison the two senior Comyns, John Comyn II, Lord of Badenoch, and John Comyn, Earl of Buchan, as well as other key prisoners, Alexander Balliol and Alexander, Earl of Menteith, after they promised to serve him overseas. Later in June, however, this plan was slightly amended as the seriousness of the revolt in Scotland became apparent – in late June, Edward asked the two senior Comyns to help him quell the revolts in Scotland. Alexander MacDougall was also released from Berwick Castle on 24 May 1297 apparently on condition that he would dissuade his son from continuing this revolt in the north. Edward also wanted John Comyn, Earl of Buchan, and his brother Alexander to help Henry Cheyne, Bishop of Aberdeen, Euphemia, Countess of Ross, and Gartnait, son and heir of Donald, Earl of Mar, to control the rebellion of Alexander Moray in the north. In the south he commanded that John Comyn II, Lord of Badenoch, should assist Brian fitz Alan in the custody of the kingdom and especially in the defence of Roxburgh. No doubt, Edward thought his hold over the Comyns was secure because important members of the family

– including John Comyn the Younger of Badenoch, and Edmund Comyn of Kilbride – were still in English custody.

The Comyns seem to have been able to deceive the English with their tacit support of the northern revolts for, as late as 26 September, the English still believed that John Comyn, Earl of Buchan, was loyal[26] – the Battle of Stirling Bridge had taken place on 11 September. By November/December 1297, Edward was clear that the Comyns were in support of the rebels as he sent out an order to his bailiff to take the Tynedale lands of John Comyn II, Lord of Badenoch, into his hands.[27] Northern English chroniclers already suspected their disloyalty as reflected in the *Guisborough Chronicle's* comments about John Comyn, Earl of Buchan, who 'at first pretended to repress rebellion but in the end changed sides and became a thorn in our flesh'.[28] Edward I's treasurer in Scotland, Hugh de Cressingham, reported his doubts on 5 August: 'the peace on the other side of the Scottish sea is still in obscurity, as it is said, as to the doings of the earls who are there'.[29] The situation Hugh reported on 24 July 1297 should have been a clue to the growing strength of Scottish resistance: 'in some counties the Scotch have established and placed bailiffs and ministers so that no county is in proper order excepting Berwick and Roxburgh and this only lately'.[30] No doubt, the Comyns were constrained by the presence of family members in the English army in Flanders but that situation changed in early March 1298 when John the Younger of Badenoch and Edmund Comyn of Kilbride, the leader of the Scottish contingent in the Flanders campaign, escaped with more than twenty others and fled to France to ask the French king to help them in their cause. The annoyance of Edward is apparent from the well-informed and contemporary chronicle of Peter Langtoft of Bridlington:

> The earl of Menteith, who was his kinsman
> And the earl of Asketil (Atholl), the Comyn likewise,
> Son of him of Badenagh, and others to the number of thirty,
> Whom king Edward without gold or silver
> Let quit out of his prison,
> Prayed devoutly to go on pilgrimage
> When they have leave, hear how
> They went treacherously to king Philip of France,
> Prayed him for succour and advancement
> Wherewith to recover Scotland
> . . .

The king sir Edward learns by hearsay
How the Scots have betrayed him often[31]

Edward I's peremptory command on 26 March 1298 to his cousin, Joan, the wife of John Comyn the Younger of Badenoch, to return to London with her children was an acknowledgement that a key Comyn hostage had escaped from his grasp and that his attempt to control the Scottish resistance through the Comyns had failed. The escape of John Comyn, the Younger, of Badenoch, was to prove a major blow to Edward I as within six months he would become the leader of Scottish resistance (a role he would retain until his murder in 1306).

John Comyn the Younger of Badenoch and the leadership of the Scottish cause

The return of the Comyns to leadership of Scottish resistance and the natural promotion of John Comyn the Younger of Badenoch, to that position have been obscured by the focus given by Scottish tradition to William Wallace in 1297 and 1298. Just as the main writers (*Gesta Annalia*, Walter Bower and Andrew Wyntoun) behind that tradition have distorted Wallace's leadership role in the 1297 rising (to the detriment especially of Andrew Moray) so they have caused more distortion to the history of the Scottish independence movement by seeking to blame the nobility (especially the Comyns) for the two low points in Wallace's career, his defeat at the Battle of Falkirk and his resignation from the Guardianship. Wallace's defeat at Falkirk is blamed, in the powerful language of *Gesta Annalia*, on the flight of the cavalry with the Comyns specifically censured:

> For, on account of the ill-will begotten of the spring of envy which the Comyns conceived towards the said William, they, with their accomplices, forsook the field, and escaped unhurt – the aforesaid victory was vouchsafed to the enemy through the treachery of the Scots.[32]

This view has been consistently maintained in Scottish tradition (and history) over the centuries, but is contradicted by the more contemporary and more detailed commentary of the Battle of Falkirk by English chroniclers.[33] No English chronicler claimed that Wallace was betrayed by Scottish magnates – they blamed Wallace himself for the defeat at

Falkirk. According to Matthew of Westminster, Wallace 'seeing that he could not resist such a mighty force . . . fled from the fight forsaking his people to the massacre of the sword', while William of Rishanger thought Wallace 'fled away, not as chief but as an absconder'. The secular chronicle, *Scalacronica*, of Thomas Gray, whose father was in the English army in this period and whose military commentary is usually precise, described how 'Wallace, who was on horseback, fled with the other Scottish lords who were there'.[34] Militarily, it was recognised by both English and Scots that the Scottish cavalry was inferior to the English and this was evident in 1296 at Dunbar, 1298 at Falkirk and 1300 at Cree. It should be borne in mind that at Bannockburn in 1314 Robert Bruce was reluctant to take on the full force of the English after having initial success in a skirmish on the first day of that battle. Bruce was prepared to adopt the 'hit and run' guerrilla-style tactics favoured by all Scottish leaders since 1298 and, according to Gray's Scalacronica, he was only persuaded to face the English army by a deserting English noble who persuaded him that the English were in disarray and that a victory over them could be gained:

> The Scots in the wood reckoned they had done well enough during the day's fighting, and were on the point of decamping and moving into the Lennox, a more defensible country, when Alexander de Seton, knight, who was of the English army, and had come there with the king, secretly left the English army, and came to Robert Bruce in the wood.[35]

Gray's father would have been well placed to comment as he was a prisoner in the Scottish camp.

The account of the Battle of Falkirk perpetuated by Scottish tradition is misleading militarily and the well-known description of Wallace's resignation from the Guardianship is as misleading politically: 'after the aforesaid victory, which was vouchsafed to the enemy through the treachery of Scots, the aforesaid William Wallace, perceiving, by these and other strong proofs the glaring wickedness of the Comyns and their abettors, chose rather to serve with the crowd, than be set over them, to their ruin'.[36] This is very much at odds with the acceptance by the Scottish political community of John Comyn the Younger of Badenoch, as Guardian 'not long after' Falkirk and in the 'same year' as Wallace's resignation from that office. The long-established picture of John Comyn as traitor to William Wallace at Falkirk, a necessary excuse for Wallace's failure in the eyes of fourteenth and fifteenth-century Scottish writers, should be expunged from the records. It distorts John Comyn the Younger's military record fighting for the Scottish cause at the outset of the wars as well as his military and political leadership of that cause from 1298 to his murder in 1306.

Fortunately, after Falkirk, it is not necessary to wrestle solely with pro-Wallace or pro-Bruce propaganda to achieve a true picture of John Comyn's achievement as leader of the patriot cause. Research has established that *Gesta Annalia* II incorporated a contemporary pro-Comyn chronicle, perhaps deriving from St Andrews, for the years 1298 (after Falkirk) to 1304.[37] That it remained within a predominantly pro-Bruce fourteenth-century narrative is perhaps owing to a lack of suitably patriotic material about Robert Bruce, the hero of the *Gesta Annalia* II after 1306, for the years 1298 to 1304.[38] This invaluable chronicle material adds to other record sources to give real insight into John Comyn the Younger's political and military leadership of the Scottish cause.

Gesta Annalia II establishes that 'John Comyn, the son [i.e. the Younger] became Guardian of Scotland; and remained in that office until the time when he submitted to the king of England [i.e. 1304].'[39] The chronicle clearly depicts John as chief political leader in Scotland in this six-year period, but an analysis of the Guardianship between 1298 and 1304 suggests a more complex political picture. Only for a period between 1302 and 1304 did John the Younger act on his own. The years 1298 to 1304 saw many changes in the composition of what was always a joint Guardianship, but there was one constant factor – the presence of John Comyn the Younger of Badenoch. It is perhaps not surprising given the history of the Comyn family, their vice-regal power over northern Scotland and their long-held position as chief pillars of the Scottish monarchy that a member of the family should take the lead at this time – through their network of lands, castles and allies, they simply had more political and military power in Scotland and greater powers of patronage (hence control) than any other family. They were the natural leaders of the Scottish political community. There were, however, two other members of that family who had seniority to John Comyn the Younger of Badenoch – his father, John Comyn II, Lord of Badenoch, who lived until 1302; and his cousin, John Comyn, Earl of Buchan, who was active in the Scottish war effort from the outset in 1296. It is not known whether John the Younger had already demonstrated superior leadership qualities to his two elders by 1298 – perhaps in his military role in the vanguard of the action in 1296 and his dramatic escape from the English army in Flanders he had shown the same fighting qualities as his grandfather: 'a keen fighter and a most outstanding participant in all knightly encounters' (*Scotichronicon of Walter Bower*).[40] His father was in ill-health by 1296 and that probably explains his lesser role in the period after 1296 until his death in 1302), but John Comyn, Earl of Buchan, was only slightly older and very active in both military and diplomatic activity until his death in 1308. Either John Comyn the Younger was seen as a stronger leader at this stage of the wars (history, albeit with hindsight, would prove this assumption to be correct) or it was simply the 'turn' of the Badenoch branch of the family to assume the political leadership role after the Buchan period of leadership under Alexander Comyn, Earl of Buchan (1258–1289). It should be remembered when the Guardianship was revived, by early 1298, it was very much a military guardianship as seen by the official title given to William Wallace in a government act of 29 March 1298: 'Guardian of the kingdom of Scotland and commander of the army, in the name of the famous prince the lord John, by God's grace illustrious king of Scotland, by consent of the community of the realm'.[41] That title followed after Andrew Moray and William Wallace (in practice, Guardians after their victory at Stirling Bridge) sealed government correspondence as 'commanders of the army of the kingdom of Scotland, and the community of that realm'.[42]

The military nature of the new Guardianship, after Wallace's defeat at Falkirk and resignation shortly afterwards, might explain the suitability of John Comyn the Younger to that office; it might also explain the somewhat surprising decision for the office of Guardian to be shared with Robert Bruce, Earl of Carrick and future king. It was an attempt, short-lived as it happened, at a government of national unity, an attempt to combine the military resources and patronage of two of the most influential families in Scotland through two vigorous younger members of those families. Scottish political leaders must have been aware that the Scottish defeat at Dunbar was not a defeat of the full Scottish host as three Scottish earls – Patrick, Earl of March and Dunbar, Robert Bruce, Earl of Carrick, and Gilbert de Umphraville – were on the English side in 1296. A number of key Scottish leaders (four earls and twenty knights) were also trapped in Dunbar Castle

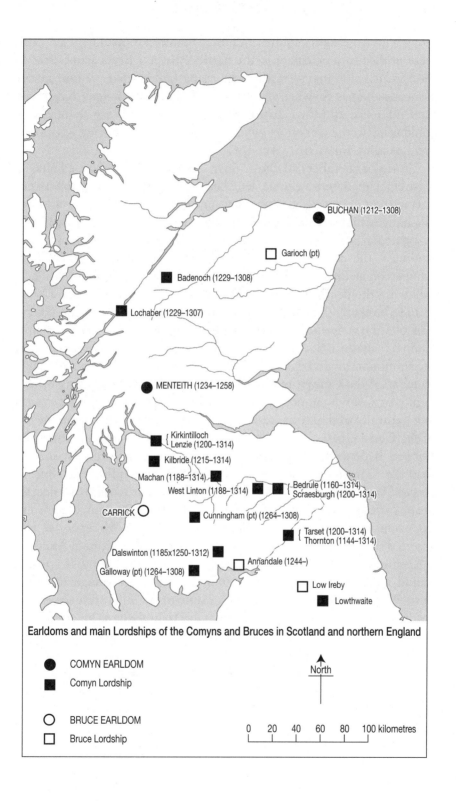

BUCHAN (1212–1308)

Garioch (pt)

Badenoch (1229–1308)

Lochaber (1229–1307)

MENTEITH (1234–1258)

Kirkintilloch
Lenzie (1200–1314)

Kilbride (1215–1314)

Machan (1188–1314)

West Linton (1188–1314)

Bedrule (1160–1314)
Scraesburgh (1200–1314)

CARRICK

Cunningham (pt) (1264–1308)

Tarset (1200–1314)
Thornton (1144–1314)

Dalswinton (1185x1250-1312)

Annandale (1244–)

Galloway (pt) (1264–1308)

Low Ireby

Lowthwaite

Earldoms and main Lordships of the Comyns and Bruces in Scotland and northern England

● COMYN EARLDOM

■ Comyn Lordship

○ BRUCE EARLDOM

□ Bruce Lordship

North

0   20   40   60   80   100 kilometres

along with over eighty squires and three hundred footsoldiers who also were unable to participate in the battle.[43] Robert Bruce came over to the Scottish side in 1297, after the rising had started, to join family associates James Stewart and Robert Wishart and it may have been their influence and their awareness of the extra military resources he could bring to the war effort which was behind Robert Bruce's appointment as joint-Guardian.

All senior members of the Comyn family and significant heirs, at least eight members in total, had been out of the country for a year during their enforced imprisonment in England after Dunbar and not all changes that had taken place in their absence were to their liking. In particular, the Comyns lost control of the important bishopric of St Andrews, the premier see in the country. The election of William Lamberton as bishop of St Andrews at the behest of William Wallace, following the death of William Fraser in France in 1297, was a blow to the Comyns. Comyn dominance of Scottish politics in the second half of the thirteenth century had been supported by a line of pro-Comyn bishops of St Andrews in mutual agreement over independence of the monarchy and the church. Gamelin (1255–71) was probably a member of the Comyn family. William Fraser (1279–97) was from a family of Comyn supporters and had been accused by the Bruces (in aid, naturally of their own candidacy for the Scottish throne on the eve of the Great Cause, 1291–2) of working closely with John Comyn II, Lord of Badenoch, as Guardians, and abusing their office. It seemed that the Comyns already had another family candidate in line to succeed William Fraser. Master William Comyn, provost of St Andrews (1287–1329), and brother of John Comyn, Earl of Buchan, objected to his exclusion from the election process and later, in 1306, it was asserted that he had, in fact, been elected to the bishopric of St Andrews but superseded by William Lamberton.[44] This allegation, if correct, would explain the animosity of John Comyn the Younger towards both William Wallace and William Lamberton. The presence of the young Robert Bruce (who was a similar age to himself) as his co-Guardian must have been a major irritation for John Comyn the Younger from the outset of the joint-Guardianship as the Bruces, from the death of Alexander III in 1286, had tried all means, both military and legal, to oust the Comyns and the Balliol monarchy (1292 onwards) which they supported.

All coalitions – especially those of national unity – have natural tensions at their heart and John Comyn the Younger had serious ones to deal with as outlined above. The animosity between Lamberton, Robert Bruce and John Comyn the Younger came out into the open, as reported by an English spy, at a baronial council meeting in Peebles in August 1299.[45] David Graham, a firm Comyn adherent, put forward a demand for 'the lands and goods of Sir William Wallace because he was leaving the kingdom without the leave or approval of the Guardians'. Sir Malcolm Wallace, William's brother, had objected to this, saying 'neither his lands nor his goods should be given away, for they were protected by the peace in which Wallace had left the kingdom, since he was leaving to work for the good of the kingdom'. A heated argument then ensued:

> At this, the two knights gave the lie to each other and drew their daggers. And since Sir David Graham was of Sir John Comyn's following and Sir Malcolm Wallace of the earl of Carrick's following, it was reported to the earl of Buchan and John Comyn that a fight had broken out without their knowing it; and John Comyn leapt at the earl of Carrick and seized him by the throat, and the earl of Buchan turned on the bishop of St. Andrews, declaring that treason and `lesemjestie` were being plotted. Eventually the Stewart and others came between them and quietened them . . . So it was ordained that that the bishop of St Andrews should have all the castles in his hands as principal captain, and the earl of Carrick and John Comyn be with him as joint-guardians of the kingdom.

The bad feeling between John Comyn, Earl of Buchan, and William Lamberton, Bishop of St Andrews, because of the exclusion of John's brother, Master William Comyn, from the election to the bishopric may have been behind the initial hostility shown; similarly, John Comyn the Younger would not have been slow to show resentment towards a member of the Bruce family who had long opposed his family's grip on power. The episode also shows the tension between William Wallace and the 'natural' leadership of the political community, i.e. the Comyns, which had reasserted itself after Falkirk. However, William Wallace and John Comyn the Younger were, at least, both vigorously in support of the Balliol monarchy as *the* symbol of the independence movement they were both fighting for.

The accusation from the Comyn side during the heated argument that 'treason and *lesemajestie* were being plotted' adds an altogether more serious note to the quarrel over land. *Lesemajestie* (literally 'replace the king') suggests that Robert Bruce had once more brought up the issue, perhaps to William Lamberton in his role as senior churchman in the country, of his family's claim to the throne being preferable to an absentee king. If this was so (as seems likely by the violence of the reaction by the two Comyns towards both Robert Bruce and the bishop of St Andrews), then it fits in with the consistent support of the Comyns for the national cause, i.e. the legitimate Balliol dynasty. It also suggests that it would be difficult for John Comyn the Younger to accept working with Robert Bruce for much longer or to accept William Lamberton as a 'neutral' voice between them. This was apparent in May 1300 at a parliament held at Rutherglen:[46]

> the bishop of St Andrews and sire John Comyn were at discord and the Stewart of Scotland and the earl of Atholl took the part of the bishop, and sire John Comyn said that he did not wish to be a guardian of the realm along with the bishop. But at length they were at accord and they elected sir Ingram d' Umphraville to be one of the guardians of the realm in place of the earl of Carrick.

Whatever opposition John Comyn the Younger faced within the nobility (and it was only from those with family connections to the Bruces) it should be noted that he won the day for the Balliol dynasty and the national cause. It is not clear whether Robert Bruce resigned (or was replaced) at this parliament or just before. There was not enough groundswell of support for the continuing presence of Bruce as joint-guardian, even with the support of the bishop of St Andrews. The new Guardian Ingram de Umphraville was a kinsman of John Balliol, having married a daughter of Ingram de Balliol and made his career in Scotland where he proved to be a staunch adherent to the national cause until 1306. He was notably pro-active in the war effort and this was a very important ingredient to have in the Guardianship – the Guardianship had to be run as a 'war cabinet'.

The new triumvirate of Guardians – John Comyn the Younger, William Lamberton and Ingram de Umphraville – was much more Comyn and Balliol-oriented and lasted until early1301, certainly no later than May. This was a period when the diplomatic efforts of the Scots in France and at the papacy seemed to be gaining some reward (see pages 149–51) and Balliol was indeed released from papal custody in the summer of 1301. His subsequent return to his family lands in Picardy suggested that, with French support, he could soon return to

Scotland. It is not known whether the increasing possibility of Balliol's return in 1300 and 1301 actually caused Robert Bruce's resignation from the Guardianship, but by late 1301 he soon showed that his priority was his own dynastic ambition – hinted at in the quarrel with John Comyn the Younger in 1299 – by returning to an alliance with the English king.

The growing likelihood of John Balliol's return to Scotland caused more changes in the composition of the Scottish Guardianship. In 1301, John de Soules was given a special role as the king's agent in Scotland by John Balliol himself. A number of official records between 10 July 1301 and 23 November 1302 refer to John de Soules acting in the name of (not on behalf of) King John or are royal acts issued by King John himself. There has been much discussion concerning the relationship between John de Soules and John Comyn the Younger but the contemporary pro-Comyn section of *Gesta Annalia* II seems to be correct in suggesting that John de Soules was acting with John Comyn the Younger rather than instead of him:

> John Comyn remained in that office [from 1298 to 1304] ... within that time John de Soules was associated with him by John de Balliol.[47]

The fact that John Comyn the Younger was sole Guardian in Scotland from the autumn of 1302, when John de Soules left Scotland to participate in the Scottish delegation to France, seems to fit with this contemporary view. It is probable that Soules (who was in fact related to the Comyns through marriage) was representing Balliol (and perhaps appointed through French influence) and was seen as a link between Balliol and the Comyn-led Scottish political community. He was an addition to the Scottish political scene – a welcome addition after his military involvement in the Scottish capture of Stirling in 1300 – rather than a replacement for John Comyn. Anyone who wanted to exert influence in the Scotland of the 1290s and early 1300s had to seek accommodation with the Comyns and, from 1298, that meant John Comyn the Younger of Badenoch. This was as true for the potential return of John Balliol in 1301 as it had been for Edward I in the 1290s and as it would be for Robert Bruce in 1306.

There has been a tendency to see the many changes in the composition of the Guardianship between 1297 and 1304 in the light of the themes highlighted by Scottish nationalist writers of the fourteenth and fifteenth centuries (and embedded since in Scottish tradition) – that faction-fighting amongst the nobility was the greatest danger to the independence of Scotland and that Scotland needed rescuing by strong leadership, i.e. Robert Bruce. With hindsight, quarrels within the leadership of the Scottish political community can be seen as leading inevitably to the coup of Robert Bruce in 1306. It has been suggested, for example, that John de Soules was 'an effective substitute for the increasingly controversial Comyn leadership of the national cause'[48] and that the numerous changes in the Guardianship after 1297 inferred that 'John Comyn was an impossible man to get on with.'[49] Yet these views distort the political reality in Scotland – a reality which is anathema to Scottish tradition – that the major self-inflicted wound on the national cause, i.e. defence of the legitimate Balliol monarchy, especially during the period 1298 to 1304, was the obsessive dynastic ambition of the Bruces. This was what John Comyn the Younger was attacking so vigorously, with the support of his cousin, the Earl of Buchan, during the quarrel at the baronial council of 1299 in Peebles. It should also be remembered that even families who had supported the Bruce claim to the throne in the Great Cause of 1290–1 were active supporters of the patriot cause, i.e. the Balliol kingship – thus John de Strathbogie, Earl of Atholl (1284–1306) was certainly a friend of the Bruces but was a consistent supporter of the national cause when war started in 1296 and was among the Scottish prisoners taken in Dunbar Castle. Donald, Earl of Mar, related to the Bruces and Atholl through marriage, had been with the Scottish forces which had raided Northumberland and then captured Dunbar in 1296. It was perfectly normal to be a consistent supporter of the patriot cause without being a Comyn partisan. That was shown too in the career of James Stewart – although he had entered a pact with the Bruces in 1286 (the Turnberry band), he still put his duties as a Guardian and the interests of national security before the interests of his allies. Stewart was ready to support the measure for the host to be placed on twenty-four-hour notice in the unsettled conditions after the death of Alexander III when the main danger to national security was the Bruces who were threatening military insurrection. In his long career, Stewart played a leading role in the Balliol government's control of northern and western Scotland and had supported the 1297 revolt of William Wallace (who was from a knightly family in his feudal following). It was the Bruces, almost solely, who were responsible for consistently subversive activity against the political establishment in Scotland after 1286 and even when the

Wars of Independence broke out in 1296. The vast majority of the Scottish political leaders supported the legitimate Balliol kingship after 1292 and were prepared to fight for that in 1296 and afterwards. This in turn meant that, whether they were Comyn partisans or not, they accepted the Comyns as leaders of the war effort.

Quarrels within the baronial councils in 1299 and 1300 have been taken (see above) by some modern commentaries to indicate the unsuitability of John Comyn the Younger for leadership. Perhaps he should be judged by the same criteria used by those fourteenth and fifteenth-century writers whose commentaries have so influenced Scottish tradition – strong leadership. When the facts are examined it will be seen that there is little evidence to suggest that John Comyn the Younger provided anything other than strong and effective political and military leadership of the national cause. It is unfortunate that in Scottish tradition, Comyn leadership was simply the *wrong* leadership because of the need to justify the illegal coup of Robert Bruce in 1306. The history of the early Scottish independence movement should concentrate on the only 'tradition' which mattered in the late thirteenth century – that the Comyns were the natural political leaders of the national cause.

The Political Achievements of John Comyn the Younger of Badenoch

The Comyns' vast influence, amounting to little less than vice-regal control in the north, contributed to the ability of the Guardianship under the leadership of John Comyn the Younger of Badenoch, to restore a semblance of sound government and administration in the area of Scotland under Scottish control. This was helped by the strategic surrender of John Balliol, under Comyn direction, in July 1296 which meant that the Comyn areas in the north were very little affected by the wars. In July 1297, Hugh de Cressingham, Edward I's treasurer in Scotland, had written: 'in some counties the Scotch have established and placed bailiffs and ministers so that no county is in proper order excepting Berwick and Roxburgh and this only lately'.[50] Also, Edward I had not been able to follow up his victory at Falkirk because of internal political problems in England in 1298 which forced him to lead his army back to England instead of consolidating control over Scotland. All this made it possible to run a very effective war administration from the Comyn-controlled north, with Aberdeen probably a key centre.[51] There is evidence that both John Comyn the Younger of Badenoch, and John Comyn, Earl of Buchan, held courts in northern Scotland. As Guardian, John Comyn the Younger held a court in northern Scotland c.1299–1300 in a case between John de Mowbray and Malise, Earl of Strathearn: 'Sir John de Mubray sued Sir Malise earl of Strathearn before Sir John Comyn guardian of Scotland [there is significantly no reference to any co-guardians] for ravaging his lands of Methven and taking the castle, because his father Sir Geoffrey had withdrawn from the King's peace in the beginning of the war'.[52] John Comyn the Younger was able, in other words, to hold to account a Scottish noble who was pursuing pro-English policies – attacking a family (the Mowbrays) who were firm adherents of the Comyns and the national cause. Comyn was free and able to execute pro-Scottish policies in support of that cause.

John Comyn, Earl of Buchan, was justiciar of Scotland, the premier administrative role in government, fittingly in as close support of his cousin's leadership in government as he was in the war effort. In 1300 in this role he was 'holding pleas of his office near Aberdeen castle, in the place called Castlesyd'.[53] Present were John, Earl of Atholl, sheriff of Aberdeen, an ally of Robert Bruce, William Meldrum, an ex-sheriff of Aberdeen and from a family long associated with the Comyns, and Alexander Comyn, brother of the Earl of Buchan (he was sheriff of Aberdeen on behalf of Edward I before 1304 though unlikely to be able to act without his brother's approval). John Comyn was therefore able to deal confidently in this north-east area with a cross-section of interests. Control over north-eastern Scotland was also significant in the war effort as the English control over Berwick and Edinburgh meant that the Scottish guardianship had to use north-eastern ports to bring in war supplies and to send off diplomats to foreign courts to argue for the national cause.

The Guardianship's administration also covered considerable areas of Scotland. The relatively scanty record evidence from the period shows that government documents were issued between 1298 and 1304 from such places as Govan, Torwood, Stirling, Rutherglen, Scone, St Andrews and Inchaffray. The Guardianship's ability to govern was also indicated by the meeting of parliaments at Rutherglen in 1300 and Aberdeen in 1302. Officials such as chancellor and sheriffs were appointed and paid. Sheriffs, key officials in local administration, are known to have been in existence at Aberdeen, Forfar, Stirling, Lanark and Roxburgh, even though there was an English officer in this latter post at the time. It may also be assumed that Comyn control of the sheriffdoms of Wigtown and Banff continued while they dominated these areas. There seems to have been an established and orderly revenue system in existence which would have allowed the important collection of revenues to take place on a regular basis. Control over sheriffdoms meant control over financial as well as military resources of the area.

The relatively few surviving government records in the period between 1298 and 1304 show that John Comyn the Younger's government was dominant in the north but had a surprising amount of influence over large areas of Scotland. There was even an attempt to spread this influence further by John Comyn, Earl of Buchan, with his mission to win over the notoriously separatist Galloway to the national cause in 1300. Effective government – the capacity to be obeyed – was important but only one aspect of good leadership. The principles which guided that leadership are probably more important when judging great patriot leaders. The explosive confrontation between John Comyn the Younger and Robert Bruce in the Peebles Council of 1299 hints at more than a petty squabble for power; it showed John Comyn willing to use force against any talk of treason – '*lesemajestie*' – against the legitimate Scottish monarch, John Balliol. A clearer depiction of the principles behind John Comyn the Younger's leadership is best illustrated in the diplomatic correspondence by which the Scottish government sought to gain support for their cause in the influential courts of the papacy and the king of France. A team of prominent Scottish churchmen and political leaders were constantly involved in putting their case – for the release of John Balliol from custody and his restoration as king in Scotland. Matthew Crambeth, Bishop of Dunkeld, seems to have been on permanent duty at the French court between 1295 and 1301. William Wallace too seems to have been heavily involved in diplomatic activity between 1298 and 1303 when he returned to Scotland to fight for the national cause. Baldric Bisset's expertise in canon and civil law was used to good effect to advocate the cause of Scottish independence in front of Pope Boniface VIII in 1301. From the autumn of 1302, diplomatic activity was stepped up with John de Soules, Balliol's representative in Scotland, returning to France and he was joined by a high-powered Scottish delegation of John Comyn, Earl of Buchan, James Stewart, Ingram de Umphraville and William Lamberton, Bishop of St Andrews. The essence of what the Scottish government stood for and believed in is well illustrated in

the supportive letter of Pope Boniface VIII to Edward I on 27 June
1299 in which he denied Edward I's right to hold Scotland:

> We may also assume that that you have not forgotten how when
> the same king of Scotland (Alexander III) was removed from
> human ken, the late Margaret was left as his heir, a girl who was
> your niece, and at that time a minor, and that the wardship of the
> kingdom did not devolve upon you, as the lord, but certain of its
> magnates were elected for its custody; and that after a dispensa-
> tion had been gained from the apostolic see for contracting a
> marriage between our beloved son, the noble Edward, your child,
> and this Margaret, during her lifetime (if the agreement of the
> nobles of the realm were forthcoming or could be had to that
> proposal), you are known to have safeguarded the interests of the
> nobles [i.e. the political community of the realm], before they
> were willing to consent to this marriage, by writing that the realm
> should remain for ever entirely free, and subject, or submitted, to
> nobody, and in no wise, and that if it should happen that there
> were no children of this contemplated marriage, this realm should
> be entirely restored to its former state, or to a similar state, and
> that it should retain its name and dignity exactly as they were
> before, both in the keeping of the laws and the appointing of the
> officials of the realm, and in the holding of parliaments, and the
> trials of causes therein, and in the summoning of none of its
> inhabitants outside for judgement; and that in your letters patent
> made on this subject these things are well known to be set out
> fully and in detail [in the document known as the Treaty of
> Birgham/Northampton].[54]

It is clear that the terms of the Treaty of Birgham/Northampton still
remained the basic political manifesto for the government led by John
Comyn the Younger. The diplomatic campaign of this government
could be said to have had a fair degree of success. John Balliol was
released from English captivity in 1299 and placed in papal custody
where, after due diplomatic pressure, he was allowed to return to
France, to his castle of Bailleul in Picardy by 1301. It was rumoured at
the time that the king of France, Philip IV, might be prepared to restore
John to Scotland by contributing significant military help. The success
of the diplomatic activity in 1300 and 1301 had been enough for
Robert Bruce to seek alliance once more with Edward I – the fear that

'the realm of Scotland might be removed from the hands of the king, which God forbid, and delivered to John Balliol, or his son'[55] was a mutual concern.

John Comyn the Younger of Badenoch and the Military Leadership of the Scottish Cause

To a large extent the lessons of Falkirk had been learned and from 1298 more harrying tactics were adopted by the Scots and strategic use made of their control of large areas of the countryside to spring surprise attacks on English forces.[56] The Scots had a great degree of success with these tactics though the weakness of the Scottish cavalry when confronted with English cavalry remained a problem as did the inability to take well-fortified English-held castles or towns when there was an English army in the vicinity. This situation was illustrated in 1299 when a force led by Ingram de Umphraville and others attacked a force under the warden of Selkirk Forest, Simon Fraser, who later went over to the Scottish side to become a hero – another unsung one – of the Scottish cause. They stayed in Selkirk Forest to await the chief political leaders in Scotland including John Comyn the Younger and John Comyn, Earl of Buchan. The Scottish leaders felt confident enough in their power to appoint Ingram de Umphraville as sheriff of Roxburgh and Robert de Keith as warden of Selkirk Forest even though these posts were held by Edward I's appointees at the time. However, the Scottish force did not have the necessary siege technology and were too wary to risk attacking the strongly fortified Roxburgh Castle. At Stirling, however, different circumstances prevailed and Scottish forces were able to lay successful siege to the castle which eventually submitted in 1300.

The two Comyns, John Comyn the Younger of Badenoch and John Comyn, Earl of Buchan, both played important roles in the campaigns of 1299 to 1303 which concentrated mainly on the south-west of Scotland. Here the castles of the Comyns of Badenoch (Dalswinton and Kirkintilloch), of the Comyn Earls of Buchan (Cruggleton) and of the Comyns of Kilbride (Kilbride) were important bases from which to attack the English. From 1300, inroads were made against the English in the south west – Kirkintilloch and Dalswinton played important roles in the conflict and changed hands on a number of occasions between 1300 and 1302. In May 1300, John Comyn, Earl of Buchan – appropriately the earl of Buchan as lord of Cruggleton and sheriff of Wigtown spent more time campaigning in the south-west than John Comyn the Younger of Badenoch – went to Galloway to try to win over the notoriously separatist leaders in the area. In the same month, John Comyn the Younger was again involved in the action when three Scottish cavalry brigades led by John Comyn, Earl of Buchan, Ingram de Umphraville and himself faced the English cavalry of the earl of Hereford, Edward I and his son at the River Cree. The Scottish cavalry chose to flee rather engage with this formi-dable force – perhaps the lessons of Scottish defeats at Dunbar and Falkirk had been learned and pragmatism, a feature of Comyn lead-ership in both politics and warfare, won the day. The defection to the Scottish side during the summer of 1301 of both Simon Fraser, warden of the strategically important Selkirk Forest for Edward I, and Herbert Morham, who had been in Edward's service in the Edinburgh garrison, certainly does not appear to indicate any pessi-mism about Scottish fortunes at the time. John Comyn, Earl of Buchan, continued to be active militarily – alongside John de Soules – in the summer of 1301 when he gathered forces at Loudoun in Ayrshire. On 7 September 1301, a large Scottish force under de Soules and Ingram de Umphraville gathered outside Lochmaben Castle. John Comyn the Younger of Badenoch had been actively involved in a largely successful Scottish military campaign from 1298 to 1301. His role as a military leader can best be judged, however, after autumn 1302 when John de Soules, John Comyn, Earl of Buchan, James Stewart, Ingram de Umphraville and William Lamberton, Bishop of St Andrews, left Scotland for an obviously important diplomatic mission in Paris. This left John Comyn the Younger as sole Guardian in charge of the Scottish military forces. The trust in his military abilities is obvious and the period 1302 to 1304 was to witness his finest achievements.

Before moving on to these achievements, it is appropriate to reveal more evidence of the solidly patriot stance taken by John Comyn the Younger in wartime diplomacy which perfectly matched his govern-ment's diplomatic activity on the Continent at the time. This is shown in the two-day peace talks which took place at Kirkcudbright in the summer of 1300 after Edward I himself led a full-scale military expedi-tion into Galloway. Edward met with the two principal Scottish lead-ers (as seen by English chroniclers reporting on the event), John Comyn the Younger and John Comyn, Earl of Buchan. No doubt, after the English had taken Caerlaverock Castle, a siege made famous by the contemporary poem about it, 'The Song of Caerlaverock', Edward, perhaps, expected a more contrite Scottish attitude in these talks (if not surrender). The Scots, under John Comyn the Younger's's leadership, remained firm in their demands[57] – the terms put forward by John Comyn the Younger (undoubtedly he would have taken the lead in these talks) consisted of the restoration of John Balliol as king and, importantly, the recognition of his son Edward as his successor. Given the Comyns' doubts about the capabilities of John Balliol as king, it was necessary to bolster the Balliol dynasty itself. This had been done previously in the terms of the Anglo-French Treaty of 1295, ratified in 1296, after the Comyn-led Committee of Twelve had taken over the executive role of John Balliol – in this treaty, a marriage union was proposed between Edward Balliol and the daughter of Charles de Valois, King Philip's brother. This, cleverly, would have given the French king a more permanent stake in the future of the Balliol dynasty. There was the suggestion during the peace talks of 1300 that these, now defunct, marriage negotiations could be resumed. These terms, as well as the right of Scottish magnates to regain their forfeited estates in England, were roundly rejected by an angry Edward I and the Scots went away but not before threatening Edward with prolonged defence of their demands. Scottish feistiness was apparent once more when a truce was agreed in the autumn of 1300 (to last until Whitsun 1301) Edward, clearly angry and impatient – he had brought an army to Scotland as large as the one he brought for the successful Falkirk campaign in 1298 and the greater part of Scotland was *still* under Guardian control – mocked the Scottish offers of peace. However, the Scottish envoy's response was again firm: 'Exert your strength and see if might will triumph over right or right over might.'[58] When Edward threatened to lay waste the whole of Scotland and force the Scots into submission, the Scottish envoys again vowed that they would fight to the end to thwart Edward. The spirit demonstrated in these reported encounters amply show the spirit and confidence behind John Comyn the Younger's leadership of the Scottish cause at this time.

Stirling Bridge, Bannockburn and . . . ROSLIN (1303)

After another truce expired in November 1302, both sides prepared for military action once again. The strengthening of the garrison at Dumfries in January 1303 and the repairs carried out to the castle and pele at Lochmaben seemed to suggest that the English, understandably, were preparing for more action in south-west Scotland where most of the fighting had taken place between 1299 and 1302. However, John Comyn the Younger took the English by surprise by switching the focus of Scottish attacks to the south-east. In the south-east, Edward I's lieutenant in Scotland, Sir John de Segrave, had been stationed at Berwick since August 1302 with William Latimer at Roxburgh. William Latimer had issued a warning to the king on 7 January, indicating the peril he was in at Roxburgh. Despite an order (on 20 January) for the archbishop of York to send reinforcements to John de Segrave, the newly built fortification at Selkirk was taken by the Scots and another new English construction, the pele at Linlithgow, came under siege. Edward I himself was not ready for campaigning in early 1303 and had summoned the host for May 1303. In the meantime he had ordered John de Segrave to send out expeditions to check Scottish strength in the Edinburgh area. According to the chronicler Walter of Guisborough, he was not ready for the 'Scottish ambush'[59] which resulted in a major military embarrassment for the English and a triumph for the military leadership of John Comyn the Younger at the Battle of Roslin on 24 February 1303.

Historians are fortunate to have a contemporary Scottish source (the pro-Comyn chronicle within *Gesta Annalia* II adds much detail from a Scottish perspective to the usually well-informed contemporary, or near-contemporary, northern English chronicles) for information on the Battle of Roslin. It is interesting to note that the *Gesta Annalia* (the basic source for much medieval history in Scottish tradition) covers the Battle of Roslin in much more detail than the Battle of Bannockburn because of the addition of this contemporary source to its narrative. There seems to be no attempt to edit it down to a smaller size to fit in with the *Gesta Annalia's* glorification of Robert Bruce as its hero. Of particular interest among the English chronicle sources for the Battle of Roslin is Thomas Gray's *Scalacronica* because the author's father was with the English army at the time, probably with Patrick, Earl of Dunbar's, force. What is still uncertain is the size of the English and Scottish forces as chronicles tend to grossly inflate the numbers involved. Later chronicles give the numbers of the two forces as approximately 30,000 English and 7,000–8,000 Scots which, while undoubtedly exaggerated, may give an indication of the relative sizes of the two armies. Modern writers have tended to minimise both the scale of the encounter and its importance: 'We should be careful not to overplay the significance of this "battle" which was little more than an ambush involving only a small English force.'⁶⁰ Elsewhere it has been described as 'probably, a mere skirmish'.⁶¹ The engagement is more fairly judged by the immediate *response* of Edward I to this surprise defeat. One eminent English historian has commented: 'The English had been extremely fortunate that the defeat had not turned into a disaster.'⁶² Edward I's rapid and forceful response to Roslin suggested that it was at least as important a defeat for him as Stirling Bridge.

Certainly the contemporary Scottish chronicle within *Gesta Annalia* II gave Roslin a very high status in the Scottish war effort:

> From the beginning of the first war which ever broke out between the Scots and the English, it is said, there never was so desperate a struggle, or one in which the stoutness of knightly prowess shone so brightly. The commander and leader in this struggle was John Comyn, the son [the Younger].⁶³

The Scottish chronicler gave the utmost praise to the harrying tactics employed by John Comyn the Younger and Simon Fraser (who had come over to the Scottish side with great effect by the summer of 1301): 'John Comyn, then guardian of Scotland, and Simon Fraser, with their followers day and night did their best to harass and annoy, by their great prowess, the aforesaid king's officers and bailiffs.' Gray's *Scalacronica* also refers to John Comyn the Younger as 'Guardian of Scotland and the leader of their cause'⁶⁴ in this phase of new fighting in the war. The chronicle gives a more specific and detailed picture of the fighting in the Border areas and refers to the roles of Ingram de Umphraville and Robert Keith, hereditary marshal of the king of Scots: 'At this time great encounters of war occurred between the marchers, and particularly in Teviotdale outside Roxburgh Castle between Ingram de Umphraville and Robert de Keith, Scots and Robert de Hastang, Englishman, keeper of the castle.' In these circumstances, it is surprising that an English army – with a large force of knights in three divisions – led by John de Segrave and accompanied by Ralf Manton, the treasurer for Edward I in Scotland and with Patrick, Earl of Dunbar, who remained loyally in the English camp, could be taken off-guard to such devastating effect. *Scalacronica* described how John de Segrave came to Roslin 'and quartered himself in the manor, with his own battle [i.e. division around him]. His vanguard was quartered a league further away, in a village.' The contemporary Scottish source within *Gesta Annalia* II showed how the English army 'pitched their tents, split up into three lines apart, for want of free camping room'. The terrain, rather than English complacency, may have contributed to the vulnerability of the English to attack at Roslin.

What is certain from both contemporary English and Scottish sources is that John Comyn the Younger showed superb tactical acumen in launching a night attack on John de Segrave's division. *Scalacronica*'s account is rather brief and to the point: 'John Comyn with his adherents marched through the night against John de Segrave, and defeated him in the night-time.' *Gesta Annalia* II added that Comyn and Simon Fraser with their abettors 'hearing of their arrival, and wishing to steal a march rather than have one stolen upon them, came briskly through from Biggar to Roslin (about 22 miles apart; Biggar was 27 miles south-west of Edinburgh) in one night, with some chosen men, who chose death before unworthy subjection to the English nation; and, all of a sudden, they fearlessly fell upon the enemy . . . some were taken, and some slain, while some fled to the other line.' It seems that John de Segrave was captured in this engagement and Ralph Manton killed. An English perspective is given of the next stage in the battle as the Scots faced the second English division: 'His (John de Segrave's) vanguard, which was quartered a league further away from him, realised he had been defeated, and in the morning, they came in battle formation to the same place that they had left their leader in the evening, intending to do their duty, but they were overrun.' This second encounter was described in *Gesta Annalia* II in more dramatic style: 'while the Scots were sharing the booty, another line [division] straightway appeared, in battle-array; so the Scots, on seeing it, slaughtered their prisoners, and armed their own vassals with the spoils of the slain; then, putting away their jaded horses, and taking stronger ones, they fearlessly hastened to the fray . . .' and this second line was overcome 'though with difficulty'. According to Walter of Guisborough, John de Segrave was rescued by his vanguard.[65] Guisborough also goes on to mention an English third division, led by Robert de Neville, and that this division had some success. The contemporary Scottish account *Gesta Annalia* II, however, describes the Scots as defeating all three English divisions in a narrative that gives the Scottish leaders almost epic status:

> When . . . the Scots thought they had ended their task, there appeared a third [line], mightier than the former and more choice in their harness. The Scots were thunderstruck at the sight of

them; and being both fagged out in manifold ways – by the fatigues of travelling, watching, and want of food – and also sore distressed by the endless toil of fighting, began to be weary, and to quail in spirit, beyond belief. But, when the people were thus thrown into bewilderment, the aforesaid John and Simon, with hearts undismayed, took up, with their weapons, the office of preachers; and, comforting them with their words, cheering them with their promises, and moreover, reminding them of the nobleness of freedom, and the baseness of thraldom, and of the unwearied toil which their ancestors had willingly undertaken for the deliverance of their country, they, with healthful warnings, heartened them to the fray. So, being greatly emboldened by these and such-like words, the Scots laid aside all cowardice, and got back their strength ... and, putting their trust in God, they and their armed vassals marched forward most bravely and dashingly to battle ... So after manifold ordeal and awful struggle, the Scots, who, if one looked at the opposite side were very few in number – as it were a handful of corn or flour compared with the multitude of the sea-sand – by the power, not of man, but of God, subdued their foes, and gained a happy and gladsome victory.[66]

This is language fitting for a patriot hero (and rather similar to the fulsome praise lavished on Robert Bruce in *Gesta Annalia* II in its later fourteenth-century rewriting of Robert Bruce's history after his 1306 coup. Perhaps the contemporary pro-Comyn source has become a little overexcited at the heroics of John Comyn the Younger. It is fair to point out, however, that John Comyn the Younger's actions at Roslin fit in perfectly with his deeds as leader of the Scottish cause since 1298. Also the sentiments of the contemporary pro-Comyn source do not stand isolated. They are supported by the Scottish diplomatic mission in Paris who wrote on 25 May to Comyn and his supporters in Scotland:

And it would gladden your hearts if you could know how much your honour has increased in every part of the world as a result of your recent battle with the English [i.e. Roslin].[67]

The diplomatic mission in Paris also encouraged John Comyn the Younger (he still seems to be referred to in narrative sources as the 'Younger' or the 'son' despite the fact that his father had died c.1302 and he was now John Comyn III, Lord of Badenoch) to continue with his military efforts:

> defend yourselves manfully and stay united, so that by your
> manful defence and with God's help you will prevail, or at least
> receive stronger support from us . . . If you have ever done brave
> deeds, do braver ones now.[68]

Edward I gave his own type of compliment to John Comyn the Younger's victory at Roslin by his military response. Firstly he held an important meeting in York on 15 March 1303[69] summoning those whom he had instructed to help John de Segrave as well as his chief officials such as the treasurer, barons of the exchequer and members of the king's council. The purpose was to discover what had caused the defeat at Roslin and no doubt to apportion blame. Then Edward launched his first full-scale campaign in northern Scotland since 1296. In particular he singled out John Comyn's centre of power in northern Scotland. His route took in key centres of Comyn influence – Aberdeen, Banff, the private Comyn of Badenoch castle of Lochindorb (which he would later use symbolically as his base for receiving the submission of the north) and the Comyn, Earl of Buchan, castle of Balvenie. Edward's awareness of the Comyn control, through strategically sited castles, of key passes in the north is particularly shown by his decision not to use the Drumochter pass. The contemporary Scottish source contained within *Gesta Annalia* II and also *Scalacronica* show the urgency and anger of Edward I's response:

> In revenge for the foregoing outrages, the king of England, with a
> very large force, both by sea and by land, entered Scotland, in the
> year 1303, with the deliberate design of once and for all fully
> bringing it, and the dwellers therin, under his yoke; or, sweeping
> out the inhabitants altogether, and reducing the land itself to an
> utter and irreclaimable wilderness.[70]

The English source, *Scalacronica*, rather more briefly commented: 'Because of this news, in the year following, Edward went to Scotland and on his first arrival, he quartered at Dryburgh.'[71]

The amount of praise heaped on John Comyn in an otherwise very pro-Bruce *Gesta Annalia* II is worthy of note. It is also interesting that the story of Roslin was repeated and added to in the Scottish nationalist writings of the fifteenth century, the very same writers who helped to establish the reputations of William Wallace and Robert Bruce in Scottish tradition. Thus Walter Bower faithfully repeated *Gesta Annalia* II's contemporary chronicle report of the victory with a few embellishments, as was his custom, for literary effect. He added that he had found a certain chronicle in which the number of English troops at Roslin was thirty thousand compared to the Scots 'scarcely eight thousand' and in *Scotichronicon* gives the following extract from this unspecified chronicle:

In the year one thousand, three hundred and two,
when dawned the day of the feast commemorating St Mathias (24
   February,
in the field of Roslin grace shone anew from on high,
for under John Comyn, leader of the Scots
the English were confounded and gave victory to the Scots'[72]

Andrew Wyntoun also celebrated the victory at Roslin:

And with them[the English] the Scotsmen
Then fiercely fought, and laid on them
Where many hard blows were seen
Many there lay dead on the green:
The Scotsmen embarrassed them so,
That many were forced on to their backs there:
They took many prisoners
And divided among them wilfully
The armour and other gear
Of war that they won from them there[73]

Wyntoun even embellished the role of John Comyn as war leader by inventing a stirring speech which he and Simon Fraser made to Scottish troops during the battle. If all the main Scottish story-tellers of the fourteenth and fifteenth centuries fully acknowledged the importance of Roslin in the Wars of Independence and the heroic leadership of John Comyn, it is to be wondered why neither John Comyn or Roslin has broken into Scottish tradition's record of famous war heroes and Scottish victories over the English. When did the censorship start if it was not there in the fourteenth and fifteenth centuries? Why is John Comyn (and Roslin) not alongside William Wallace (and Stirling

Bridge) and Robert Bruce (and Bannockburn) in the Scottish hall of fame for war heroes and famous victories over the English?

Nor could it be said that John Comyn's victory at Roslin was a flash in the pan. His fight for the Scottish cause continued after Roslin even after Edward I brought his full force into Scotland and even when Scotland had lost its greatest ally, France. Despite the high-profile Scottish diplomatic presence in France from the autumn of 1302, following the surprise defeat of the French army by a Flemish force at Courtrai on 11 July 1302, Scotland lost France as its significant ally by May 1303. An Anglo-French peace was made on 20 May 1303 which specifically excluded the Scots despite the best diplomatic efforts of their representatives. This was, potentially, a demoralising blow – the prospect of future French military assistance must have been a real encouragement to Scotland's military leaders since 1300. Thomas Gray's *Scalacronica* (his father was in the English army which came into conflict with John Comyn in 1303) gives graphic detail, however, of John Comyn's continuing military activity after Edward I came back to Scotland. In *Scalacronica* he tells of a force of sixty men-at-arms led by Hugh de Audley in support of Edward I who was quartered at Dryburgh. Audley's force could not be quartered near to the king and therefore moved to Melrose to stay at the abbey:

> John Comyn, then guardian of Scotland, was in Ettrick Forest with a good band of men-at-arms. Seeing Hugh's encampment at Melrose in that manner, he marched through the night against him, and had the gates broken; and while the English within the abbey were arraying and mounting their horses in the middle of the courtyard, the gates were thrown open. The Scots entered on horseback in great numbers, forcing the English (all of whom were few) to the ground, taking or killing them all. At the same time he was struck down, Thomas Gray, knight [the chronicler's father] had seized the house outside the gate; he held it in the hope of rescue, until the house began to burn down over his head, and he was taken along with the others.[74]

This episode, along with the successful tactics adopted at Roslin, clearly shows John Comyn's shrewd use of the type of surprise attacks normally associated in Scottish tradition and history almost exclusively with William Wallace and Robert Bruce.

While Edward I was pressing north to target Comyn centres of power, Scottish campaigns (perhaps as diversionary attacks) took place in the south. In June, a large Scottish force under Simon Fraser and Edmund Comyn of Kilbride was reported crossing the Border into Annandale and Liddesdale and causing destruction to land around Carlisle. Another Scottish force under John de Mowbray, one of John Comyn's closest supporters, and William Wallace (now back in Scotland after his long spell on the Continent) marched through Galloway to raise support there. They then threatened the area around Caerlaverock and Dumfries and, it was feared, would move into Annandale and join up with Simon Fraser's forces.

John Comyn too was still campaigning further south in the autumn of 1303, with as many as 100 mounted men and 1,000 footsoldiers, a force which so alarmed the Countess of Lennox (in Edward's service at this time) that she appealed to Edward I for his help:

> We make known to your highness and dignity that sir John Cumyn has sent a part of his host across the Forth into Lennox to destroy and ruin those persons who have come to your peace Whereupon we pray your lordship humbly and devoutly that you would deign to send us your counsel, together with succours hastily for their deliverance, and for the governance and support of those who have come to your peace. And as it is reported, they have come with a hundred mounted men and a thousand footsoldiers, and reached Drymen in Lennox on the Sunday next after Michaelmas.[75]

A Principled and Honourable Surrender

Edward I's determination to defeat Scottish resistance by wintering in Scotland 1303–4 must have been a blow to John Comyn. As seen by the Countess of Lennox's letter, a number of Scots had now come into the English king's peace. Importantly, a number of Comyn allies had chosen to come to terms with Edward between 1301 and 1304, for example the MacDougalls in 1301, Alexander Balliol in 1301, Alexander de Abernethy in 1302 and William, Earl of Ross, in 1303. Another important Scot, not a Comyn partisan but a significant supporter of the Scottish war effort, John, Earl of Atholl, would be received in the king's peace in January 1304. No doubt, this steady stream of defections and the scale of Edward's campaign prompted Comyn as Guardian and military leader in Scotland to start negotiations for the wholesale submission of the Scots in February 1304. According to *Scalacronica*: 'John Comyn, realising that he could not stand against the power of the King of England, put himself at the king's mercy, on condition that he and all his adherents should have back their rightful possessions.'[76] Other English contemporary English sources, for example Peter Langtoft of Bridlington, naturally give the impression of an abject Scottish surrender:

> the lord of Badenagh goes skulking about,
> Fresel [Fraser] and Wallace go with him robbing
> Henceforth they have nothing to fry, or drink, or eat,
> Nor power remaining wherewith to manage war;
> They are come to the king to solicit his peace.[77]

The decision by John Comyn to seek a formal submission should not be viewed from a triumphalist English perspective. It should be seen from the position of a shrewd leader of the Scottish political community. The surrender terms which Comyn sought were not the surrender terms of a defeated military leader and the negotiation period was long – from the autumn of 1303 to the final submission on 9 February 1304 – which suggests a degree of mutual respect. John Comyn was in a position of relative strength after his famous victory at Roslin in February 1303 and was seeking to secure the best terms. Like other Scottish leaders in the period, including Robert Bruce who was naturally inclined to flight after his first day success in a skirmish at Bannockburn, Comyn realised the disparity in military resources between England and Scotland and the most probable outcome should Edward I focus his resources fully on conquest. John Comyn had learned well from his family's leadership in military and political matters since 1286. The Comyns led Scotland into war with England in 1296 but it is noticeable that both their submissions in 1296 and 1304 were completed without their (and their associates) wholesale defeat in battle and importantly without the destruction of their castles and lands in the north. There was no resistance to Edward I's progress through Scotland after the capture of key members of the Balliol/Comyn government at Dunbar in April 1296. Similarly, there was little resistance to Edward I's next major military expedition north of the Forth in 1303 – there was little resistance beyond Brechin though Scottish campaigning was still taking place in the south. It was a time for pragmatism and realism.

To the Comyns, in particular, the desire to protect their lands was not a purely selfish act. Their lands were the key to their political power and their power of patronage, and therefore control, so it is perfectly understandable that they should seek to protect these in their submission terms.[78] The first clause of the preliminary terms of submission put forward by Comyn concerned securing life and limb, freedom from imprisonment and the confirmation of lands and property in Scotland. The Comyns in particular had suffered much from the imprisonment forced on eight key members of their family in 1296 and they, and their associates, had also suffered from the confiscation of their lands. That John Comyn sought to protect his landed interests and those of his chief allies, the Mowbrays, is demonstated by one particularly blatant clause: John Comyn and John de Mowbray asked Edward I if he would grant them the lands which John Balliol as Scottish king had given to both of them and their fathers before them. Edward refused these specific demands pointing out that they 'have been more concerned to harm and travail the king and his people and have done worse than others, wherefore they should be more humble'.[79] The answer shows a recognition that John Comyn and his allies had formed the backbone of Scottish resistance to Edward I. The question itself shows that Comyn had the confidence of a leader who had not suffered the ignominy of disastrous defeat. There was a more optimistic, certainly a more dignified, air about the Scots in 1304 than there had been in 1296. John Comyn was putting forward firm demands in the negotiations 'on behalf of the community of Scotland'.

John Comyn never forgot, however, that he was representing the political community of the realm, including the important political delegation at the French court. So he required that, in return for submission, all the laws, usages, customs and franchises should be kept in all points as they were in the time of Alexander III. An important supplement to this negotiating position was that amendment to these laws, usages, customs and franchises could only be made with the advice of the 'bones gentz' of the land.[80] Such terms have been recognised as being 'the language of the Treaty of Birgham'.[81] This fits in appropriately with the Comyns' consistent role as chief pillars of monarchy in Alexander III's reign and, after his death, with their leadership within the Guardianship which produced the Treaty of Birgham/ Northampton (1290) with its clearly stated defence of Scotland's independence. John Comyn III, Lord of Badenoch, showed in his negotiations of 1304 that he was imbued with the spirit of Birgham.

Edward I's reaction to John Comyn's negotiating stance is interesting. Surprisingly, in view of John Comyn's leadership and determined, persistent opposition to him between 1298 and 1304, his treatment of Comyn was not ungenerous – indeed, John Comyn was treated more generously than others such as James Stewart, John de Soules, Simon Fraser and Robert Wishart, Bishop of Glasgow, in the initial terms which Edward put forward. John Comyn was allowed to 'retain the lands of his ancient heritage provided he be exiled for one year outside Scotland'.[82] James Stewart and John de Soules (in their absence in France and perhaps because of it) were to receive two years' exile outside Scotland and south of the Trent; Simon Fraser and Thomas Bois were to receive an exile period of three years not only outside Britain and Gascony but outside the lordship of the king of France. Robert Wishart, Bishop of Glasgow, 'for the great evils he has caused' was to be exiled for two or three years outside Scotland. While John Comyn was leading negotiations for a general submission in January and February 1304, a number of matters still had to be settled – there were Scots on the Continent who had not submitted (they should have submitted by 12 April but James Stewart, John de Soules and Ingram de Umphraville still had not done so); Stirling Castle, under William Oliphant, did not surrender until 24 July 1304; while negotiations were taking place, William Wallace and Simon Fraser were still in active resistance though in February 1304 they suffered defeat at Happrew in Stobo, near Peebles, by an English force under Segrave, Clifford and Latimer with Robert Bruce also with them; William Wallace's last known skirmish in September 1304 was below Earnside by Abernethy and Lindores.

Edward I's patience was stretched by the prolonged defiance of both William Oliphant and William Wallace. On the day after the siege of Stirling had ended, Edward I ordered John Comyn, Alexander de Lindsay, David Graham and Simon Fraser (who must have come into the English king's peace by this time), all of them with sentences of exile pending, to prove their loyalty to him in very practical terms. They were given an ultimatum: 'to make an effort between now and the twentieth day after Christmas to take Sir William Wallace and hand him over to the king, who will watch to see how each of them conducts himself so that he can have better regard towards the one who takes him with regard to exile or ransom or amend of trespass in anything else in which they are obliged to the king'.[83] It was not until October 1305, i.e. after Wallace's capture and death, that final details covering the terms of submission were finalised. Terms of exile were replaced by a system of fines. Those who had submitted with John Comyn, i.e. in February 1304, were to pay the value of the rents of their lands for three years; those who submitted before Comyn were to pay the value of rents for two years; the Scottish clergy were to pay the value of rents for one year. There were a number of exceptions – Robert Wishart, Bishop of Glasgow, had to pay three years' rent; Ingram de Umphraville, because of his late submission to Edward, had to pay five years' rents. In addition, James Stewart's lands were not restored to him until November 1305.

In terms of property and land, John Comyn and his family had emerged very favourably from the surrender negotiations considering their dominant role in defiance of Edward I since 1296. They were treated more leniently than James Stewart, Simon Fraser, John de Soules, Robert Wishart, Bishop of Glasgow, Alexander de Lindsay, Ingram de Umphraville, Thomas Bois, Herbert Morham and certainly more leniently than William Wallace. It can be argued that the Scots singled out for harsher treatment were chiefly those who had been in Edward's service and betrayed that trust – this applied to Simon Fraser, Herbert Morham, Alexander de Lindsay and Thomas Bois. However, John Comyn the Younger, and Edmund Comyn of Kilbride had deserted Edward's campaign in Flanders in 1298 and fled to Edward's enemy, the king of France. John Comyn had been one of the military leaders of Scottish forces at the outset of the wars in 1296 and had led Scottish resistance from 1298 to 1304. Unlike William Wallace and Simon Fraser, John Comyn and other members of the Comyn family were never declared outlaws. Among the charges levelled against William Wallace at his trial was that he convened parliaments in Scotland and that he sought to promote the Franco-Scottish alliance. During John Comyn's leadership (1298–1304), a number of parliaments were held in Scotland and the Comyns had been leading proponents of the Franco-Scottish alliance between 1295 and 1304. Edward treated John Comyn and his family in a special way despite, or, indeed, because of, their leadership of the Scottish cause.

It should be remembered that Edward I had not achieved a total victory over Scottish forces in 1303. The north of Scotland, Comyn-dominated territory, was largely out of English control between 1297 and 1303 even after English success at Falkirk in 1298. A consolidation of that victory was not possible because of Edward's priorities in the south. To achieve consolidation in 1298 or 1303 would have required a large and permanent English presence and new fortifications similar to those built in North Wales in the 1270s and 1280s. As Professor Prestwich has pointed out, Edward I was 'not in a financial position to build new fortifications in Scotland on the scale that he had done in Wales'.[84] The final commutation of provisional sentences of exile for his Scottish enemies into large fines based on value of land rents showed his financial priorities. It is understandable in these circumstances that he continued with his policy – trying to control Scotland by controlling the Comyns – despite the lessons of 1292–1303. The years 1296–1303, in particular, showed the importance of the Comyn network of influence in the political and administrative control over Scotland north of the Forth. Edward I still hoped he could reach some *modus operandi* with a family who had important English marriage connections – in addition to John Comyn of Badenoch's marriage to Joan de Valence, Edward's cousin, there was Alexander Comyn of Buchan, the Earl of Buchan's brother, who was married to William de Latimer's sister Joan, and Alexander's daughter Alice, married to Henry Beaumont from another prominent English family.

As part of the submission of 1304, the Scots had to agree to the Ordinances of Edward with regard to the future government of Scotland. The lessons of the period 1296 to 1303 – when the administrative system run by the Scottish guardianships (under the leadership of John Comyn of Badenoch from 1298 to 1303) had been much more effective, especially in northern Scotland, than any structure Edward tried to impose in 1296–7 – had been learned. More Scots were involved in local administration than in 1296 as the final structure for Scottish government was revealed in 1305. The 1305 Ordinances[85] could be said to fulfil key aspects of John Comyn's submissions of 1304 – the retention of the laws, usages and franchises of Scotland as they had been in Alexander III's time, with amendments being made only with the advice of the 'good men' of the land. Edward I's plans for Scottish government emphasised much continuity with the administration which had been under John Comyn's leadership. Many families who had been traditionally associated with previous Comyn-led regimes appeared in the list of sheriffs of 1305. These included the names of Lochore (Fife), Siward (Dumfries), Sinclair (Lanark), Mowat (Cromarty), Ros, Barclay and Airth. A number were seen prominently in Comyn's council at the time of the submission of 1304.[86] Two members of the Ros family were in this council, Geoffrey and James.

Geoffrey, who had been sheriff of Lanark under John Balliol, was to be sheriff of Ayr in 1305 (incidentally replacing Robert Bruce in this office). Two members of the Airth family were in John Comyn's council in 1304 – this family, long associated with the Comyns of Badenoch, were rewarded in 1305 with the sheriffdom of Forfar. Walter Barclay, also in Comyn's council of 1304, gained the sheriffdom of Banff in 1305, a sheriffdom long associated with the Comyns of Buchan.

As for the central administration of the new government structure in Scotland, Robert Bruce, Robert Wishart, Bishop of Glasgow, and John de Mowbray (one of John Comyn of Badenoch's closest allies) were used as advisers for the new Scottish constitution. Following their advice, a Council of Ten[87] was elected by the Scottish community of the realm to advise the English parliament in framing the Ordinances. The Comyns retained a strong presence through John Comyn, Earl of Buchan, and John de Mowbray. Also present were a number of individuals who had played roles in the Scottish cause against Edward I. According to the 1305 Ordinances too, a council of twenty-one Scots was to advise Edward I's new lieutenant of Scotland John of Brittany. This council would act alongside Edward's chancellor, chamberlain and a team of justiciars who were to cover four regions of Scotland (one Englishman and one Scotsman to be responsible for each region). The Council of Twenty-One[88] reflected Edward's recognition of who comprised the political community of Scotland in 1304–5 – it reflected the strong presence of the Comyn family with John Comyn III, Lord of Badenoch, John Comyn, Earl of Buchan, and their family associates William, Earl of Ross, John de Mowbray and Alexander MacDougall, Lord of Argyll. The list included Henry Cheyne, Bishop of Aberdeen (from a family associated with the Comyns). Among the fourteen secular lords represented in the list, the earls of Buchan, Atholl, Ross had been actively involved for most or part of the period after 1296 in opposition to English overlordship, though the earl of Dunbar had been consistently on the English side and Robert Bruce, Earl of Carrick, had only been on the Scottish side between 1297 and 1300. Of eight Scottish nobles, John Comyn III, Lord of Badenoch, John de Mowbray, Alexander of Argyll, Robert de Keith, Adam de Gordon and John de Inchmartin had been mainstays of the Scottish opposition to Edward.

Edward was, above all, intent through the Ordinances on 'the keeping of the peace and the quiet of the land' and tried to ensure more continuity in government than he had done in 1296 by the involvement of Scots at a number of levels. In effect, he had taken over the local administrative system run by John Comyn as Guardian. However, while fulfilling some of John Comyn's submission demands in 1304, such as the retention of the laws, customs, usages and franchises of Scotland as they had been in Alexander III's time, it was clear from the Ordinances that Edward I no longer regarded Scotland as a kingdom as it was consistently referred to in the Ordinances as 'the land of Scotland'. It was clear too that the real reins of power were in the hands of Englishmen through the offices of lieutenant, chancellor and chamberlain.

John Comyn III, Lord of Badenoch – Pillar of 'Legitimate' Kingship

The 1304 submission itself and Edward I's arrangements for a new Scottish government in the period 1304–5 affected the chief political figures in Scotland in a number of different ways. English overlordship was about to become a reality when the new constitution was put into effect. What did this mean for the Scottish cause and its leaders? Was it the end of the fight for the Balliol kingship, that all-important symbol of Scottish independence in the period from 1292 to 1304? Not all Scots welcomed the submission itself. John de Soules, one of the strongest defenders of the Balliol kingship after 1301, 'refused the conditions' in 1304 and does not appear to have returned to Scotland from his diplomatic mission in France. Others probably felt aggrieved by the final submission terms. Robert Wishart, a fervent supporter of the cause of Scottish independence from the time of the Treaty of Birgham/Northampton (1290), was punished (despite being involved as adviser to Edward I in 1305) rather more harshly than others in the surrender terms. Simon Fraser, having at one stage been declared an outlaw, was sent into exile after his eventual submission. William Wallace's capture ended in his savage execution on 23 August 1305. James Stewart did not have his lands restored to him until November 1305. A number of Scots, who had submitted early in the hope of better treatment and were initially rewarded with posts of responsibility, must have felt aggrieved that they were deprived of any responsibility in the final Ordinances. This applied to Alexander de Abernethy, William, Earl of Ross, John, Earl of Atholl, and Robert Bruce, Earl of Carrick.

There has been tendency at this point for historians, with the benefit of hindsight, to concentrate on Robert Bruce and the inevitability (with hindsight!) of his coup in 1306. It has been pointed out that

Robert Bruce must have felt aggrieved by his treatment at the hands of Edward I after he had submitted to him (before February 1302) almost exactly two years before John Comyn had led the vast majority of the Scots to submission. Bruce had fought for Edward I after 1302 – this included action against William Wallace and Simon Fraser and he also helped the English king in the siege of Stirling Castle in 1304 – and had been made sheriff of Ayr and Lanark. In the Ordinances of 1305, he had lost these sheriffdoms and was not even rewarded with land for the support he had given the English king. The Bruces had hoped, since Alexander III's death in 1286, that they would gain Edward's support for their long-held claim to the Scottish throne. They needed outside help for this as they had little support within the Scottish political establishment. The Ordinances of 1305 demonstrated forcibly that, whatever the promises made in their agreement of February 1302, Edward had his own plans for Scotland and these did not include a Bruce kingship. The change in Robert Bruce's personal circumstances in 1304 may have pushed him into finding his own means of satisfying his family's dynastic ambitions. On 21 April 1304, Robert Bruce's father died and he therefore inherited the family claim to the Scottish throne. He also inherited more resources (and power) as he gained the lordship of Annandale to add to the earldom of Carrick and part of Garioch. He was also acting guardian for his neighbour Donald the young earl of Mar, and this brought another important earldom within his control. Robert Bruce soon acted on his new power and position and he took advantage of the unrest at the time of the submission. On 11 June 1304, he made a secret bond of mutual alliance with William de Lamberton, Bishop of St Andrews, 'conferring on mutual dangers and wishing to avoid them as far as possible and to resist the strivings of rivals, they entered a treaty of friendship in the following form, namely that they will faithfully consult mutually in whatever their business and dealings at whatever times and against whatever persons, and bring aid or help by themselves and their men with all their strength for ever and without dissembling'.[89]

Plots seemed to be in the air and the savage execution of William Wallace on 23 August 1305 undoubtedly raised the political temperature further – when William Wallace was captured in August 1305, documents were found in his possession allegedly showing that he had been plotting with the magnates of Scotland. It is not known if Bruce was involved with Wallace (it is unlikely as Wallace was always one of

the most fervent upholders of the Balliol kingship) but Bruce's pact
with Lamberton showed that Bruce certainly was seeking wider
support in the Scottish political community. This is the usual background given to the seemingly inevitable coup by Robert Bruce in
1306. His murder of John Comyn is almost slipped in, with due literary embellishments, as an unavoidable consequence of Robert Bruce's
journey to the Scottish Crown.

Yet there is nothing in the history of the period to suggest that
Robert Bruce's seizure of the Scottish throne was inevitable between
1304 and 1306. There was no groundswell of support in Scotland for
Robert Bruce to become king in 1306 just as there had been no support
for his restoration as Guardian when he resigned, or was removed,
from the Guardianship in 1300. If hindsight shows that Robert Bruce
did become king in 1306, hindsight also reveals that he did not have
anywhere near majority support in Scotland for his coup, that his
support within Scotland was not secure until after Bannockburn (1314)
and that even after this, a serious plot to replace him could still be
made between 1318 and 1320. All this suggests that Bruce's coup was
neither inevitable, or, indeed, necessary, and that a basic assumption
about the period between 1304 and 1306 – that support for the Balliol
kingship had collapsed completely – should be re-examined. This
assumption, of course, supports the view in Scottish tradition that
Robert Bruce rescued Scotland from chaos in 1306. This, in itself,
should be enough reason to pause for further reflection. Most historians seem to assume that support for the Balliol kingship simply dissi-
pated.[90] A number of issues are cited as evidence that hopes for a Balliol
restoration ceased – the defeat of the French forces at Courtrai in July
1302 and the subsequent loss of Scotland's key ally when England and
France made a peace treaty in May 1303, a treaty which excluded
Scotland; alongside this was King John's apparent disinterest in
proceeding with his own restoration as seen in his letter of 21 November
1302 authorising Philip IV of France to act on his behalf to settle his
affairs with King Edward:

> you have had, and still have, our affairs at heart, and we have
> hope that you will be so always in time to come; it pleases us, we
> will, and we consent for you to prosecute, or cause to be prose-
> cuted, our said affairs, especially those which we have against the
> king of England, in the way which shall seem good to you, either
> in conjunction with your own matters, which you have against

the said king, or separately, . . . and to bring it to an end in the way you best may.[91]

All of these factors plus the submission of the Scots under John Comyn in February 1304 seem to suggest that the Balliol kingship was over and the time was ripe to find a suitable successor. This is, however, far too neat a picture to accept quite as readily as most historians have done.

The submission in February 1304 was not neat and conclusive, and was certainly not the end of the Scottish cause – defence of the Balliol monarchy was central to the Scottish cause after 1292. William Wallace and Simon Fraser continued to fight on in the name of John Balliol; William Oliphant stubbornly resisted at Stirling Castle; John de Soules did not accept the submission terms and stayed in France. As for John Balliol himself giving up on his restoration altogether in November 1302, his letter should be placed alongside other submissive words and deeds since his accession in 1292. His executive power was taken from him by the Comyn-led Council of Twelve in 1295 *after* he failed to defy Edward I's demand for personal military service in Edward I's army and he was weak in not defying Edward's demand to hear appeals from Scotland in the English king's court. It was the Council of Twelve who promoted and acted out policies to maintain Scottish independence – the treaty with France in 1295, the declaration of war on England and the papal absolvement from those oaths (forcibly gained, it was argued) by which Balliol acknowledged English overlordship to Edward I – in the name of John Balliol their king. In April 1298, too, John Balliol (in English custody) seems to have abjectly confessed to his wrongdoing as king and given up hope of returning to Scotland:

John . . . uttered a statement in French, to this effect: namely, that when he possessed and ruled the realm of Scotland as king and lord of the realm, he found in the men of that realm much malice, deceit, treason, and treachery, arising from their malignity, wickedness, and stratagems . . . that it is not his intention to enter or go into the realm of Scotland at any time to come, or to interfere in any way with it, or its appurtenances, through his own agency, or through that of any other person or persons, or even (for the reasons given and for many others) to have anything to do with the Scots.[92]

While it is probable that this letter was, in effect, English propaganda rather than a reflection of John Balliol's true position, it has still helped to add to the sense that John Balliol wanted to dissociate himself from his duties as king (it should also be pointed out that John Balliol's powerful letter of defiance to Edward I in 1296 was more the work of his Comyn-led government than himself). On his release from English captivity in 1299, however, the evidence[93] suggests that he had every intention of continuing to rule Scotland, even if that meant ruling from exile in France. English chroniclers reported that, when he was searched at Dover, his gold crown and the Great Seal were found on him. He clearly intended to perform royal duties again after his release in 1299 – and came close to realising this in 1301–2 with French and papal support. It would, therefore, be unwise to take too literally another letter from John Balliol (November 1302) showing apparent disinterest in returning to the Scottish throne as the end of the Balliol kingship. John Balliol continued to use the title 'King of Scots' for various acts while in France and he was still recognised by Phillip IV in 1309 at the same time as he was acknowledging Robert Bruce as king.[94] If there was still some doubt in the French king's mind in 1309, surely the situation in 1302 was rather less final than most historians seem to think.

Given John Balliol's role as a figurehead king, not fully cognisant of the independence movement in his 'new' kingdom (and his role within that movement) it is important to establish the attitude of his chief political advisers. In particular, what was the attitude of John Comyn III, Lord of Badenoch, to the Balliol kingship after the submission (which he had led) in 1304? Was he compliant with Edward I's vision of Scotland, i.e. Scotland without a king? Was he content to lose the long family tradition of holding power at the centre while retaining vast lands and influence in the localities?

An argument has been put forward recently that not only was John Comyn prepared to abandon the Balliol dynasty but that he had his own agenda for putting forward his claim to the Scottish Crown[95]. It is certainly true that not enough focus has been placed on how close John Comyn III was to the Scottish succession and the consequences of this. His closeness to the throne surely consolidated his political status in Scottish government and the war effort and may have been reflected in his intolerance to opposition during the Guardianships of 1298–1302. The fact that his family was conscious of its royal connections was revealed in the Great Cause of 1291–2 when his father, John Comyn II,

Lord of Badenoch, put forward the family's claim. To put forward a claim was to preserve that claim for the future '. . . if the main claim of the Balliols died out, his own descendants by Eleanor [Mary or Marjorie] Balliol would have a double claim to the throne, and it was important that the Comyn side of it be put on the record now'.[96] But did he actively pursue this option in the period between the submission of 1304 and his fateful (and fatal) meeting with Robert Bruce in the Greyfriars Church at Dumfries on 10 February 1306? It has been suggested that contemporary evidence in 'The Scottish Poem' appended to *Liber Extravagans* of Walter Bower's *Scotichronicon* implies a 'Comyn for king sentiment'.[97] This very interesting poem, written between 1296 and 1306 (probably 1304–6), has been interpreted as being anti-Bruce and anti-Balliol with the suggestion of a pro-Comyn (St Andrews) authorship (Master William Comyn, brother of John Comyn, Earl of Buchan, was provost of St Andrews and rival to William Lamberton as bishop of St Andrews). However, it should be noted that William Lamberton, Bishop of St Andrews, was far from being a friend of John Comyn, and the poem could, in fact, be interpreted as being in support of a Bruce claim. The poem certainly gives mixed messages as in places it gives support to the Balliol claim over the Bruce claim in the Great Cause but also is critical of John Balliol's capacity as king 'for ruling the Scots whom he did not rule as subjects well known to him'.[98] The poem certainly promotes a strong message for an independent Scotland and a Scottish king and it is curious, as the editor of the poem points out,[99] that Balliol is not mentioned by name. But does this suggest an anti-Balliol sentiment or does it merely suggest that the poem was written in a period of great uncertainty about the Balliol kingship, i.e. some time between the Scottish submission of February 1304 and the Bruce coup of 1306? There is no hard evidence that a Comyn claim for the throne is being promoted here nor strong evidence that the poem is so strongly anti-Balliol that it rules out a continuation of the Balliol dynasty (thus opening the way for a possible Comyn claim). The section of the poem which has been seen as ruling out the Balliol candidacy is very much open to interpretation:

Thus far these [kings] had all been Scots like their people,
and if God grants it, it may be henceforth just as it was before.
When a body has an alien head, it is all filth;
So a people is defiled when a foreigner becomes its king

The king referred to has been interpreted by the editor of the poem as Edward I[100] and by Dr Grant as John Balliol[101]. It seems more probable that the invective – criticism of Balliol elsewhere in the poem is quite mild – is aimed at Edward I. Edward I, though never referring to himself as king of Scotland, was still *in effect* king over the land of Scotland. The appeal for a Scottish king in the poem could be a desperate plea for a Balliol kingship or an even more desperate plea for a Bruce kingship in support of the Bishop of St Andrews' accord with Robert Bruce in June 1304.

John Comyn's own attitude to the possibility of a 'Comyn for king campaign' in 1304 is best judged by his, and his family's, long record in support of legitimate Scottish kingship than by 'The Scottish Poem'. John Comyn had come to terms with Edward I in 1304 without suffering military defeat and without harm to his vast landholding base and the castles which dominated strategic communication routes especially in the north. He was, therefore, still in a position to influence events and his past history surely suggests that he would want to do that. The loss of Scottish kingship must have been a bitter personal blow to the family who had been pillars of Scottish kingship for Alexander III and John Balliol and foremost proponents of the independence which legitimate monarchy represented even when there was not a monarch in place (1286–92) or when the monarch was a minor (1249–58). The Comyns had engineered strategic withdrawals from conflict with Edward I in 1296 in order to fight another day (they were secretly supporting rebellion in the north in 1297and they were openly doing this by 1298). It is most probable that the strategic surrender of 1304 had a similar purpose in mind. As a practical and pragmatic politician, John Comyn, 'perceiving that he could not withstand the might of the King of England'[102] in 1304, felt that the time was not right to renew the fight for the restoration of the Scottish monarchy. The Comyns had more to lose than any family in Scotland by an early military attempt to restore Scottish kingship and as leader of the military campaign for most of that period, John Comyn was probably in the best position to judge. A 'wait and see' approach must have seemed the wisest policy at the time. Edward I was elderly and the political situation might change on his death and on the succession of a son who had shown little of the character of his father. The diplomatic situation with the French king and the papacy could also change for the better – after all a combination of military success in Scotland against Edward I, or at least an effective nullifying of English campaigns in Scotland between 1298 and 1303, together with French and papal support had come very close to achieving the restoration of John Balliol to Scotland in 1301 and 1302. The proximity to success here must still have been a source of some encouragement to the Scots in 1304.

It is therefore extremely improbable that John Comyn would have taken part in any bond or agreement (regarded as a fact by some historians)[103] such as the one which Robert Bruce made with William Lamberton in June 1304 – certainly none which implied support for the Bruce claim to the throne. Here again it has proved too easy with hindsight for historians to stray from the reality of politics in 1304 into the traditional 'Bruce-centred' picture of Robert Bruce's inevitable rise to power. A 'Comyn-centred' view of the years 1304–6 – what John Comyn III, Lord of Badenoch, hoped to achieve after the submission of 1304 – is more likely to come closer to historical reality than the Bruce view. It bears repetition that Robert Bruce did not have majority support for his coup in 1306 and for many years after.

In this light, what options faced John Comyn, who was accepted in 1304 as the 'man most widely recognised as the true leader of the Scottish political community'?[104] It should be remembered that the Comyns, both John Comyn's father (John Comyn II, Lord of Badenoch) and his uncle (John Comyn, Earl of Buchan) had deceived Edward I and his officials for a considerable time in 1297 when the English king released them from English captivity and sent them to quell the rebellions of Andrew Moray, William Wallace and others in Scotland. John Comyn the Younger of Badenoch, had himself deceived Edward when he secured release from his own captivity in England in 1298 in return for service in the English king's campaign in Flanders, only to desert this force and make his way to the king of France to seek his help for the national cause. The Comyns still had their castles and lands intact in 1304 and so could enjoy a great deal of freedom from English supervision as they had done between 1298 and 1304 as well as a certain amount of trust from an English king keen to secure stability in Scotland rather than attempt a thorough conquest and consolidation, as achieved, at great cost, in Wales. That would give John Comyn invaluable time. The Scottish king was still alive in France and he had a son and successor Edward (at that time still in English 'custody' – another important reason for a cautious approach). Added to this, Edward I was aged and his death could cause uncertainty on the English side. From a Comyn perspective, there was every reason to wait for a better opportunity to restore the legitimate Scottish monarchy.

The Bruce-centred view of the years 1304–6 pays too little heed to the essential conservative nature of Scottish political society. A number of historians have noted this but it has not been sufficiently applied to the political situation that Scotland found itself in at this time, and especially John Comyn's attitude to the Balliol dynasty. Fiona Watson has wisely commented: 'It is difficult for modern observers to accept that the existence of medieval Scotland was so dependent in the minds of its leaders on the maintenance of a "legitimate" kingship.'[105] In similar vein, Robin Frame has written of 'the Scottish sense of national identity . . . the response of a small, conservative society . . . that drew strength from a widespread awareness of the antiquity of the native monarchy'.[106] To this society, national identity, and the national cause, was still synonymous with the kingship of John Balliol. It was hardly surprising, therefore, that the majority of the Scottish political community was slow to overthrow the Balliol dynasty as the limited support for the Bruce coup showed in Scotland in 1306. The Comyns themselves, more than any other family in Scotland, had everything to gain from continuing in their role as pillars of the Scottish monarchy and John Comyn is, surely, best seen in an historical sense as looking out, and waiting, for the best opportunity to regain that role which he and his family regarded as traditionally theirs by right.

John Comyn had nothing to gain from being party to the overthrow of the 'legitimate' monarchy and his apparent readiness, according to Scottish tradition, even to consider a pact with Robert Bruce which involved a 'lands or crown' deal is also not in keeping with the family's traditional role in Scottish political society. It could be said that the Comyns' leading role in separating John Balliol from his executive power through the Council of Twelve in 1295 was a step towards removing Balliol from the throne. It was certainly quite a revolutionary move. However, in 1295 the Comyns were very conservative revolutionaries – their actions in 1295 simply reflected their lack of confidence in John Balliol's personal capacity to carry out royal executive duties (he had demonstrated this frequently in the trying political circumstances after 1292) and to put into practice the principles established by them and other members of the Scottish political community in the Treaty of Birgham/Northampton in 1290. The terms of the treaty with France (1295) clearly show the significance of the Balliol kingship to the Council of Twelve who sought to enhance and consolidate the Balliol dynasty through a marriage alliance between John Balliol's son and heir Edward and the daughter of Charles de Valois, Philip IV's brother. In 1299, John Comyn had reacted violently, along with his cousin, John Comyn, Earl of Buchan, when treason or talk of treason – *lesemajestie* – against the Balliol kingship had arisen. Further, in 1300, during peace talks with Edward I, John Comyn specifically asked for the restoration of John Balliol and recognition for Edward Balliol as his successor as well as the possibility of this marriage alliance being revived. As for John Balliol, despite appearing not to relish the forceful guidance of both the Comyns and Edward I, he too seems to have promoted the succession of his son whenever possible. In 1299, for example, shortly after release from English power, he 'freely and willingly declared that if his lordship the most Holy Father, Lord Boniface VIII, should not take order anent him and the affairs relating to him and to the kingdom of Scotland, that his successor or successors shall be able, until the matter is finally determined, to take order therewith according to their pleasure'.[107]

In the period 1304–6, there was a 'legitimate' Scottish king still alive in France (and still acknowledged in France as the Scottish king), who had come close to being restored only two years previously. John Balliol had a successor in his son Edward. The family's claim to the throne was still intact and had not been nullified, for example, by conviction in a trial for treason. John Balliol had proved to be an unsatisfactory king at a time when very firm leadership was required. He had to be guided by the Comyns and their associates. He had, however, provided Scotland with a legitimate, male successor, Edward, who was about fourteen years of age in 1296 and in English custody and about twenty-two years of age in 1304 and still resident in England. Edward Balliol was a king in waiting and close to reaching his majority. The Comyns had shown their expertise in Guardianship, securing the rights of legitimate Scottish rulers through the 1250s, between 1286 and 1291 and between 1296 and 1304 and could continue in that role. John Comyn III, Lord of Badenoch, had been a bold defender of the Balliol dynasty and the principles of Birgham. He had the respect of Edward I in 1304 which gave him time to consider the best way forward and he retained much power through vast landholding and control over key areas of Scotland. He could wait for better political and diplomatic circumstances to resume his role as pillar of the legitimate Scottish royal dynasty, the Balliols.

Support for this dynasty was still present in Scotland, and was still present after Bruce's coup of 1306, and, dare it be said ... after the Battle of Bannockburn! John Comyn could wait, but history tells us that Robert Bruce, desperate to fulfil his family's twenty-year search for the Scottish throne, could not!

The Murder of John Comyn III, Lord of Badenoch

ANALYSED FROM A MEDIEVAL CANON LAW PERSPECTIVE

G.A. Cumming[1]

Summary

This chapter attempts to demonstrate that the murder of John Comyn III, Lord of Badenoch, by Robert Bruce, Earl of Carrick, on 10 February 1306 in the church of the Minorite Friars in Dumfries, took place intentionally. Contrary to the traditional[2] position of Scottish historiography,[3] it is contended herein that Robert Bruce intended to kill his distant relative, John Comyn. Perhaps the classic statement, in this regard, is that of Barrow[4]: 'It is contrary to everything we know about Bruce's character that he should have called Comyn to the Greyfriars' church with the secret intention of killing him.' With due respect to the greatest contemporary biographer of Robert Bruce, one could say the very opposite: namely, that Bruce was fundamentally a brilliant tactician whose primary objective was to achieve his personal ambition. Robert Bruce coveted the throne of Scotland in defiance of stronger claims thereon by Edward Balliol, later King Edward, son of King John Balliol deposed by Edward I of England, and by Comyn himself and oblivious to the eventual consequences of the realisation of such illegitimate ambitions: excommunication for the murder of an innocent man in a church; renewal of war between Scotland and England but, above all, a form of civil war within Scotland itself between his supporters and his opponents; the creation of an ongoing system of propaganda to sustain and legitimise his usurpation of the throne and create the basis for a dynasty composed of his heirs and successors, ultimately the Stewarts.[5] In short, all means to obtain the throne of Scotland were considered by Bruce to be justified ranging from murder and the variation of alliances to temporary rapprochements with Edward I himself prior to the latter's foreseeable death from old age and illness. For Robert Bruce, who would usurp the throne of Scotland, the end justified the means. Thus, in analysing this extraordinary man, who, in truth, possessed marked courage coupled with substantial military and political abilities but all the while being consumed by his own personal ambition to accede to the throne of Scotland, it is clearly necessary to adopt the following approach: namely, to use the most objective method possible in order to establish the real state of mind at the time he, Bruce, killed Comyn rather than to rely upon the traditional speculative and hypothetical character analysis such as that of Barrow and traditional Scottish historiography. In reality, the analysis of the murder of John Comyn proposed here seeks to establish *how* this assassination took place factually and legally as opposed to *why* it may have occurred.

An attempt will be made to establish or reconstruct by means of Roman Catholic medieval canon law[6] the state of mind which, arguably, animated Robert Bruce when he killed John Comyn. The canon law to be used and in particular the rules of procedure are those recorded by the monk Gratian[7] and applied by the Catholic Church at the time of the murder in 1306. However, in order to facilitate quotations in English in this text, the analysis is based upon commentaries of Gratian's work by two nineteenth-century canonists who wrote in English: O.J. Reichel[8] (barrister) and Rev. S.B. Smith[9]. In brief, the canon law analysed by Smith and Reichel in English is indeed that of Gratian and therefore represents the rules which were applied to Robert Bruce during the relevant period commencing in 1306. The focus of the analysis will be two crimes committed by the Bruce: homicide, that is, his intentional killing of John Comyn, on the one hand, and on the other, sacrilege[10] to holy goods. Bruce committed both sins by entering the Franciscan church when armed and again through his actual murder of Comyn in that church. Unfortunately, the church in which Comyn was murdered happened to have been constructed by his grandmother, Dervorguilla of Galloway.

Further, as regards the canon law analysis it is to be noted that only two documents will be used and none of the numerous chronicles currently in existence and traditionally used by Scottish historians, given that the chronicles are composed essentially of what might be termed non-contemporaneous hearsay[11] whose original source is unknown and unverifiable. The two documents which will be used are: first, the papal bull of commission dated May 1306,[12] the objective of which is to prepare a declaration of excommunication[13] of Robert Bruce; and second, the letter of commission for granting absolution[14] to Robert Bruce dated 1310.[15]

The essence of the Bull of 1306 for our purposes is as follows:

> It has come to our notice through a reliable report that Robert, Earl of Carrick with a few of his followers from that area, having come armed to the church at the place of the Friars Minor of Dumfries, in the diocese of Glasgow violated with temerity the immunity of the said church by committing within it sacrilege by homicide against the indults conceded to the said brothers by the Apostolic See to the peril of his soul and to the scandal of many people: for this it is declared that he has incurred the sense of excommunication.[16]

The most important part of the second document dated 1310 is as follows:

> A petition sent to us states that he, once persuaded [by the devil], with several accomplices, killed John and Robert Comyn, knights, and others joined against him, in the church of the Friars minor in Dumfries, . . .[17]

Further, the essence of the legal analysis will be based on what might be termed the elements of the crime of homicide in medieval canon law coupled with, in particular, the procedural defences which could be raised through appeal in the context of punishment for the crime, that is the commission to investigate whether or not Bruce[18] had as a matter of fact and law committed homicide and above all sacrilege by entering the church of the Minorite friars armed constituted the procedural forum in which an appeal could be made by him against any finding of his guilt as regards the homicide or the sacrilege. It is appropriate to note with respect to the commencement of the analysis of intention on the part of the Bruce that the bull of 1306 uses the term 'violating recklessly the immunity of the said church' in describing his 'armed' entrance to the church:

> Upon our hearing a reliable report that Robert, Earl of Carrick with a few of his followers from that area, having come armed to the church at the place of the Friars Minor of 'Dumbres' in the

diocese of Glasgow, violated recklessly the immunity of the said church by committing within it sacrilege by homicide, against the indults/permissions of the privileges conceded to the said brothers by the Apostolic See.

The term 'immunity' is significant in so far as its violation could lead during the medieval period to an excommunication automatically pronounced. The following note from the *Catholic Encyclopedia*[19] is of assistance as regards the understanding of an immunity, notably a local immunity, and the consequences of its violation:

> An immunity according to its object, is local, real, or personal. Local immunity refers to places consecrated to Divine worship, to churches; local immunity withdraws places dedicated to Divine worship from secular jurisdiction and preserves them from acts that would profane the respect due to holy places. It implies like-wise the right of a person to remain in a place consecrated to God, so that the public authorities may not remove delinquents there-from. This is the right of asylum (q.v.); it was greatly restricted by canon law, and is now abandoned everywhere without any formal protest from the Church. As local immunity arises from a place or building being dedicated to Divine worship, it must be considered as attaching not only to churches that have been solemnly conse-crated, but also to those that have merely been blessed, and to chapels and oratories legitimately erected by ecclesiastical author-ity; it extends likewise to the accessory buildings, sacristy, porch, yard, belfry, and to the neighbouring consecrated ground and the burial ground (ch. ii, 9, De immunit. eccles. lib. III, tit. 49). Among the profane acts forbidden in churches by canon law, not to mention those that are prohibited by their very nature, we may cite: the employment of force to enter sacred places, breaking down doors, interrupting or preventing Divine service, are viola-tions of local immunity. This crime was formerly punished with excommunication *ipso facto* incurred, but this is no longer enforced by the Constitution 'Apostolicæ Sedis'.

It is submitted that the basis for the automatic excommunication – *latae sententiae* (defined later in this chapter) – suffered by King Robert for having entered the church armed is desecration or violation of a sacred object which sounds like the violation of a civil immunity. This

violation of the civil immunity or defilement of a sacred object constituted one of the two grounds upon which Robert was excommunicated automatically, that is, *latae sententiae*. The other ground was, of
course, the homicide of John Comyn. It is however, the violation of the
civil immunity by King Robert, namely, the entering of the church with
arms which, in itself, explains the reason why Pope Innocent V was
directly involved in the excommunication and above all the absolution
of King Robert Bruce. The gravity of the sacrilege was such that for
sovereign policy reasons of the Vatican, the discipline of the sinner was
remitted to the pope which notably entailed his exclusive jurisdiction
as regards both the excommunication and the absolution.[20] Such policy
therefore reduces the probative value of the letter referred to by
Lawlor:[21]

> John and Robert Comyn were murdered on 10th February, 1306;
> *and* it is well known that Bruce was absolved a few days later
> apparently on Saturday, 12th February (*Registra Joh.
> JVhethamstede*, etc, ed. H.T. Riley (R.S.) ii. 352; cf. Eng. Hist.
> Rev., xxxiii, 1918, p. 366). But the absolver was Robert Wischard,
> Bishop of Glasgow, Bruce's whole-hearted admirer. It is quite
> probable that a few years later he thought it well to secure an
> absolution that would carry more weight.

The relevant part of the letter reads as follows in English translation:

> The Saturday before this letter was made the Earl of Carricke
> came to Glascu and the Bishop gave him plenary absolution ...
> and made him swear that he would stand by the ordinance of the
> clergy and ... as ... well to gain his heritage in all the manners
> that he might;[22]

The editor, Riley, notes: 'There is no indication by whom or to whom
this letter is addressed.'[23]

This absence of the identity of both the author and the destined
recipient arguably fundamentally undermines the probative value of
the document. While it may be the expression of the truth, the letter in
reality may constitute also nothing other than a report of unfounded
and oft repeated rumours. The essential difficulty in terms of medieval
canon law is that even if it were true that the Bishop Wishart had
endeavoured to absolve King Robert, at a minimum the purported

absolution would have been void by want of the authority or jurisdiction.[24] Moreover, the text of the letter of commission of 1310 specifically states that Robert Bruce affirmed that he was unable to contact the bishop of his diocese which was apparently Glasgow, who would be Bishop Wishart: 'because of the murderous enmity and war and other considerations could not approach the Holy See, or even his diocesan bishop or his vicar, to make humble supplication on behalf of himself and of his accomplices ...' Arguably, to the extent that the letter might have probative value which is not yet clear in terms of the rules of evidence of medieval canon law, its significance lies in a possible use in an attempt to establish the role played by Bishop Wishart as an eventual co-conspirator in the murder of John Comyn. This subject will however be explored in a later book. Having excluded the use of the chronicles for the purposes of analysing the murder, it therefore becomes necessary to focus in particular upon the recitation of facts which appear in two documents: first, in the papal bull of commission of May 1306 and second, in the letter of commission addressed to the abbot of Paisley. The existence of both of these documents is extremely important for the following reasons: the bull of 1306 commissioned two leading ecclesiastics, the archbishop of York and the bishop of Carlisle, to investigate whether Robert Bruce had indeed committed the crimes enumerated therein. Of substantial significance from the point of view of the rights of the defence is the following: that this commission leading to judicial inquisition undertaken by the two bishops provided Bruce with the possibility of appealing the publication of the declaration of excommunication very simply on the grounds he did not commit the homicide or the sacrilege. However, from the absence of any documents establishing such a recourse to establish his innocence, the conclusion can be drawn that Robert Bruce did not launch an appeal against the public declaration of his excommunication for both the homicide and the sacrilege. Rather Bruce, as established in the document of 1310, admitted commission of the crimes of murder and sacrilege and promptly sought absolution and forgiveness by the Church in the name of God. This leads us, procedurally, to focus on the document of 1310. This document was a letter sent on behalf of Pope Innocent V by the head of the Roman Curia to the abbot of Paisley.[25] The letter enjoined the abbot to investigate whether Robert Bruce had atoned for his sins subsequent to his making a complete and private confession of the murder and the sacrilege. In the event that the relevant degree of atonement had been achieved, the abbot of Paisley was authorised to absolve King Robert (by this time enthroned) of his sins. However, this process of absolution in itself presupposes the admission through private confession by the king, as a son of the Church, that he had committed the homicide and the sacrilege. It is for this reason that contained within the letter of commission preparatory for absolution is to be found the essence of his admission which bears citation a second time:

> A petition sent to us states that he, once persuaded [by the devil], with several accomplices, killed John and Robert Comyn, knights, and others joined against him, in the church of the Friars minor in Dumfries . . .

Basically, the procedural context here is a petition to the Roman Curia for absolution. Accordingly, the petitioner must set forth an admission of the sins committed and for which absolution is being sought in order to activate the procedure leading to absolution. In his supplication or petition, Robert Bruce explicitly admits the essence of his sins which were homicide and sacrilege: first, there was the homicide, namely that 'he . . . killed John and Robert Comyn'; second, brief allusion to the motive, namely something sinful – 'once persuaded [by the devil]' as opposed to a reason justifying the murder such as self-defence. Therefore Robert Bruce had an evil motive or intent as regards the killing of John and Robert Comyn; and third, the commission of the sacrilege 'in the church of the Friars minor in Dumfries'.

The most striking element of this document is that it arguably constitutes, in very rudimentary form, an admission, by Robert Bruce that he had killed John Comyn in a church for evil and therefore for sinful reasons. It was for this killing that King Robert sought the absolution from the pope. The importance once again of this document is that it forms part of the canon law criminal procedure activated in order to obtain absolution for the sins of homicide and sacrilege: the obtaining of absolution required the admission of the sins in this case by Robert. The king complied and gave his admission which constitutes, as noted previously, the minimum requirement in order to commence the process to obtain absolution. Ultimately, this document signals the commencement of a process by Robert whereby he confesses, in private, his sins through admission to his confessor. In order for it to be effective, in the sense of leading to an absolution, the confession was to consist necessarily in a recitation of the true facts: that is that he, Robert Bruce, while armed, committed for evil reasons, the murder of John Comyn in the church of the Minorite Friars. Therefore, the aforementioned constitutes a brief synopsis of the canonical analysis of the events which occurred in the church of the Minorite Friars on 10 February 1306. The matter now becomes one of demonstrating in more detail how the procedure of medieval canon law applied to the analysis of the homicide and to the sacrilegious violation of the church can establish the existence of irremediable intention on the part of Robert Bruce to kill his unarmed cousin in the church constructed by the latter's grandmother, Dervorguilla de Galloway Balliol.

Relevant Facts

Before commencing the legal analysis based upon the actual crimes of homicide and sacrilege it is also useful to note once again that the above analysis is based upon very limited facts. This analysis takes as fundamental facts the descriptions notably in the bull of commission of 15 May 1306 of Pope Clement coupled with the letter of commission for the absolution in 1310. Arguably, the truth of the words in these documents is procedurally verifiable in the manner just described: as an admission of their truth by the king in the procedural context of his attempt to obtain absolution for homicide and for sacrilege which required a truthful admission through confession of his acts. Ultimately, however, it is the omission by King Robert Bruce to appeal the declaration of his excommunication on those facts and in turn his supplication for absolution and penance which required admission through confession of the true event those basic facts surrounding the murder which can be taken as an admission by silence of their truth. The basic facts are taken to be that Robert Bruce killed John Comyn in a church with some degree of assistance from what might be termed supporters. Corroboration of the basic elements of the murder are to be found in the letter of commission to investigate the granting of absolution of 1310 in that they reproduce in essence the fundamental elements of the crimes of murder and the sacrilege of defilement of sacred objects. There is, accordingly, no need to refer to speculations as in the chronicles concerning the reason for the meeting of Comyn and Bruce or whether indeed a dispute took place and, if so, the reason for it. Finally, it is submitted that the wording of, certainly, the bull of 1306 coupled with operation of the canon law itself precludes the possibility that John Comyn was armed himself: firstly, the bull of 1306, while very clearly specifying that Bruce was armed, which fact was necessary in order to establish the sacrilege of violating a holy place, makes no such mention with respect to Comyn. Indeed, had John Comyn been armed, he too would have committed a sacrilege of defiling holy buildings; secondly, had Comyn been armed, it would have been possible for Robert Bruce to raise legitimate self-defence. Bruce, as noted earlier, never raised any defence either to the murder or to the sacrilege of violating holy objects, among which, of course, was legitimate self-defence. Accordingly, both the wording of the bull of 1306 coupled with the operation of the crimes of sacrilege and defilement of holy objects and in particular their defences preclude the possibility that Comyn, unlike Bruce, was armed.

It is useful at this point, having examined very briefly the relevant facts, to relate the above analysis to some of the rules of evidence used in canon law. Following Reichel, proof for the purposes of medieval canon law may be defined in the following manner:

> Proof is defined to be the establishment by evidence or demonstration of a doubtful matter or disputed matter in judgment in order to enable a judge to determine a controversy pending between two parties. It involves a) producing proper and trustworthy evidence meeting or rebutting all exceptions taken to the evidence and b) the publication of sufficient evidence before the judge.
>
> Judicial proof is made firstly by evidence of the fact and secondly by the confession of the opposite party or thirdly by the deposition of two or more credible witnesses.[26]

Reichel then observes:

> Evidence of a fact is such evidence as is firstly, either 'notorious' or most evident; secondly, manifest or most evident; or thirdly, simply clear. Notorious evidence is that which is known to all men in the sense that it is information or a fact which is known to all men such as St Paul's stands in London. Manifest evidence is that which has been openly done and can be proved by any number of witnesses although it is not known to all men or when a criminal has been caught in the act of a crime. However, the best kind of proof is that of a confession to the adverse party.

Reichel concludes by affirming that a confession occurs effectively in two circumstances: first when the accused does not deny a notorious crime or second when he has publicly been condemned for it.[27]

Overall it is submitted that Robert Bruce confessed the crimes of intentional homicide and sacrilege. The reasoning here is straightforward and based upon the criminal canon law procedure which was utilised by Bruce in order to obtain absolution for the aforementioned crimes and sins. The procedural chain of the criminal canon law which linked Robert Bruce beginning with his murder of John Comyn is basically as follows: the procedural event of the investigation undertaken by the archbishop of York and the bishop of Carlisle by its nature gave Robert Bruce the possibility to appeal the decision to publish and declare publicly the excommunication both of himself and certain of his followers. In short, Bruce had been automatically excommunicated because he had murdered Comyn in a church. In so doing, the king had committed a sacrilege and therefore attracted a particular sanction, namely automatic excommunication which took effect privately the moment that he committed all of the legal elements of the crime of homicide and the sin of sacrilege of defilement of holy objects. However, before declaring publicly this private and automatic excommunication, the normal procedure required an investigation through inquisition which was delegated by Pope Innocent V to the archbishop of York and the bishop of Carlisle. The two bishops were to investigate specifically the veracity of the facts enumerated in the bull of commission as regards the murder and the sacrilege. At the present time it is not clear exactly on what date the two bishops would have procedurally dealt with the matter or whether the king appeared before them in person. It is clear, however, that no document exists in which Bruce indicated or declared his intention to appeal a declaration of his notorious crime. In short, at no time did the king or his supporters ever deny precisely the events which are described in the bull of 1306 as he and they were procedurally entitled. The essence of what might be termed the informal defence of Robert Bruce by his supporters over several hundred years consists in allegations that somehow Comyn provoked or deserved being killed in a church. In reality this attempt at a defence is spurious in the extreme: first, Bruce and his followers at no time sought to appeal the automatic excommunication as one which he and they had not committed among other things because the requisite intention was lacking. No document exists in this regard; second, by failing to appeal the automatic excommunication on the basis of non-commission of the murder and the sacrilege Bruce, as noted earlier, publicly admitted the truth of the declaration which ultimately was made by the two bishops: that the facts contained in the bull of 1306 as regards the automatic excommunication were accurate and true. By deciding therefore not to challenge and to appeal the public accusation resulting from the declaration of the automatic excommunication Robert Bruce can be said to have admitted having committed not only the intentional homicide of Comyn but also the commission of the sacrilege in the church of the Minorite Friars in the specific sense presented by Reichel just cited: that is, 'when the accused does not deny a notorious crime or second when he has publicly been condemned for it'. This analysis is in turn strengthened by additional procedural steps which were involved by the letter of 1310. It is clear that this letter contains not a denial but an express admission by Bruce and its significance is increased because it constitutes a step in the procedure required in order to achieve absolution. Absolution for the crime was required by canon law, as the letter itself indicates that Bruce should make a confession. As noted earlier, the confession necessarily would contain a private and never to be publicly divulged confession. Once again, it is clear that at no point in the procedure leading to the obtaining of absolution for his crimes did Robert Bruce ever deny having specifically committed murder and specifically the intention which that included. Above all, at no time did Bruce ever interpose the argument made over the centuries by supportive chronicles of purportedly provocative and above all treacherous behaviour by Comyn. Rather it is submitted that at all times by reason of his failure to specifically appeal the public declaration of his excommunication for the murder in the church of his cousin John Comyn, Robert Bruce can for procedural reasons be taken to have admitted in the two senses described by Reichel and just cited, his commission of that intentional murder.

Accordingly, the aforementioned facts contained within these two documents of 1306 and 1310 coupled with the procedural process of a supplication for absolution which requires admission and formal confession in the absence of any attempt at contestation by Robert Bruce serve as follows: they constitute the facts which were admitted by the king in order to obtain absolution and therefore can be arguably considered as true.

It is, however, necessary to consider the elements of the offence notably of homicide as well as that of sacrilege in order to understand clearly the following: first, why Robert Bruce can be said to have intended to kill John Comyn; and second, to identify the points at which the king could have appealed in order to have his innocence established and the consequences of his having failed to so do.

Applicability of Canon Law

Overall, medieval Roman Catholic canon law constituted the only legal system which was applied to Robert Bruce as regards his murder of John Comyn: that is, King Robert Bruce was never tried under the penal law of either the Kingdom of Scotland or the Kingdom of England such as they existed.[28]

Bruce was however excommunicated and then ultimately reintegrated to the Roman Catholic Church by means of medieval Roman Catholic canon law, specifically absolution. Herein lies the primary justification for the use of this system of canon law: namely, the fact that Robert Bruce was a Roman Catholic who submitted to the application of the canon law to himself. The fact that King Robert submitted to the application of canon law to him and notably the imposition of one of its most grave punishments, namely excommunication, also establishes very clearly the following. First, Bruce was a Catholic. The system of canon law, being the internal law of the Church, once again following Reichel, only applied to Roman Catholics. Second, the application therefore was predicated upon putative acceptance given by the infant at the time of baptism. Third, Robert Bruce, who had entered in a personal bond of support with Wishart, Bishop of Glasgow prior to the killing of John Comyn,[29] can be deemed in those circumstances of pre-Reformation Scotland to have possessed the requisite knowledge of certain of the major canons of the Roman Catholic canon: that is the two which will be utilised in this analysis, the crime of homicide and that of desecration of sacred objects such as churches.

HOMICIDE

According to Reichel homicide in terms of medieval Roman Catholic canon law may be defined in the following manner:

> Homicide consists in intentional take the life of another (note 161 Augustin ap Gratian Caus XXIII) or doing so unintentionally and accidentally if the act was the result of carelessness or doing any other criminal act. It includes aiding and abetting in murder.[30]

Significantly, Reichel adds:

> It is however not homicide when another is accidentally killed
> through no fault of the slayer whilst doing a lawful act nor if he is
> killed by a defendant against his master's prohibition nor if he
> were killed in lawful warfare by an official at the command of a
> superior or in necessary self-defence. (Note *Decre lib* V, Tet XII
> C2)[31]

There are no *per se* exemptions but rather examples of where the
requisite state of mind or *mens rea*, specifically intent, is absent.
Accordingly where all of the elements of the crime and sin do not exist,
notably that of intent, the crime of homicide is not established.
Therefore, clearly, the existence of intent is necessary in order for the
elements of the crime of homicide to be fulfilled.

Further, culpability may be either culpable ignorance of the law or
culpable negligence. Although it is *per se* a lower degree of guilt than
malice, it may be gravely imputable. The violation of a law which is
not known or is not imputed at all if there was ignorance was incul-
pable. Otherwise, imputability is diminished more or less in proportion to the culpability of the ignorance. Ignorance of the penalty alone
does not remove imputability but diminishes it somewhat. Finally,
passion if voluntarily and deliberately aroused or nourished rather
increases imputability. Otherwise, passion diminishes imputability
more or less in proportion to the heat of the passion and it entirely
removes imputability if it precedes and prevents all deliberation and
consent.

Thus, one can see that the operation of the crime of homicide in
medieval canon law turns very much upon precisely the matter of the
state of mind. This state of mind in turn has enormous procedural
consequences: that is, the possibility for an individual to prevent
himself or herself from being punished for a crime such as homicide or
sacrilege when there is no foundation in fact.[32]

SACRILEGE OF DEFILING HOLY OBJECTS

The second crime[33] is that of sacrilege against things: according to
Reichel 'the treatment of sacred persons and things as unsacred or the
attributing of sanctity to profane persons and things constitutes the
crime of sacrilege'.[34] Reichel mentions in particular the following:
violating the precincts of a church (synod Rom AD 878 op Gratian

Caus XVII). It is submitted that the carrying of weapons in a church would violate the sanctity of the church and therefore constitute a sacrilege. The analysis is substantiated by the papal bull dated 18 May 1306, a translation of which is: 'violated with temerity the immunity of the said church by committing within it sacrilege against indults of the privileges conceded . . .'.

Further, this crime of sacrilege against things can be viewed in the following manner under the heading of an Immunity[35] which is specifically cited in the text of the bull of excommunication:

> Immunity means an exemption from a legal obligation (*munus*), imposed on a person or his property by law, custom, or the order of a superior (lex 214, sqq. De verb. signif., 1. 50, tit. 16) . . . Local immunity withdraws places dedicated to Divine worship from secular jurisdiction and preserves them from acts that would profane the respect due to holy places . . . As local immunity arises from a place or building being dedicated to Divine worship, it must be considered as attaching not only to churches that have been solemnly consecrated, but also to those that have merely been blessed, and to chapels and oratories legitimately erected by ecclesiastical authority; it extends likewise to the accessory buildings, sacristy, porch, yard, belfry, and to the neighbouring consecrated ground and the burial ground (ch. ii, 9, De immunit. eccles. lib. III, tit. 49). Among the profane acts forbidden in churches by canon law, not to mention those that are prohibited by their very nature, we may cite: criminal secular trials (c. v, *h. t.*) even under penalty of excommunication; civil secular trials (c. ii, *h. t.* in VI); but acts of ecclesiastical jurisdiction (even judicial) are not forbidden. Commerce and trading are prohibited, likewise fairs, markets, and in general all purely civil meetings, as secular deliberative assemblies (*parlamenta*), unless permission has been granted by the ecclesiastical authorities, whose rights are thus safeguarded. The employment of force to enter sacred places, breaking down doors, interrupting or preventing Divine service, are violations of local immunity. This crime was formerly punished with excommunication *ipso facto* incurred.

It is submitted that the carrying of arms into a church is the equivalent of entering a sacred place 'with force' and would therefore be punished by automatic excommunication.

Rights of the Defence

INFLICTION OF PUNISHMENTS GENERALLY

Reichel notes:

> Canonical punishments whether vindicatory or correctional can be inflicted only for crime and for no other cause. Hence no person can be punished save where he has committed a crime. This truth is founded in the very law of nature and is also repeatedly and solemnly inculcated by the law of the Church as a fundamental and essential condition of all punishments.[36]

In addition Reichel observes:

> Where is a censure *ipso jure* null and void: . . .
> (c) in the absence of canonical proof of crime sufficiently grave to warrant the infliction of censures although in reality the crime has been committed.[37]

Accordingly, in principle at least if not in practice, it is submitted that every effort would have been made by the Curia to ensure that Robert Bruce was indeed culpable to the crimes before publication of the excommunication.

It is extremely important, particularly in a matter such as the case involving Bruce, to note that there exist specific limitations upon the scope of the application of the canon law dealing with crimes. In short, if these limitations are violated, they may serve to protect or vindicate the rights of the defence, in this case, those of Robert Bruce, through the mechanism of appeal. These are described by Smith as follows:

> a) A crime in the canonical sense of the term is an act or omission contrary to the law of the Church and imputable to its author. Where an act is not wilful, that is, done without due knowledge or free will it is not a human act and is not imputable to its author and, therefore, is not punishable. Hence a violation of a law which proceeds from want of knowledge, or from grave fear or from violence is but a material and not a formal violation of the law and therefore not a crime.[38]

It is clear therefore that the essence of the operation of the criminal sections of the canon law is predicated upon the element of the will, that is, on intention of the perpetrator. Smith very clearly gives examples of what might be termed exceptions to the scope of a crime which is duly constituted: namely those instances where the will or intention is absent as, for example, 'want of knowledge' or 'fear'. It is here that the rights of the defence require that a crime may only be punished if it is fully constituted notably with regard to the will or the *mens rea*.

b) A crime must be external. For it is manifest that internal acts or mere thoughts and consequently offences which are committed merely in thought cannot be proven externally and therefore lie beyond the pale of the Church's external tribunal. 'The crime must be personally committed. In other words a person can be punished only for a crime which he himself committed and not for a crime which another person has perpetrated. Our natural sense of justice tells us that the punishment should not extend beyond the criminal himself to a third party who is innocent. Thus Pope Boniface VIII expressly enacts that excommunication should not be inflicted upon a whole body corporate or a community but only upon such members of the said body who have been duly convicted of the crime lest the innocent suffer with the guilty.[39]

Here once again the essence of the rights of the defence intervene in the sense that only a party who has committed a crime and who has either been proved to have committed it or admitted its commission may be punished.

c) The crime must be mortal or grievous. Not only the law of the Church but the very law of nature tells us that there should be a just proportion between the crime and its punishment and that therefore if the punishment be severe the crime must also be grievous. Thus Pope Benedict XIV speaking of censure writes 'If according to the opinion of all canonists a grievous and heinous crime is required in order to authorise the Superior to inflict a censure which is merely ferendae it is manifest that a far greater and more execrable crime is necessary in order that a person may be punished with a censure latae sententiae.[40]

This expresses one of the reasons why the pope had reserved to him the treatment of crime of sacrilege given that it affected notably the physical church itself. Such crimes came to be sanctioned automatically upon commission without the pronouncement of a tribunal: that is through the mechanism of automatic excommunication following commission of the requisite elements of the crime of sacrilege.

d) The crime must be complete. Hence a person who strikes another person with intent to kill does not incur the penalty of murder if he merely wounded him or broke his arm but did not really kill him. Consequently also the sole attempt to commit a crime or the mere co-operation to commit a crime or the mere co-operation whether by advice command or otherwise cannot be punished with the punishment decreed by the law for the crime itself unless the law expressly states that those who commit the crime itself but also those who give aid counsel etc shall incur the same penalty as though they had perpetrated the crime itself.[41]

Smith resumes the constituents which must be present in the commission of a crime for it to be visited and in so doing provides a summary of the above elements in the following manner:

Three things are required to constitute a human act which may form a crime susceptible to punishment: knowledge, will and liberty. The will presupposes knowledge: since a person cannot will something which is unknown to him. Freedom in its turn presupposes both knowledge and will: for liberty is the power of choosing between several things. Now a person cannot choose between two or more objects unless he wills one or the other: and he cannot will unless he knows. Opposed therefore to a human or imputable act are ignorance or the absence of due knowledge, grave fear or the apprehension of serious evil for a person acting from grave fear against his will. Violence of force that is external or physical compulsion actually inflicted upon a person by a third party.[42]

Finally, Smith mentions specifically the right of appeal which procedurally serves to ensure compliance with the above mentioned principles in their application:

It is superfluous to say that it is allowed to appeal against all censure or correctional punishments whether of excommunication suspensions or interdict no less than against other punishments and grievances: upon this point there is no dispute whatsoever. This right of appeal is not only conceded by the express law of the Church as in force at present but is moreover based on the very law of nature. Or it is part of a just self-defence. In fact the object of an appeal is to prevent an innocent person from being visited with punishment injustice or wrong . . . Finally when the correction punishment is inflicted *a jure* and is *latae sententiae* it is incurred as we have seen in the internal forum by the very commission of the crime itself, i.e. ipso facto without any juridical formality. But in the external forum a declaratory sentence is required. Against this declaratory sentence it is allowed to appeal . . . so that the appeal in the case suspends the effect of the declaratory sentence and hinders its publication. This has reference to a declaratory sentence after it is pronounced.[43]

In this regard Reichel observes:

To prevent injustice being done by hasty or ill considered sentences or by the prejudice and imperfect knowledge of a judge the remedy of appeal is provided (Note 120 p 322m pseudo Isidor ap Gratian Caus ii QU VI c 1) In the first three centuries what would be properly called an appeal was unknown. There were no regularly constituted courts. Christian principles had not as yet settle down into uniform law and the practices of different churches varied. Some bishops then made an excessive use of excommunication with the result that application was made to a neighbouring bishop to procure a rectification of their sentences (note 121 Council Chalcedon ap AD 451) Thus was established a kind of informal appeal from the individual bishop to the church of the province.

Of note is the element of intent with the crime of homicide: the intent is necessary before the delict of homicide is fully consummated. In the absence of intent no delict or crime of homicide can be imputed to an individual.[44]

As regards the consequences, Reichel notes:

The discipline awarded for the homicide depends upon the circumstances and it is more leniently dealt with when committed by an avenger of blood or in anger than in other circumstances.[45]

TYPES OF CENSURE OR PENALTY IMPOSED FOR THE COMMISSION
OF HOMICIDE AND SACRILEGE: EXCOMMUNICATION

As regards the imposition of the censure of excommunication, this could be done either *latae sententiae* or *ferendae sententiae*. The latter was imposed by a judge following a trial with witnesses and evidence. The former was incurred automatically on the commission of the crime on the acts. Further these censures operated in two different domains: the first was *forro interno* which was the domain of the conscience and God. The second domain was that of the material world and third parties.

Smith observes as follows:

> A censure *a jure* which are *latae sententiae* is incurred in the *forro interno* even though the crime is not judicially proved it has really been committed. But in *forro externo* there punishments are not incurred until the Bishop or his Superior has given the accused a trial and pronounced declaratory sentence. In other words the Bishops cannot pass a declaratory sentence or publish the censure in the case unless the crime is juridically proven or so completely notorious that it is proved through notoriety. Now a person who has incurred a censure in *forro interno* must indeed admit – indeed observe it in *forro interno* in conscience and before God ... We say who has really incurred it for if a person commits the or crime to which the censure is *ipso jure* but has acted from ignorance and from fear or inadvertence he does not incur the censure even in *forro interno* and hence need not observe it publicly or privately.[46]

Finally, having examined the elements of both homicide and the sacrilege of defiling holy objects as well as the possibility of an appeal on the grounds of non-commission of the crime of homicide as described in the bull of commission of investigation and the letter of commission for an absolution, it is appropriate to consider proof: what constitutes the best type of proof under the precepts of canon law.

It is necessary, however, to consider one other aspect which has been raised by historians. It is claimed that, in reality, Bruce was animated not by intention but rather by anger. According to Sellar,[47] the anger arose in the context of an argument between the Bruce and Comyn. With due respect, the argument is most appropriately analysed in the following manner: first, its existence is not attested by any contemporaneous witness; second, it would seem that the presence of anger would not prevent the application of the requisite state of mind or *mens rea* in the circumstances, namely that Robert Bruce intended to kill John Comyn. Rather the presence of anger if there were any resulting from a dispute would serve to reduce the penalty. Thus Reichel observes:

> The discipline awarded for homicide depends upon the circumstances and it is more leniently dealt with when committed by an avenger of blood or in anger than under other circumstances. (Note 180 Tehodare poenit I IV If homicide is the result of anger let him do penance of three years: if of accident one year if affected by drugs or . . . four years or more. if the result of strife ten years. Gratian Caus XXII)[48]

According once again to Reichel, the requisite elements which ensure the commission of the crime of homicide or *a contrario* prevent its commission are the following:

> Homicide consists in intentionally taking the life of another or doing so unintentionally if the act was the result of careless or doing any other criminal act. It is not however homicide when another is accidentally killed through no fault of the slayer whilst doing a lawful acts nor if he were killed by a dependent of his masters nor if he were killed in lawful warfare.[49]

The aforementioned analysis in which the Bruce could not have intended to murder Comyn, however, has an additional hurdle: it does not take account of the fact set forth in the papal bull and which was never denied: specifically that Bruce never denied the description set forth therein that he was armed when he arrived in the church. It is to be recalled that the fact that he was armed served as the basis for the imputation of the sacrilege of defiling blessed property, i.e. the church. This argument of absence of intention on the part of Bruce arguably fails on the reasonable observation that the fact that Bruce arrived at the church armed and entered it armed knowing that it would be a sacrilege to enter the church in such a state arguably establishes to the requisite standard that he intended to kill the unarmed Comyn in the church. Once again, therefore, the commission of the sacrilege of defilement of a sacred object by means of a weapon carried into the church which constituted the reason for the intervention of the pope once more was, of course, never denied by Bruce. It is submitted, there-fore, that failure to deny the sacrilege which consisted in carrying the arm or weapon into the sacred church coupled with a failure to deny the commission of intentional homicide is yet additional manifest proof that Bruce intended to kill Comyn in the church. This conclusion is also coherent with the concept of proof by admission presented by Reichel and as applied earlier herein. Further, the forensic utilisation of an unproved dispute between these two competitors for the throne does not in itself undermine intentional homicide as noted earlier: it affects only the gravity of the punishment given its factually unsub-stantiated existence in no way assists the legal explanation of the murder. Accordingly, no use is made of the unproved altercation between Bruce and Comyn.

Investigation

It is to be noted that the papal bull of 1306 was not only a commission to the archbishop of York and the bishop of Carlisle to investigate the facts contained therein in order to ascertain whether Robert Bruce had in law and fact committed homicide and sacrilege before declaring publicly his excommunication. Rather, in addition the papal bull had two other effects: first, as noted earlier, the investigation would have presented the king with another occasion to establish his innocence and seek to have it recognised notably by the two bishops and ulti-mately Pope Innocent V; second, this bull set into motion a legal cause or action which would have proceeded by means of a special process of investigation known as inquisition. According to Reichel 'the aim of an inquisition is to ascertain whether a particular person is guilty of offences of which he is suspected or denounced'.[50] Reichel goes on to note the following:

> Whenever presentment is made of common fame only and not of facts known to the denouncer or wherever there is grave suspicion of the existence of some crime a case arises for inquisition. Inquisition is the judges' act of setting inquiry on foot either *ex mero motu* [of its own will] as it is in the interest of the church to ascertain whether the rules of the Christian Church are being observed or else the result of the presentment is to ascertain whether a report on the suspicions are true. Before a particular inquisition is resorted to there should exist either strong grounds

for suspecting crime or the presentment of some informer who is himself above suspicious and public infamy or scandal.[51]

It would appear that the letter of Edward I[52] would fall into this category. Further, it is known that Edward did commission the Franciscan friars at Oxford to compile a report of what had occurred to be based on interviews with the friars who were present in the church of the Minorite Friars on 10 February 1206.[53] Reichel goes on to note some of the practical prerequisites necessary before an inquisition would take place which once again serve to protect the rights of defence of King Robert:

> Without ill fame preceding a particular inquisition ought not to be made at least publicly ... since the rule of charity enjoins respect for another reputation and secondly publicity in such case may do more harm than good to the Church. Particular inquisitions may however privately and preparatorily or by way of summary information be undertaken in order to ascertain (1) whether there exists probably proof of the alleged offence and (2) whether the accused is defamed in consequence of it. Should the latter admit the offence or ... be notorious he may be dealt with summarily by the mere office of judge. Should he deny it the matter may be referred for judicial discussion in plenary proceedings by promoting the judges office. If as a result of solemn inquisition no adequate proof is forthcoming of the existence of the crime denounced or suspected it is incompetent for the prelate or judge to administer the oath of purgation and thus establish the innocence of the accused. In purgation the defamed person appears before the prelate or judge within the prescribed number of compurgators ... and swears upon the Gospels not only that he is innocent of the crime alleged but also that he has not committed it. His compurgators then declare that they believe that what he says is the truth. As the object of purgation is not merely to show that the crime is not proven but to establish the innocence of the defamed person before all, it should be made in the place where the accused is defamed.[54]

It is clear as a result of this description of the procedure of the inquisition which would have been initiated by the complaint of Edward I to Pope Innocent V that the inquisitors, the archbishop of York and the bishop of Carlisle, would have proceeded in summary fashion: arguably, King Robert, having been notified of inquisition, would have admitted his crimes of both homicide and sacrilege given that the objective which he sought to obtain was not a defence but rather absolution and the removal of the public declaration of his automatically imposed excommunication *latae sententiae*.[55] This arguably is demonstrated in the text of the letter of letter of commission of 1310.

Infliction of Punishments Generally

As noted earlier, Reichel observes that canonical punishments whether vindicatory or correctional may be inflicted only for a crime actually having been committed.[56] No person may be punished unless he has committed a crime.

In addition Reichel notes:

> Where is a censure *ipso jure* null and void: [in the following cases]
>   (c) In the absence of canonical proof of crime sufficiently grave to warrant the infliction of censures although in reality the crime has been committed.[57]

Accordingly, in principle at least if not in practice, it is submitted that every effort would have been made by the Curia to ensure that Robert Bruce was indeed culpable to the crimes before publication of the excommunication.

Conclusion

As Grant noted, there are very few facts concerning the murder of John Comyn by Robert Bruce which are known:

> All we know for certain about what happened is that Comyn and Robert Bruce were together in the church of the Franciscan Friary at Dumfries, that Comyn and his uncle Sir Robert Comyn were killed, and that Robert Bruce was responsible.[58]

Notwithstanding, as observed earlier, that the purpose of this analysis has been to establish what facts do exist concerning the manner in which the murder took place particular as regards intentional homicide as opposed to the reason that the murder took place in the sense of a dispute for which no documentary evidence exists. Arguably, as noted in the initial summary, the necessary facts are to be found in the text of the papal bull of 1306 and the letter of 1310. The relevant extracts of the two documents are as follows commencing with the bull of 1306:[59]

> because with some followers ... approaching the Franciscan church at Dumfries ... with arms at hand, he audaciously violated its immunity, committing the sacrilege of homicide within it.[60]

and the letter of 1310 (see endnote 15):

> A petition sent to us states that he, once persuaded [by the devil], with several accomplices, killed John and Robert Comyn, knights, and others joined against him, in the church of the Friars minor in Dumfries ...

It is recalled that the essence of the facts here deal with the intentional homicide and the sacrilege: the letter of 1310 largely repeats the facts stated in the bull of 1306 with respect to both the homicide and the sacrilege.

Nevertheless, the real forensic strength of the two documents is to be found in their status as legal documents which form part of a process in the context of a procedure which sought firstly, by means of a public declaration of excommunication incurred automatically, whether in fact King Robert had committed the two crimes. As noted earlier, the bull of commission of 1306 sought in truth to establish by means of inquisition whether or not Robert Bruce had committed the crimes before a public declaration of such was made. This is the first point at which the king was able to exercise his rights of defence and repudiate through imposition upon him of the commission of the crimes of homicide with intent as described within the bull as well as sacrilege. Once again it is recalled that Bruce is described as having entered the church armed which provides not only the basis for the sacrilege of defilement of holy objects but perhaps above all the imposition of the crime of intentional homicide. It was noted subsequently in the discussion of the elements of the crime of both sacrilege but above all that of homicide that the establishment of intent was crucial to the proof of commission of those two crimes. The reaction of Robert Bruce was to not avail himself of the possibility of appealing the publication of the public declaration of the excommunication. In short, Bruce did not deny the crimes of intentional homicide and sacrilege. Nor did he repudiate his public condemnation for them through the public declarations of his excommunication *latae senten-tiae*. Rather, according to the document of 1310, the letter prepara-tory to the granting of absolution, the king, as it were, reinforced his confession of having committed both the crime of homicide with intent and sacrilege by introducing a supplication for absolution instead of by launching an appeal. Clearly the letter confirms the admission made through the failure to appeal the public declaration of the automatic excommunication *latae sententiae*. Accordingly, it is submitted that it is through something of an unique combination of the rules dealing with the nature of proof through admission and appeal against condemnation for commission of crimes that the following becomes clear: that Robert Bruce possessed the requisite state of mind, specifically intention, to murder John Comyn by reason of the uncontested fact that he committed the sacrilege of entering a church symbolically by force with arms, knowing or being quite certain that John Comyn would be unarmed within the church. Clearly this was not murder in hot blood. Otherwise Bruce would have contested the matter before the pope. This was homicide, that is murder in cold blood. This was a straightforward and undisputed murder in the church. The analysis is once again sustained by the fact that neither Robert Bruce nor his supporters nor subsequent genera-tions of Scottish chroniclers ever seek to deny that he murdered John Comyn with the requisite intent. Rather, the efforts through the chroniclers have always been directed at justifying the murder but by means of unsubstantiated allegations against Comyn, alleging, with-out a tissue of evidence, a compromise with Edward I whose forces were defeated soundly by John at the Battle of Roslin in 1303.

In terms of general consequences of this murder one must note the description used by Grant of John Comyn: basically as a man whose murder was necessary for the greater good of Scotland and, it must be said, for Bruce. This analysis is regretfully and, with due respect, profoundly flawed. Grant observes firstly:

Perhaps, therefore, from the long-term point of view (and echoing the narrative constructed by the author of *Gesta Annalia* II); John Comyn has to be regarded as an unfortunate yet essential sacrifice on the altar of Scottish history.

Then he states his premise:

> Therefore he [Bruce] was forced to commit himself to a fight to
> the death, which he eventually won. And having won his fight, he
> managed – through highly effective kingship – to establish the
> essential foundations for the Bruce/Stewart regime, which shaped
> Scotland throughout the rest of the Middle Ages and the early
> modern period. That is Robert I's great achievement – but, in a
> sense, it could not have been achieved without John Comyn,
> whose own royal descent is surely what made their co-operation
> impossible and his killing inevitable.[61]

The major difficulty, of course, with Grant's aforementioned conclusion is that it is devoid of any basis of fact in the sense of facts
marshalled to an acceptable level such as on the probabilities. Rather,
upon examination the phrase 'essential sacrifice on the altar of Scottish
history' is predicated upon a value judgement alone: that the creation
of the Bruce/Stewart regime was desirable or, more particularly, more
desirable than the Balliol/Comyn as a means of retaining the independence of the kingdom of Scotland at specific points in time. Regretfully,
it has never been demonstrated as a matter of fact that Bruce ever
defended the vital interests of the kingdom of Scotland in the most
effective manner possible. This would include the establishment of
peaceful relations with England as well as strengthening the legitimacy
of the Scottish kingship and ensuring harmony within Scottish society
and the exclusion of civil war. Therefore, as regards John Comyn III,
Lord of Badenoch, it is both logically and, as a matter of factually
based historiography, impossible to seriously argue that the interests
of Scotland as an independent kingdom, as distinct from the personal
interests of Robert Bruce, led to the murder of Comyn being not only
inevitable but justifiable as a means to an end.

Further, it is necessary to deal with some concerns regarding notably
the truth of the admission made by Robert Bruce: firstly, those
expressed by Lewis,[62] concerning what might be a procedural truth
which is devoid of any factual basis and which results simply by reason
of the application of the rules of procedure of canon law. However,
arguably, the dangers of such a procedurally based truth are eliminated by virtue of the points in the procedural chain in this particular
case where King Robert could have appealed but omitted, on the basis
of extant documents, to so do; secondly, there are the concerns of

Shoemaker[63] which are something of a refined version of the concerns of Lewis. Basically, did Bruce simply admit to having committed the murder because it was the most convenient way to extract himself from a difficult situation irrespective of the real truth? Shoemaker makes his point as follows:

> It is possible, one might argue, that Bruce accepted the canonical proceedings because the canon law offered him an easier and more politically expedient path than either Scottish or English law of the fourteenth century – under which a conviction, failing a pardon, would mean loss of lands and life. This of course does not excuse the Bruce, but it may explain why he didn't fight the canonical conviction, preferring absolution to secular proceedings.

It is clear that the matter of strategy was essential. It is also clear that for political reasons Bruce would not have submitted himself to Edward I and his courts in England. Further, it is difficult to see how Robert, particularly after he had been enthroned, would submit himself or could submit himself to the ordinary courts of justice of Scotland such as they were. Therefore, the question becomes less the choice of the legal system, given that the civil systems were *de facto* eliminated, and rather more the following: given that Robert submitted himself to the application of medieval canon law, why did he choose effectively to admit the truth rather than to appeal? In one sense, Shoemaker must be correct here: admitting guilt as regards the commission of the murder of John Comyn was the easiest option available. In this regard, Reichel observes:

> After lengthy dispute in the third century as to the possibility of sins unto death being forgiven at all by the Church after baptism it was finally ruled that even idolatry, murder, adultery and other crimes to which the civil law attached the penalty of death might be forgiven by the aid of the collective prayers of the faithful but not without a sharp discipline and satisfaction ... Confession must be followed by satisfaction which may be the humble submission to the discipline of severity rendered necessary by the circumstances of the excess or sin. Properly satisfaction includes three things: (1) atonement or satisfaction to God for the guild of sin which places man in a state of enmity to God and therefore entails

on him eternal punishment; (2) amendment or satisfaction to Go's justice for the injury done to holiness which requires temporal punishment to undo it; (3) restitution or satisfaction to man when any one has been injured by the excess or sin.[64]

As regards satisfaction Reichel observes the following:

> Whenever an injury has been done to another satisfaction must also be made to the injured person either by restitution or compensation for the sin is not forgiven until what has been taken away is restored.[65]

There is no evidence to suggest that King Robert Bruce ever paid the Comyn family money to compensate them for the killing of Robert Bruce.

Therefore, as Shoemaker observes, by reason of what one might term the wide scope of the availability of the remedy of absolution as described by Reichel, the easiest course for Robert, particularly once he was enthroned, was to avail himself of absolution as provided by the Church and its canon law provided that he accepted the penance required. He would not be confronted by either the death penalty or forfeiture of his lands. Rather, the pardon could be forthcoming in the form of absolution coupled with penance. Thus, at least in one sense, it was easier for Robert to tell the substantive truth as opposed to what one might call, as per Lewis, merely a procedural truth. However, it is suggested that the situation was somewhat more complicated than that. It may have been that an appeal was precluded by reason of a different method of proof provided by medieval canon law: that of the public knowledge or notoriety of what had happened. It was for this reason either as opposed to mere simplicity or rather in combination with that motive that Robert Bruce came to admit the substantive truth, that he had killed John Comyn with intent. Concerning the methods of proof involved in canon law at the time of the murder, Smith observes:

> In other words, the Bishop cannot pass declaratory sentence or publish the censure in the case unless the crime has been judicially proven or is completely notorious.[66]

Reichel defines notorious evidence in the following manner:

Notorious evidence is that evidence which is known to all men. Manifest evidence is that which has been openly done and can be proved by any number of witnesses although it is not known to all men as when a criminal has been caught in the act of committing a crime.[67]

As regards proof through notoriety of a crime, it is clear that Robert Bruce never denied publicly having entered the church whilst armed and killing John Comyn therein.[68] The uncontested fact of having entered the church in itself eliminates the defence proposed by Sellar.[69] Arguably, the three facts, that Robert, whilst armed, killed John Comyn in a church, were of such notoriety or, following Reichel, so manifest in the sense of being known to some witnesses that they would have prevented any serious attempt to appeal on a ground of absence of the requisite state of mind or *mens rea* by King Robert. More specifically, knowledge of the relevant facts, the killing of Comyn by Bruce in the church of the Minorite Friars with an arm, was apparently possessed by Edward I as demonstrated by his letter to Pope Clementine V,[70] who in turn presented the same facts but added thereto the crucial fact of Bruce arriving at the church armed in his bull of commission of 1306 requesting verification thereof.

What appears to be the case is that King Robert opted for admission of the crime in part through opportunism, that is he had been advised that even murder could be forgiven through confession absolution and penance, no doubt by Bishop Wishart[71] and secondly, because certain fundamental facts were already too well known publicly or notorious such that they precluded an appeal by the king. Accordingly, it is submitted that for those reasons the tacit admission by Robert Bruce of intentionally killing John Comyn was first, factually and forensically true in nature and second, was attributable to the procedural structure and the substantive nature of the crime of intentional homicide and proof within medieval canon law. However, in truth, although the strategy of using the canon law absolution does indeed reveal itself as being the simplest and most advantageous for Bruce, nevertheless it does comport very substantial difficulties: specifically, a confession of intentionally murdering John Comyn in order to usurp the throne could undermine the moral and legal credibility of Bruce if considered in its own right. This matter therefore required in reality obscuring the truth of the events but without directly denying the intentional homicide. It is submitted that the confession of the substantive truth by the enthroned monarch, concerning the murder of Comyn, explains the inception of a determined and vigorous campaign by the king and continued throughout his entire reign: specifically, the need to consolidate both his own personal position as monarch and that of his dynasty, the Bruce/Stewarts. Arguably, this campaign was executed in the following manner: through the concealment and obfuscation of the full truth concerning the murder by means of dissemination of spurious justifications such as treachery on the part of John Comyn;[72] by means of the physical elimination of members of the Comyn family and destruction of their property in the devastation of Buchan in 1308; through the preparation of documents such as the Declaration of Arbroath; by means of the vilification and erroneous portrayals of both the Balliols and Comyns as either traitors or incompetents controlled by the English, by chroniclers as detailed by Young.[73] Therefore, while the application of medieval canon law led to admission by Robert Bruce of his crime of intentional homicide in particular in addition to that of sacrilege, ultimately the application of this legal system eventuated in the following: Bruce and his supporters created and sustained a whole series of myths, in some cases extant at the present time, devoid of any factual basis but designed and communicated in order to justify the usurpation of the throne of Scotland by Robert Bruce and to sustain his dynasty, the Bruce/Stewarts. One might say that had Robert Bruce not murdered John Comyn intentionally, as argued herein, then there would have been conspicuously no need for the falsification of historical facts concerning the Comyns, notably as analysed and described by Young. The existence of such historical distortions might be taken almost as indirect proof of the intentional murder of Comyn by Bruce. Finally, it is hoped that this chapter will lead to further study and investigation of the Comyn family of that period and in particular of John Comyn III, Lord of Badenoch.

6

The Comyn Legacy

In Scottish tradition, the Comyn legacy has been a reputation for treachery because of their so-called 'betrayal' of William Wallace at the Battle of Falkirk (1298) and of Robert Bruce in 1306. Furthermore, tradition has accepted the depiction of the Comyns – as overmighty subjects from the 1240s onwards – by pro-Bruce writers of the fourteenth and fifteenth centuries. In the search for examples of 'evil counsellors' for the thirteenth century to act as 'dire warnings' from history to those threatening royal authority (and national independence) during the political instability of the fourteenth and fifteenth centuries, they naturally turned to the Comyns as easy targets for their venom in a pro-Bruce age.

The Comyn family's reputation in history has, therefore, suffered a double distortion by fourteenth and fifteenth-century Scottish writers with curiously contradictory aims. On the one hand, they championed William Wallace and Robert Bruce as if they were the only patriot heroes of the early Scottish independence movement, even if this meant using a literary device to give the appearance that Wallace and Bruce were kindred spirits and fought for the same Scottish cause. On the other hand, as a basic aim of their 'propaganda' they sought to bolster royal authority, that premier symbol of Scottish independence in the Middle Ages, by warning their fourteenth and fifteenth-century audiences of the dangers of 'evil counsellors' and overmighty subjects. However, by casting the Comyns as the premier example of the threat to royal authority (and national independence) they have stood thirteenth-century Scottish history on its head. The Comyns had been the premier agents, and allies, of royal authority in thirteenth-century Scotland – they had been, literally, 'Guardians' of that royal authority after Alexander III's death in 1286 – while the Bruces had been the principal opponents of that Guardianship and the 'legitimate' monarchy represented by it. While tradition has Robert Bruce rescuing Scotland and its monarchy from twenty years of baronial faction-fighting between 1286 and 1306, the historical reality suggests it was the Bruce family which brought Scotland to near civil war between 1286 and 1306 in the narrow pursuit of their own dynastic ambitions.

This is not the only contradiction between Scottish tradition and Scottish history. The pro-Bruce Scottish writers of the fourteenth and fifteenth centuries heightened Alexander III's reign as a 'Golden Age' in order to portray Robert Bruce, and not John Balliol, as the successor to Alexander III and restorer of an 'ideal' kingship. Yet the Comyns, Alexander III's chief political advisers and partners in government – responsible for defending Scotland's integrity against Henry III's interference during Alexander's minority years and consolidating his monarchy's independence in his majority, as well as helping to define the kingdom geographically and administratively especially in the north and west – were written out of the achievements of Alexander III's reign.

Dr Cumming's forensic legal investigation of the murder of John Comyn III, Lord of Badenoch, by Robert Bruce in the Greyfriars Church at Dumfries on 10 February 1306 has starkly underlined the inescapable conclusion from canon law evidence that the murder was premeditated and that it was committed by an armed Robert Bruce against an unarmed John Comyn in a holy place. This, in turn, set off a relentless chain of further violent Bruce behaviour aimed at removing the Comyns from Scotland's physical landscape as described by John Barbour in his narrative poem 'The Brus':

[1308, the 'herschip' (harrying) of Buchan]
Now let us go to the king again, who was well pleased at his victory [Inverurie], and had his man burn Buchan from end to end, sparing none. He harried them in such a way that a good fifty years afterwards people bemoaned the devastation of Buchan.[1]

Even Bruce's famous biographer does not hide the hero of his epic poem from the sacrilegious murder of John Comyn III:

He acted wrongly there, without doubt, [for he did] not respect sanctuary at the altar. Because of it such misfortune befel him that I have never heard tell in a romance of a man so hard beset as he was.[2]

This, however, hardly compares with the misfortune of the Comyns. Their base in Buchan was utterly destroyed and the physical symbols of their presence there – the castles of Dundarg (New Aberdour), Slains, Cairnbulg (Philorth), Rattray, Kingedward and Ellon, their manor house at Kelly (now Haddo) and their religious centre, the Cistercian abbey of Deer – almost entirely wiped from the Buchan landscape. This destruction was matched by an equally thorough attempt through the fourteenth and fifteenth centuries to remove the Comyn name from Scottish history on a bogus charge, described by Walter Bower in *Scotichronicon*:

> As I said earlier, these Comyns were in the lead among those who rose against the king [1257]: as a consequence their name is now, so to speak, obliterated in the land, despite the fact that at that time they were multiplied beyond number in the ranks of the magnates of the kingdom.[3]

The nature of Robert Bruce's crime made the international recognition of his illegal 'coup' very difficult for many years. The determined resistance – even after the murder of 1306, the 'herschip' of Buchan (as well as Galloway in 1308), and even after the Battle of Bannockburn in 1314 – of many families associated with the Balliol/Comyn government of the 1290s meant that a long-term propaganda campaign was needed by the Bruce government and by the pro-Bruce narratives of the fourteenth and fifteenth centuries to bolster the Bruce/Stewart dynasty and vilify its enemies. It should be remembered that the Declaration of Arbroath of 1320, apart from being the most famous and most articulate expression of Scotland's independent status, was also a propaganda exercise putting forward Robert Bruce's case at Avignon and trying to persuade the pope to accept his kingship as legitimate. It seems that much of Robert Bruce's reign was almost obsessively concerned with the justification of a sacrilegious murder and an illegal 'coup' which led to bloody civil war in Scotland. This interrupted and distracted Scotland from the pursuit of a political and military campaign for Scottish independence – already well-established before 1306. It was some time after his murder of John Comyn III, Lord of Badenoch, that Robert Bruce would be accepted as the leader of a united Scottish independence movement. Even Bruce's speech before the Battle of Bannockburn (as recreated by Abbot Bernard) seems to give as much priority to his dynastic right to the kingdom as the Scottish cause of independence:

> we have struggled for eight years now for [our] right to the king-
> dom, for the honour of freedom.[4]

The Battle of Bannockburn in 1314 was as much a part of the civil war that Robert Bruce had instigated by his actions in 1306 as the fight against England.

So powerful has been the championing of Robert Bruce and William Wallace by *Gesta Annalia*, Walter Bower's *Scotichronicon*, Andrew Wyntoun's *Orygynale Cronykil of Scotland*, John Barbour's *The Brus* and Blind Harry's *The Wallace* (and in the case of the latter two, so widespread the circulation) that it is not surprising that few historians, until recent times, have gone against the pro-Bruce and pro-Wallace line and highlighted the Comyns' achievements for the national cause. The views of William Fraser (1880) on Walter Comyn, Earl of Menteith, and James Ferguson (1914) on the Comyn family in general stand out as small islands of praise in a sea of hostility:

> [Walter Comyn] was the head of a large and powerful family, the
> chief of numerous vassals possessed of high talents, and a strong
> love of his country, which enabled him to direct the great power
> thus lying in his lands for what he considered the interest of
> Scotland . . . the patriotism of the Earl of Menteith was devoted to
> the preservation of the liberties of his country.[5]

A detailed and underestimated overview of the Comyns by James Ferguson – to be presented originally to the Buchan Field Club, appropriately at the Abbey of Deer, on 29 July 1914, but postponed owing to the gravity of international affairs on the eve of World War I, declared on 4 August 1914 – argued that the murder of John Comyn and the charges of treachery made by Robert Bruce and his supporters in the following centuries:

> have undoubtedly obscured the great qualities and services of
> their [John Comyn III, Lord of Badenoch, and John Comyn, Earl
> of Buchan] family, and the facts that they were the loyal servants
> of the Scottish dynasty of Malcolm Canmore, and the chief lead-
> ers of the national party that under William the Lyon and the later

Alexanders resisted the persistent encroachments of the Norman and early Plantagenet Kings of England. The chief men of the Comyn race were capable commanders in the field, sage statesmen and administrators, and active agents in the promotion of civilisation and Christianity in Scotland. They were the right hand men of the 'Kings of Peace' whose reigns were looked back to with regret in the troubled times that followed.[6]

This judgement seems all the more perceptive before the publication of so many of the government records of Scottish kings of the twelfth and thirteenth centuries in modern editions.[7] These published records have confirmed the Comyn family's immense influence on Scottish government and politics in the twelfth and thirteenth centuries and their major contribution to an increasingly mature and independent Scottish kingship. In their service to successive Scottish monarchs in the twelfth and thirteenth centuries as well as through periods of Guardianship – under David I, William the Lion, Alexander II, Alexander III, under the Guardianship 1286–92, under the kingship of John Balliol and under the Guardianships between 1298 and 1304 – the Comyn family provided one chancellor, three justiciars of Scotia, one justiciar of Lothian, one (possibly two) justiciar of Galloway, two constables, three Guardians, a 'Guardian' of Moray, sheriffs of Ayr, Forfar, Dingwall, Banff, Wigtown and Aberdeen, and 'baillies' (in time of crisis) at Inverie (Knoydart), Jedburgh, Dull, Kilbride, Kirkcudbright and Barburgh (Dumfriesshire). When dominance over offices of state by Comyn allies is taken into account, this list is extended to offices such as chamberlain, additional influence over the justiciarships of Scotia, Galloway and Lothian, as well as the sheriffdoms of Fife, Roxburgh, Kincardine, Elgin, Berwick, Cromarty, Edinburgh, Linlithgow and Haddington. Most impressive of all, however, was the fact that the Comyns (three successive Comyn earls of Buchan) occupied the most senior political and administrative office in Scottish government, the justiciarship of Scotia, for sixty-six out of a hundred years between c.1205 and 1304. Truly, the hundred years before 1306 deserve to be described as the 'Comyn century' when the family were the very pillars of Scottish monarchy, integral to major political and constitutional developments and major contributors to the Scottish 'cause'. Comyn activities in thirteenth-century Scotland 'stitched them . . . into the very fabric of Scotland'.[8]

In view of the overwhelming record evidence which is testimony to Comyn achievement and to the development of a mature, self-consciously independent kingdom, it is somewhat surprising that there is not an accompanying, contemporary pro-Comyn, government-supported narrative for the 'Comyn century' proclaiming Comyn achievements and championing Comyn 'Patriot Heroes'. If there was one, it has been submerged under the pro-Bruce narratives of the fourteenth and fifteenth centuries. However, the fine work of Professor D.E.R. Watt and his team with their forensic study of Walter Bower's *Scotichronicon*[9] has revealed some of the contemporary thirteenth-century influences on the major strands of medieval Scottish narrative history – the *Gesta Annalia* and Walter Bower's *Scotichronicon*. It is clear that these two sources, and also Andrew of Wyntoun, did have access to a lost *St Andrews Chronicle* which was pro-Comyn. This is hardly surprising because the Comyns, as well as controlling the chief political offices in Scotland during the thirteenth century, especially the second half of the century, also controlled the main ecclesiastical offices in this period, especially the bishopric of St Andrews. Gamelin, a Comyn relative, was bishop of St Andrews from 1255 to 1271; William Wishart, from a family prominent among Comyn supporters in the 1250s, was bishop of St Andrews from 1271 to 1279; William Fraser, also from a family with close association with the Comyns, was bishop of St Andrews from 1279 to 1297. The prospective bishop of St Andrews in 1297, at least as far as the Comyns were concerned, was Master William Comyn, brother of John Comyn, Earl of Buchan. Although unsuccessful, due to William Wallace's favouring of William Lamberton, William Comyn remained provost of St Andrews from 1287 to 1329, and thus St Andrews still retained a Comyn presence.

The now lost *St Andrews Chronicle* seems to have covered the twelfth and thirteenth centuries, continuing until at least 1321, and informed both Walter Bower's *Scotichronicon* and Andrew Wyntoun's *Orygynale Cronykil*. *Gesta Annalia* only appears to have used material from the *St Andrews Chronicle* from 1285. As seen in Chapter 4, pro-Comyn material from this St Andrews source has been used for the period 1298 to 1304 by *Gesta Annalia*. This has shed invaluable light on the role of John Comyn the Younger of Badenoch in this vital period of the early Scottish independence campaign. This glimpse of the worth of the now missing *St Andrews Chronicle* only suggests what would have existed if such a pro-government, i.e. pro-Comyn, source was still available to shed light on the thirteenth century as a whole.

The excellent forensic work of the editorial team behind the recent editions of Walter Bower's *Scotichronicon* has uncovered further hints in places of pro-Comyn sentiment found in later chronicles such as *Gesta Annalia*, Bower's *Scotichronicon*, and the *Book of Pluscarden*, some of it deriving from the pro-Comyn *Melrose Chronicle*, the only extant chronicle of the thirteenth century.[10] In places it has been shown that material deriving from one of the pro-Comyn contemporary sources has been used by Bower, but with the pro-Comyn sentiment edited out. A.A.M. Duncan has studied the relationship between the *Melrose Chronicle* (and Melrose-related texts) and *Gesta Annalia*[11] and noted that it is clear that a Melrose-related text was used by the compiler of *Gesta Annalia* though *Gesta* had access to other chronicles too. He notes too, however, where Melrose text was used, that pro-Comyn material was probably edited out 'for they were a non-family in the fourteenth century'.[12] This editing out of pro-Comyn evidence confirms the findings of the editorial team of Walter Bower's *Scotichronicon* who comment at one point that Bower appears 'to summarize the long account in *Melrose* though without the pro-Comyn sentiment of that chronicle'.[13]

As seen in Chapter 2, coverage of the Comyn family from the 1230s to 1260s by the *Chronicle of Melrose* gives a very different picture of the family's role in Scottish politics of that period than the one presented by Scottish tradition. Surely the narrative of the only extant Scottish chronicle of the thirteenth century (the *Melrose Chronicle* was a contemporary chronicle until 1263) should be preferred to the fourteenth and fifteenth-century Scottish chronicles which have so largely contributed to the 'impudent success of the Bruce and Stewart dynasties in seizing the national past for themselves'.[14] Thirteenth-century narrative sources need to be freed from the shackles of a fourteenth and fifteenth-century overview. The contemporary narratives of the thirteenth century, the *Melrose Chronicle* and the rare survivals from the lost *St Andrews Chronicle*, should be allowed to represent thirteenth-century views in their own right. It is hard to imagine that an extant *St Andrews Chronicle* alongside the *Melrose Chronicle* would *not* have made 'Patriot Heroes' out of members of the Comyn family and other families who supported 'the free status of the kingdom and . . . hatred of English domination'[15] under the legitimate regimes of Alexander II, Alexander III, the Guardianships 1286–92 and 1297–1304, and John Balliol's kingship 1292–1296 (and afterwards). Their narrative story would have matched perfectly with the increasing record evidence of Scottish governments in the thirteenth century which shows political maturity and constitutional awareness with government families such as Comyns, Morays, Frasers and Stewarts contributing substantially to the Scottish cause. Contemporary or near-contemporary English chronicle sources such as Matthew Paris's Chronicle, Walter Guisborough's Chronicle, the *Lanercost Chronicle* and Thomas Gray's *Scalacronica* (which uses contemporary evidence from his father who fought in the War of Independence) reinforce the reality of the picture presented by thirteenth-century Scottish sources and further expose the false re-editing of thirteenth-century history by the fourteenth and fifteenth-century Scottish narratives.

The criteria used by fourteenth and fifteenth-century sources, and Scottish tradition to judge thirteenth-century history, and thirteenth-century 'Patriot Heroes', are, of course, valid for all centuries covered – the growth of the Scottish nation, the need to keep it independent and the importance of the monarchy in attaining these two objectives are at the heart of the analysis. Events relating to the extension and definition of the kingdom, the threat of revolt and their suppression and the fight against English interference were carefully selected. However, it has been seen that *Gesta Annalia* and Walter Bower's *Scotichronicon* have laid much greater emphasis on the threat of revolts and the dangers posed by evil counsellors than other aspects and have highlighted this theme in their coverage of thirteenth-century Scottish politics. This emphasis reflects fourteenth and fifteenth-century concerns and perhaps stems from the insecurities caused by Robert Bruce's murder of John Comyn III, his illegal coup and the bloody civil war that was unleashed in 1306. Preoccupation with threats to the Bruce/Stewart dynasty has naturally led fourteenth and fifteenth-century commentators to dwell on internal threats when compiling information about the thirteenth century. The elevation of Robert Bruce as 'Patriot Hero' at the end of the thirteenth century and the beginning of the fourteenth century was, of course, in complete contradiction to the theme emphasised most – the dangers of internal revolt and faction-fighting. The Bruces, including the future king, were the 'overmighty subjects' threatening the political stability and integrity of Scotland between 1286 and 1306. Robert Bruce's linkage with William Wallace, who had been a staunch defender of the kingship of John Balliol, fervently opposed by the Bruces, was another contradiction imposed by fourteenth and fifteenth-century writers seeking to rewrite thirteenth-century Scottish history.

The choice of William Wallace and Robert Bruce as 'Patriot Heroes' of late-thirteenth-century Scottish history was a rather narrow and artificial one set against the criteria used by fourteenth and fifteenth-century commentators. It has been seen, however, that the themes of extending and defining the Scottish kingdom, defending the monarchy from internal as well as external threat from England and Norway, were no better exemplified than by the Comyn family's role as pillars of Scottish monarchy under Alexander II, Alexander III, John Balliol and the Guardianships 1286–92 and 1297–1304. Particularly notable contributions were made by Walter Comyn from the 1230s to 1258, Alexander Comyn from the 1250s to 1289 and John Comyn III from the 1290s to 1306.

Walter Comyn was involved as Alexander II's main trouble-shooter in those areas where royal authority needed most reinforcement – Moray and Caithness in the north and Galloway in the south-west – while his involvement in the Border areas provoked an angry response from Henry III. Walter Comyn was also notably persistent during the minority of the young Scottish king, Alexander III, in reducing to a minimum Henry III's attempt to control Scottish government, ostensibly while protecting the interests of his daughter, Alexander III's wife. These years have been rather underestimated by Scottish tradition (and the fourteenth and fifteenth-century narratives behind it) as a period when the Scottish kingdom and its political integrity were under threat. The contemporary Scottish and English chronicles, the *Melrose Chronicle* and Matthew Paris's *Chronica Majora*, do not miss the period's significance or the pivotal role of Walter Comyn. The importance of Alexander III's minority was not lost on either Alexander III or his main government adviser/counsellor Alexander Comyn, justiciar of Scotia. He had lived through the 1240s and 1250s, and learnt the lessons of two decades when Border issues and English interference had threatened the integrity of the Scottish kingdom. This was immediately obvious in 1260/61 when the constitutional significance of the young Scottish queen going to England to give birth to the Scottish heir was fully appreciated by Alexander Comyn as leader of the Scottish political community. Appropriate constitutional measures were made to deal with the situation. Similar political maturity was shown again in 1278 when Alexander III swore fealty to Edward for his English lands (but not for Scotland). Scotland had been well prepared for the constitutional crisis which befell the kingdom on Alexander III's unexpected death in 1286. Alexander Comyn was the most experienced of the six Guardians who took political management of the kingdom and responsibility for the succession. He had contributed substantially to the definition of the Scottish kingdom and the protection of the Scottish cause against English interference. Although Alexander Comyn died in 1289, the definition of Scottish independence contained within the Treaty of Birgham/Northampton of 1290 was a fitting testimony to his experience gained during Alexander III's minority, the Scottish queen's confinement (1260/61), Alexander III's swearing of fealty to Edward I (1278) and the Guardianship following Alexander III's sudden death in 1286. It represented fifty years of mature political and constitutional thinking.

Patriot heroes are most often made from those fighting for a cause rather than from those forging and defining that cause. Alexander Comyn was certainly a major practical contributor to Scotland's greater sense of political and constitutional identity and independence, but he also played a major role in defending Scotland from a Norwegian threat in the dispute over the Western Isles. While the Scottish victory at the Battle of Largs (1263) was not the result of a major pitched battle – victory was largely brought about when the Norwegian fleet was blown aground and Norwegian forces subsequently defeated in the ensuing fighting – the ceding of the Western Isles and the Isle of Man to Scotland (in return for a payment of 4,000 marks and an annual rent of 100 marks) by the Treaty of Perth (July 1266) was a major enhancement to the Scottish kingdom. Alexander Comyn played a major role as jointly responsible (with Alan Durward) for the kingdom's defence against the Norwegians. However, in his role as justiciar of Scotia, sheriff of newly created sheriffdoms at Wigtown in the south-west and Dingwall in the north, as well as baillie of Inverie, he played a wide-ranging role in the assertion, and reorganisation, of royal authority in the south-west and north of the kingdom.

It has always been war with England rather than with countries such as Norway which has defined Scotland's 'Patriot Heroes'. In particular, the Wars of Independence have been traditionally seen as Scotland's finest hour and the best (some would say only) source for Scotland's 'Patriot Heroes'. However, the impact of the fourteenth and fifteenth-century Scottish narratives has been to limit the war heroes in Scottish tradition to William Wallace and Robert Bruce. It should now be asked why John Comyn III, Lord of Badenoch, is not ranked alongside Wallace and Bruce as a war hero. He was one of the first Scots to strike a blow against the English when the War of Independence broke out in 1296; he escaped English custody in 1298 to return to Scotland and become the chief Scottish political and military leader against the

English between 1298 and 1306; his leadership, alongside his cousin, John Comyn, Earl of Buchan, based on Comyn strength across northern Scotland, consistently frustrated English forces and he won a significant victory over the English at the Battle of Roslin in 1303. This victory, underestimated in Scottish tradition, deserves much higher status in Scottish history – the sharp reaction to it by Edward I shows Roslin should be judged to be as important as the Battle of Stirling Bridge (1297) in Scottish folklore. The story of John Comyn of Badenoch in the early Scottish independence movement is as worthy of praise in epic form as that of William Wallace. Wallace, of course, received epic treatment both in medieval times (through Blind Harry's *The Wallace*) and in modern times (through the film *Braveheart*). If John Comyn had been murdered by someone *other than* Robert Bruce, surely he would have become as much, if not more, of a martyr to the Scottish national cause as William Wallace.

The hundred years prior to Robert Bruce's coup in 1306 have been fairly judged by some historians as 'the Comyn century'.[16] The Wars of Independence, starting in 1296, are also acknowledged at their outset as being the 'War of the Comyns'.[17] The Comyns were behind the forging and definition of Scotland's political independence during the thirteenth century – the Treaty of Birgham/Northampton (1290) contained an articulate summary of the Scottish cause, the result of fifty years of mature political leadership. The Wars of Independence were caused by the need to preserve and defend the political manifesto for an independent Scotland as contained in the Treaty of Birgham/Northampton. It has been seen that the Comyns, especially Walter Comyn, Earl of Menteith (d. 1258), Alexander Comyn, Earl of Buchan (d. 1289) and John Comyn III, Lord of Badenoch (d. 1306) were integrally involved in both the definition of the Scottish cause and its defence and protection. Their roles in the early Scottish independence movement should now be fully acknowledged even if this involves a battle with the Scottish heritage industry itself.

Scottish history has room for more 'Patriot Heroes' from the Middle Ages than William Wallace and Robert Bruce. The 'Comyn Century' and the 'War of the Comyns' surely deserve to have Comyn 'Patriot Heroes' acknowledged in the public domain. Thirteenth-century Scottish history and traditions are incomplete without the Comyns. The early Scottish independence movement cannot be understood without the Comyn contribution. The Comyns should be as closely associated with the expressions of Scottish nationalism within the

Treaty of Birgham/Northampton (1290) as Robert Bruce is associated with the expressions of Scottish nationalism in the Declaration of Arbroath (1320). Professor Cowan is quite right to declare boldly that: 'it is difficult to resist the conclusion that John, the Red Comyn, has suffered, at the hands of posterity, one of the greatest betrayals in all of Scottish history',[18] but the same sentiments could equally be applied to Walter Comyn, Earl of Menteith, and Alexander Comyn, Earl of Buchan.

The nature of the murder of John Comyn's III, Lord of Badenoch, by Robert Bruce in the Greyfriars Church, Dumfries, on 10 February 1306 has meant that it has been much more than 'convenient forgetfulness about history that is uncomfortable'[19] that has distorted the Comyns' contribution to the Scottish independence movement. A concerted propaganda campaign by the Bruce government after the defeat of the Comyns in Buchan in 1308 was followed by Scottish narrative accounts of the fourteenth and fifteenth centuries which favoured the Bruce/Stewart dynasty of their day. The uncritical repetition of their accounts by most later historians, the popularity through the centuries of John Barbour's *The Brus* and Blind Harry's *The Wallace*, and the nineteenth-century need to raise monuments and memorials to William Wallace and Robert Bruce make it more difficult to give the Comyns their rightful place as heroes of the early Scottish independence movement.

There is a case, however, for both Scottish tradition and the Scottish heritage industry to be updated. There was a political necessity in the fourteenth and fifteenth centuries to suppress the Comyn achievements of the thirteenth century, *but* should modern Scottish governments not now embrace the historical reality that Scotland's sense of its own political independence was already well established before the Wars of Independence and before the involvement of William Wallace and Robert Bruce? Should they also actively acknowledge that there were other medieval patriot heroes as worthy as Wallace and Bruce? How can these 'unsung' heroes reach the popular mind? As seen in Chapter 1, mass circulation has particularly helped to promote Shakespeare's historical heroes and villains, Blind Harry's picture of William Wallace, John Barbour's portrait of Robert Bruce and Henry Stanley's idealised view of David Livingstone. Their views have tended to be repeated in modern times through film. Historians can always dream that new ideas can also achieve mass circulation and that their views could receive further attention through the medium of popular television documentary or feature film. However, to make three members of the Comyn family into popular 'Patriot Heroes' perhaps requires more practical, achievable solutions. It would, naturally, be good if modern patrons were as ready to fund suitable statues to Comyn 'Patriot Heroes' as were nineteenth-century patrons who rushed to fund statues and memorials for William Wallace and Robert Bruce. There are still real opportunities to represent Comyn heroes (and Scotland's thirteenth-century achievements) rather better than at present in museums, both national and local, at sites of Comyn castles and abbeys and at places particularly associated with Comyn achievement in the national cause, for example the Battle of Roslin.

The ferocious 'harrying' of Buchan in 1308 has left few visible remains of the Comyns' secular lordship in Buchan with which to commemorate the Comyn achievement and leadership of the national cause, but the Comyn story could be told from Deer Abbey in Buchan. Buchan should celebrate Comyn achievement in the thirteenth century rather than Comyn defeat by Bruce in 1308. The Comyn contribution to the Scottish independence movement can be told, however, elsewhere in northern Scotland at Historic Scotland's Balvenie Castle and Inverlochy Castle (if not so easily at Lochindorb Castle). The Comyn story can, and should, be told at accessible Comyn sites as well as museums in northern Scotland. Northern Scotland was as important for the Scottish independence movement as northern Wales, especially Snowdonia, was for the Welsh independence movement in the Middle Ages. Further south, another Comyn site at Historic Scotland's Inchmahome Priory offers an opportunity to present the story of Walter Comyn as founder of a religious house but also to show him as one of Alexander III's key royal trouble-shooters and a major contributor to the forging and defining of an independent Scottish kingdom. There is thus an opportunity at Comyn sites and at national and local museums to present the public with a more rounded view of the Scottish independence movement than revealed by fourteenth and fifteenth-century propaganda and nineteenth-century memorials. Only then will 'the best of men' be known as Scottish 'Patriot Heroes'.

Notes

Preface

1. Scottish Association of Teachers of History, *History Teaching Review* (September 1998).
2. 'The Cult of Victorian Celebrity', *Daily Telegraph*, 16 March 2013, Weekend, p. 17.

Chapter 1

1. Quotation from M.J. Cohen and John Major (eds), *History in Quotations: Reflecting 5000 Years of World History* (London, 2004), Chapter 5, p. xxi.
2. Allen Massie, 'Shakespeare's Histories are No More Legends, but They Live', *Daily Telegraph*, 14 September 2012.
3. G. Morton, *William Wallace, Man and Myth* (Stroud, 2001), p. 6.
4. Andrew Fisher, 'William Wallace', *Oxford Dictionary of National Biography* (hereafter *ODNB*), vol. 56, p. 953.
5. Tim Jeal, *Livingstone*, revised biography (Yale 2013). His reflections on the reputation of David Livingstone are contained in his article 'The Cult of Victorian Celebrity', *Daily Telegraph Weekend*, 16 March 2013.
6. Morton, *William Wallace*, p. 11.
7. Sydney Wood, *Wallace, Bruce and the Wars of Independence 1286–1328* (Glasgow, 1999), p. 6.
8. Marinell Ash, 'The Strange Death of Scottish History', quoted in David McCrone, 'Scotland – the Brand: Heritage, Identity and Ethnicity', *Images of Scotland*, The Journal of Scottish Education, Occasional Paper Number One (Dundee, 1997), p. 50.
9. Thomas Smith Hutcheson, *Life of Sir William Wallace; or Scotland Five Hundred Years Ago* (Glasgow, 1858), vii, as cited in Edward J. Cowan, 'William Wallace: 'The Choice of the Estates', in Edward J. Cohen (ed.), *The Wallace Book* (Edinburgh, 2007), p. 18.
10. G.W.S. Barrow, 'Robert Bruce', *ODNB*, vol. 47, p.107.
11. Andrew Fisher, 'William Wallace', *ODNB*, vol. 56, p. 953.
12. Cited in Cohen and Major, *History in Quotations*, p. xxi.

13. John of Fordun, *Johannis de Fordun, Chronica Gentis Scotorum* II, ed. W.F. Skene (Edinburgh, 1871–2), p. 321 (hereafter *Chron. Fordun* II).

14. *Scotichronicon by Walter Bower*, 9 volumes, general editor D.E.R. Watt (Aberdeen and Edinburgh, 1987), VI, p. 317 (hereafter *Chron. Bower* (Watt)).

15. Cited in A. Fisher, *William Wallace* (Edinburgh 1986), p. 132.

16. *Chron. Fordun* II, p. 300.

17. *Chron. Fordun* II, p. 330.

18. *Chron. Bower* V, p. 385.

19. *Chron. Bower* VI, p. 301; VI, p. 319.

20. John Barbour, *The Bruce*, ed. and notes A.A.M. Duncan (Edinburgh,1997).

21. E.J. Cowan, 'William Wallace: The Choice of the Estates' in Cowan (ed.), *The Wallace Book*, p. 13.

22. Cited by Elspeth King (ed.) in *Blind Harry's Wallace* William Hamilton of Gilbertfield (Edinburgh, 1998), p. xiv.

23. Andrew Fisher, 'William Wallace', *ODNB*, vol. 56, p. 953.

24. Morton, *William Wallace*, p. 31.

25. G.W.S. Barrow, 'Robert Bruce', *ODNB*, vol. 47, p. 107, citing Andrew Lang's *History of Scotland* I, pp. 188, 236.

26. Morton, *William Wallace*, p. 31 (my italics).

27. Ibid., p. 99.

28. *Chron. Fordun* II, p. 323.

29. *Chron. Bower* VI, pp. 95–7.

30. Andrew Fisher, 'Wallace and Bruce', *History Today*, vol 39, February 1989, p. 18.

31. James Goldstein, *The Matter of Scotland* (Lincoln and London 1993), p.18; see also pp. 1–19.

32. A. Grant, 'Bravehearts and Coronets: Images of William Wallace and the Scottish Nobility' in Cowan (ed.), *The Wallace Book*, p. 101. *Gesta Annalia* II covers the period after 1285.

33. The Bruce questioning of the Comyn leadership of the political community of the realm was clearly stated in the Appeal of the Seven Earls (1290–1).

34. N. Reid, 'Crown and Community under Robert I', in A. Grant and K.J. Stringer (eds), *Medieval Scotland: Crown, Lordship and Community* (Edinburgh 1993), pp. 203–7.

35. E.L.G. Stones (ed.), *Anglo-Scottish Relations 1174–1328 – Some Selected Documents* (London, 1963), p. 281.

36. J. Fraser, 'A Swan from a Raven, William Wallace, Brucean propaganda, and *Gesta Annalia* II' *Scottish Historical Review* 81 (2002), pp. 1–22.

37. *Chron. Fordun* II, p. 292.

38. *Chron. Bower* V, p. 323.

39. *Chron. Fordun* II, pp. 323–4.

40. *Chron. Bower* VI, p. 305.

41. *Chron. Fordun* II, p. 315.

42. Ibid., p. 320.

43. Morton, *William Wallace*, p. 20.

44. As cited in Morton, *William Wallace*, p. 59.

45. As cited in Grant 'Bravehearts and Coronets' in Cowan (ed.), *The Wallace Book*, p. 94, where there is excellent discussion of this theme.

46. Cited in Barrow, 'Robert Bruce', *ODNB*, vol. 47, p. 107.

47. J. Stevenson (ed.), *Documents Illustrative of the History of Scotland 1286–1306*, vol. I (Edinburgh, 1870), p. liii.

48. Agnes Muir Mackenzie, *Kingdom of the Scots* (Edinburgh, 1948), pp. 67, 113.

49. Lord Hailes (Sir David Dalrymple), *Annals of Scotland from the Accession of Malcolm III to the Accession of the House of Stewart* (Edinburgh, 1819) I, p. 205.

50. J. Horne (ed.), *The History of Kirkintilloch* (Kirkintilloch, 1910).

51. D.E.R. Watt, 'The Minority of Alexander III of Scotland', *Transactions of the Royal Historical Society*, 5th series, 21 (1971), p. 2.

52. Alan Young, *Robert the Bruce's Rivals: The Comyns 1212–1314* (East Linton, 1997, 1998), especially Chapter 1 'Heroes and Villains in Scottish Tradition'; G.W.S. Barrow, *Robert Bruce* (3rd edition, Edinburgh, 1988), p. 80, described the notion of the medieval nobility as traitors as 'one of the hardest-dying half-truths of Scottish history'; Fiona Watson, 'The Enigmatic Lion: Scotland, Kingship and National Identity in the Wars of Independence', in Dauvit Broun, R.J. Finlay and Michael Lynch (eds), *Image and Identity: the Making and Re-Making of Scotland Through the Ages* (Edinburgh, 1988), p. 23; Fiona Watson, 'The Demonisation of King John', in E.J. Cowan and R.J. Finlay (eds), *Scottish History: the Power of the Past* (Edinburgh, 2002), pp. 44–5; Grant, 'Bravehearts and Coronets', in Cowan (ed.), *The Wallace Book*.

53. Barrow, *Robert Bruce*, p. 145.

54. Edward J. Cowan, *'For Freedom Alone': The Declaration of Arbroath 1320* (East Linton, 2003), pp. 31–2.

55. A. Grant, 'The Death of John Comyn: What was going on?' *Scottish Historical Review* 86 (2007), pp. 31–2.

56. Robin Frame, *The Political Development of the British Isles 1100–1400* (Oxford, 1990).

57. As cited in Norman H. Reid, 'Alexander III: The Historiography of a Myth', in Norman H. Reid (ed.), *Scotland in the Reign of Alexander III 1249–1286* (Edinburgh, 1990).

58. Neil Cooney, *The North-East and Scottish Wars of Independence*, Aberdeen Town and County History Society (Aberdeen, 2008).

59. Dauvit Broun, 'A New Look at *Gesta Annalia* attributed to John of Fordun', in Barbara E. Crawford (ed.), *Church, Chronicle and Learning in Medieval and Early Renaissance Scotland* (Edinburgh, 1999), pp. 9–21.

60. D. Broun with A.B. Scott (eds), 'Liber Extravagans' (Supplementary Book), in D.E.R. Watt (ed.) *Chron. Bower* IX, pp. 54–119.

61. Alexander Grant, 'The Death of John Comyn: What was going on?' *Scottish Historical Review* 86 (2007), part 2, pp. 202–7. See discussion in Chapter 4, pp. 172–4.

62. Grant, 'The Death of John Comyn', pp. 182, 191, 195, 215, 219.

63. Fiona Watson 'The Demonisation of King John', in E.J. Cowan and R.J. Finlay (eds), *Scottish History: the Power of the Past* (Edinburgh, 2002), pp. 29–41.

64. M. Lynch, *Scotland, a New History* (London, 1991, 1992), especially pp. 96–8, 112, 121–2; G.W.S. Barrow, *Robert Bruce*, pp. 80, 114, 128; Cowan, 'For Freedom Alone', pp. 30–2.

65. Broun, Finlay and Lynch (eds), *Image and Identity*, p. 1, especially Fiona Watson, 'The Enigmatic Lion: Scotland, Kingship and National Identity in the Wars of Independence', pp. 19–37.
66. Morton, *William Wallace*, p. 31.
67. Barrow, *Robert Bruce*, p. 84.
68. R. James Goldstein, *The Matter of Scotland: Historical Narrative in Medieval Scotland* (Lincoln, Nebraska, 1993).
69. *Chron. Fordun* II, p. 304.
70. *Chron. Bower* V, p. 424.
71. A. Young, 'Noble Families and Political Factions' in Norman H. Reid (ed.), *Scotland in the Reign of Alexander III 1249–1286* (Edinburgh, 1990), pp. 1–30.
72. B. Webster, 'Anglo-Scottish Relations, 1296–1389: Some Recent Essays', *Scottish Historical Review* 74, No. 197, April (1995), pp. 1–23.
73. G.W.S. Barrow, *Robert Bruce*, p. 78; Young, *Robert the Bruce's Rivals: the Comyns*, p. 143; Cowan, *'For Freedom Alone'*, p. 20.
74. Morton, *William Wallace*.
75. Cowan, *'For Freedom Alone'*, p. 32.

Chapter 2

1. Matthew Paris, *Chronica Majora* V (Rolls Series 57, London, 1872–83), p. 656, trans. in A.O. Anderson (ed), *Scottish Annals from English Chronicles 500 to 1286* (London, 1908, reprinted 1990), p. 376. The notion was *embellished* in W. Fraser, *The Red Book of Menteith* (Edinburgh, 1880), p. 18.
2. *Chron. Fordun* II, p. 292.
3. Ibid., p. 293.
4. *Chron. Bower* (Watt) V, p. 181.
5. Ibid., pp. 321–3.
6. J. Aikman, *History of Scotland, translated from the Latin of George Buchanan* I (Glasgow and Edinburgh, 1827–9), p. 240
7. Ibid. I, p. 387 (as cited in Norman H. Reid, 'Alexander III: The Historiography of a Myth', in Norman H. Reid (ed.), Scotland in the Reign of Alexander III 1249–1286 (Edinburgh, 1990), p. 196.
8. Lord Hailes, *Annals of Scotland*, p. 205.
9. D.E.R. Watt, 'The Minority of Alexander III of Scotland', *Transactions of the Royal Historical Society*, 5th Series XXI (1971), pp. 1–23; an alternative view is given in A. Young, 'The Political Role of Walter Comyn, Earl of Menteith, during the Minority of Alexander III of Scotland', in K.J. Stringer (ed.), *Essays on the Nobility of Medieval Scotland* (Edinburgh, 1985), pp. 131–49.
10. *Chron. Bower* (Watt) V, pp. 307–17.
11. A number of excellent books and articles have illustrated this point. See particularly Keith Stringer, 'Social and Political Communities in European History: Some Reflections on Recent Studies', in Claus Bjorn, Alexander Grant and Keith J. Stringer (eds), *Nations, Nationalism and Patriotism in the European Past* (Copenhagen, 1994), pp. 9–27; Susan Reynolds, *Kingdoms*

and Communities in Western Europe 900–1300 (2nd edition, 1997), pp. 251–3, 262; M.T, Clanchy, *England and its Rulers 1066–1272* (2nd edition, Oxford, 1998), pp. 180–6.

12. R. James Goldstein, *The Matter of Scotland: Historical Narratives in Medieval Scotland* (Lincoln and London, 1993), pp. 7, 23–4.

13. Norman Reid, 'The Kingless Kingdom: the Scottish Guardianship of 1286–1306', *Scottish Historical Review* 61 (1982), p.129, as cited in Goldstein, *The Matter of Scotland*, p. 29.

14. Goldstein, *The Matter of Scotland*, p. 30; see also pp. 31–2.

15. As cited in Keith Stringer, 'Social and Political Community in European History: Some Reflections on Recent Studies', in Bjorn, Grant and Stringer (eds), *Nations, Nationalism and Patriotism*, p. 23.

16. For more detail see AIan Young, *Robert the Bruce's Rivals: the Comyns, 1212–1314*, Chapter 2, 'The Foundation for the 'Comyn Century', pp. 14–33.

17. G.W.S. Barrow, *The Kingdom of the Scots* (London, 1973), Chapter 3.

18. G.W.S. Barrow, *Regesta Regum Scottorum* II, p. 5.

19. A.A.M. Duncan, *Scotland, The Making of the Kingdom* (Edinburgh, 1975), p. 595.

20. See Alan Young 'The Earls and Earldom of Buchan in the Thirteenth Century', in Alexander Grant and Keith J. Stringer (eds), *Medieval Scotland: Crown, Lordship and Community: Essays presented to G.W.S. Barrow* (Edinburgh, 1993), pp. 174–202.

21. Alan Young, 'The Comyns to 1300', in Richard Oram and Geoffrey Stell (eds), *Lordship and Architecture in Medieval and Renaissance Scotland* (Edinburgh, 2005), pp. 69–73.

22. *Chron. Bower* (Watt) V, pp. 142–5.

23. G.W.S. Barrow, 'Badenoch and Strathspey 1130–1312: I. Secular and Political', *Northern Scotland* 8 (1988), pp. 1–15.

24. Young, 'The Comyns to 1300', pp. 74–6.

25. G.W.S. Barrow, 'Badenoch and Strathspey', p. 8.

26. Barbara E. Crawford 'The Earldom of Caithness and the Kingdom of Scotland, 1150–1266' in K.J. Stringer (ed.), *Essays on the Nobility of Medieval Scotland* (Edinburgh, 1985), pp. 25–43.

27. Ibid., p. 34.

28. E.L.G. Stones, *Anglo-Scottish Relations 1174–1328* (Oxford, 1965), pp. 35–7.

29. R. Fawcett and D. Breeze, *Inchmahome Priory* (Edinburgh, 1986), pp. 15–16.

30. J. Stevenson (trans.), 'The Chronicle of Melrose', in *The Church Historians of England: Chronicle of Melrose* IV, pt. I (London, 1835–8), p. 179.

31. F.M. Powicke, *King Henry III and the Lord Edward* (Oxford, 1947), p. 744.

32. G.W.S. Barrow (ed.), *Regesta Regum Scottorum* II: *The Acts of William I, 1165–1214*, p. 45.

33. For general discussion of the north and Anglo-Scottish relations in the period see Alan Young 'The North and Anglo-Scottish Relations in the Thirteenth Century', in John C. Appleby and Paul Dalton (eds), *Government, Religion and Society in Northern England 1000–1700* (Stroud, 1997), pp. 77–89.

34. Alan Orr Anderson, *Early Sources of Scottish History, AD 500 to 1286* II (Edinburgh, 1922), p. 530; M. Paris, *Chronica Majora* IV, pp. 192–3, cited in Anderson, *Scottish Annals*, p. 349.

35. Anderson, *Scottish Annals*, pp. 352–3.

36. *Calendar of Close Rolls 1242–47*, p. 122.

37. Young, 'The Comyns to 1300', pp. 75–6

38. *Calendar of Close Rolls 1242–47*, p. 222; *Calendar of Documents Relating to Scotland* V (Edinburgh, 1986), no. 12 (herefter Cal. Docs Scot.); G.W.S. Barrow, 'Frontier and Settlement: Which Influenced Which? England and Scotland 1100–1300', in Robert Bartlett and Angus MacKay (eds), *Medieval Frontier Societies* (Oxford, 1981), p. 11.

39. Keith J. Stringer, *Earl David of Huntingdon 1152–1219: A Study in Anglo-Scottish History* (Edinburgh, 1985), Chapter 9; G.W.S. Barrow, *The Anglo-Norman Era in Scottish History* (Oxford, 1980); Keith J. Stringer, 'The Scottish Foundations: Thirteenth-Century Perspectives', in A. Grant and K.J. Stringer (eds.), *Uniting the Kingdom? The Making of British History* (London, 1995), pp. 85–96.

40. *Chronicle of Melrose*, cited in Anderson, *Early Sources* II, p. 538.

41. Matthew Paris, cited in Anderson, *Scottish Annals*, p. 351.

42. *Cal. Docs. Scot.* I, nos 2671–2.

43. Anderson, *Scottish Annals*, p. 350; F.M. Powicke, *King Henry III and the Lord Edward*, p. 744. Geoffrey de Marisco was, apparently, the nephew of the Archbishop of Dublin, John Comyn, and this explains the presence of a Maurice and Eustace Comyn in his company. There is no direct evidence to link the Irish Comyns with Scottish affairs.

44. *Chron. Bower* (Watt) V, p. 161.

45. D.E.R. Watt, 'Minority of Alexander III', pp. 1–23. For an alternative view see A. Young, 'Walter Comyn, Earl of Menteith', in K.J. Stringer ed. *Essays on the Nobility of Medieval Scotland* (Edinburgh, 1985), pp. 131–49.

46. Matthew Paris, in Anderson, *Scottish Annals,* p. 349; *Chronicle of Melrose,* in Anderson, *Early Sources*, p. 530.

47. Matthew Paris, in Anderson, *Scottish Annals*, pp. 349–50. The first group to make a response against the Bissets was the one led by Patrick, Earl of Dunbar, the king's cousin.

48. For general discussion of the incident see Young, *Robert the Bruce's Rivals*, pp. 37–43.

49. Anderson, *Early Sources*, pp. 536–7.

50. Anderson, *Scottish Annals*, pp. 350–1 (my italics)

51. *Calendar of Close Rolls* (1242–47) (London 1892–), p. 221 (hereafter *Cal. Close Rolls*).

52. Anderson, *Scottish Annals*, p. 350.

53. *Cal. Docs Scot.* I, nos 2671–2.

54. Grant G. Simpson, 'A Seal of Minority of Alexander III', in Grant and Stringer, *Medieval Scotland*, pp. 134–5; Duncan, *The Making of the Kingdom*, p. 559.

55. Barrow, *Kingdom of the Scots*, p. 85 and no. 11; *Chron. Fordun* II, p. 289.

56. Anderson, *Early Sources*, p. 571.

57. Watt, 'Minority of Alexander III', pp. 6–7.
58. *Chron. Fordun* II, p. 289.
59. *Chron. Bower* (Watt) V, p. 293.
60. M. Ash, 'The Church in the Reign of Alexander III', in Reid, *Scotland in the Reign of Alexander III*, p. 37.
61. *Chron. Fordun* II, p. 291.
62. M. Lynch, *Scotland: a New History* (London, 1995), p. 101; see Ash, 'The Church in the Reign of Alexander III'.
63. M. Lynch, *Scotland: a New History*, p. 112.
64. Anderson, *Scottish Annals*, pp. 365–6.
65. Ibid.
66. Ibid., pp. 368, 370.
67. *Chron. Fordun* II, p. 292; Grant G. Simpson, 'Kingship in Miniature: A Seal of Minority of Alexander III, 1249–1257', in Alexander Grant and Keith J. Stringer (eds), *Medieval Scotland: Crown, Lordship and Community* (Edinburgh, 1993), pp. 134–5.
68. *Cal. Docs Scot.* I, no. 2013, *Chron. Fordun* II, p. 292; cf. *Cal. Docs Scot.* I, nos 2671–2.
69. Anderson, *Scottish Annals*, pp. 370–4.
70. Ibid., p. 369.
71. *Chron. Fordun* II, p. 292.
72. *Chron. Bower* (Watt) V, p. 303.
73. *Chron. Fordun* II, pp. 292–3.
74. *Chron. Bower* (Watt) V, p. 317.
75. Stones, *Anglo-Scottish Relations*, pp. 61–9.
76. Anderson, *Early Sources*, pp. 581–3 (my italics).
77. Ibid., pp. 585–9.
78. *Chron. Bower* (Watt) V, p. 363; p. 381: The same source adds more praise on Gamelin's death: 'He was a man of weighty counsel [and fair judgement], the defender of generosity and courtesy in the church'.
79. *Foedera, Conventiones, Litterae, e Cuiuseunque Generiis Acta Publica* I, ed. Rymer, T. (Record Commission edition, London, 1816–1869), p. 353 (hereafter *Foedera* I).
80. *Cal. Docs Scot.* I, no. 2080.
81. Young, 'The North and Anglo-Scottish Relations', p. 87.
82. *Chron. Fordun* II, p. 293.
83. *Chron. Bower* (Watt) V, p. 319.
84. Ibid., p. 323.
85. *Liber Pluscardensis* II, ed. Skene, F.J.H. (Edinburgh, 1877–80), p. 67.
86. Ibid.
87. *Chron. Bower* (Watt) V, p. 317.
88. Anderson, *Early Sources*, pp. 589–90.
89. Anderson, *Scottish Annals,* p. 376.
90. *Foedera* I, I, p. 370.
91. Translation taken from G.W.S. Barrow, 'Wales and Scotland in the Middle Ages', *Welsh Historical Review* 10 (1980–81), pp. 311–12 (my italics).

92. Anderson, *Scottish Annals*, p. 376.
93. *Chron. Bower* (Watt) V, p. 323, repeating *Gesta Annalia* (*Chron. Fordun* II, p. 293).
94. As cited in Reid, *Scotland in the Reign of Alexander III*, p. 196.
95. Lord Hailes (David Dalrymple), *Annals of Scotland* (Edinburgh, 1819), p. 205.
96. Cited in Reid, *Scotland in the Reign of Alexander III*, pp. 200–2.
97. William Fraser, *The Red Book of Menteith* I (Edinburgh, 1880), p. 18.
98. *Chron. Bower* (Watt) V, p. 323 (my italics).

Chapter 3

1. *Chron. Bower* (Watt) V, p. 303.
2. *Chron. Fordun* II, p. 292.
3. Ibid., p. 293.
4. *Chron. Bower* (Watt) V, pp. 319, 321.
5. Ibid., p. 303.
6. Ibid.
7. For much of what follows see A. Young, *Robert the Bruce's Rivals: the Comyns*, especially Chapter 3, 'A Responsible, Aristrocratic Governing Community c1260–186'.
8. Watt, 'The Minority of Alexander III', p. 20.
9. Duncan, *Scotland, the Making of the Kingdom*, p. 589.
10. Watt, 'The Minority of Alexander III', p. 20.
11. Michael Brown, 'Henry the Peacable: Henry III, Alexander III and Royal Lordship in the British Isles, 1249–1272', in Bjorn K.U. Weller (ed.) with Ifor W. Rowlands, *England and Europe in the Reign of Henry III* (1216–1272) (2002), pp. 55, 65 note 34, shows continued Comyn dominance of the king in May and October 1258.
12. He was for instance a royal messenger to England in 1259, as well as a member of the provisional regency council set up in 1261, and was actively involved in royal missions to counter the Norwegian military threat in 1263 and 1264.
13. *Liber Cartarum Prioratus Sancti Andree in Scocia* (Bannatyne Club, 1842), p. 346.
14. See pp. 66–8. For lists of the Comyn 'party' in 1244 see *Cal. Docs Scot.* I, nos 2671–2; in 1255, *Cal. Docs Scot.* I, no. 2013; in 1257, *Chron. Bower* (Watt), p. 320; in 1258, *Foedera* I, I, p. 370.
15. C.A. Malcolm, 'The Office of Sheriff in Scotland', *Scottish Historical Review* 2 (1922–3).
16. Norman H. Reid and G.W.S. Barrow (eds), *The Sheriffs of* Scotland *(An Interim List) to c.1306* (University of St Andrews Library, The Scottish Medievalists, 2002).
17. D.E.R. Watt, *Fasti Ecclesiae Scoticanae Medii Aevi* (2nd draft) (Scottish Record Society New Series, Edinburgh, 1969), pp. 2, 39, 126, 293.
18. *Regesta Regum Scottorum* IV, pt. 1.
19. *Chron. Bower* (Watt) V, p. 423.

20. *Regesta Regum Scottorum* IV pt 1.
21. See especially Geoffrey Barrow and Ann Royan, 'James Fifth Stewart of Scotland, 1260(?)–1309', in K.J. Stringer (ed.), *Essays on the Nobility of Medieval Scotland* (Edinburgh, 1985), pp. 166–87.
22. A.M. Mackenzie, *The Kingdom of Scotland* (Edinburgh, 1948), p. 113.
23. Anderson, *Early Sources*, pp. 592 (my italics).
24. Anderson, *Scottish Annals*, p. 377 (my italics).
25. Ibid., pp. 377–8.
26. For valuable discussion of the impact of Henry's political problems on English relationships with all neighbouring countries see Brown 'Henry the Peacable'.
27. Anderson, *Scottish Annals*, p. 378.
28. *Cal. Docs Scot.* I, no. 2157.
29. Ibid., nos 2205 and 2206.
30. *Flores Historiarium*, in Anderson, *Scottish Annals*, p. 379.
31. *Cal. Docs Scot.* I, no. 2229.
32. Ash, 'The Church in the Reign of Alexander', pp. 43–5; M. Brown, *The Wars of Scotland 1214–1371* (Edinburgh, 2004), pp. 122–6; Brown, 'Henry the Peacable', pp. 49–50.
33. Ash, 'The Church in the Reign of Alexander', p. 31.
34. W.R. MacDonald, *Scottish Armorial Seals* (Edinburgh, 1904), nos 943–4, as cited in Ash, 'The Church in the Reign of Alexander', p. 47.
35. Lynch, *Scotland, a New History*, p. 97
36. E.L.G. Stones and G.G. Simpson, *Edward I and the Throne of Scotland* II (Oxford, 1978), pp. 84–5.
37. Brown, 'Henry the Peacable', pp. 47–61.
38. Anderson, *Early Sources*, p. 607; *Chron. Fordun* II, p. 295.
39. *Exchequer Rolls of Scotland* I, ed. J. Stuart and others (Edinburgh, 1878–1908), p. 20.
40. *Chron. Fordun* II, p. 296; *Exchequer Rolls* I, p. 11.
41. Young, *Robert the Bruce's Rivals*, pp. 78–9, with details from *Exchequer Rolls* I, pp. 18, 19, 22, 30–3.
42. *Acts of the Parliaments of Scotland*, ed. Thomson, T. and Innes, C. (Edinburgh, 1814–1875), pp. 78–9 (hereafter Acts. Parl. Scot.); *Chron. Fordun* II, p. 297.
43. National Archives (NA). SCI 16/93; NA SCI 20/158.
44. Anderson, *Scottish Annals*, p. 382.
45. See A. Young, 'The Earls and Earldom of Buchan in the Thirteenth Century', in Grant and Stringer, *Medieval Scotland*, especially pp. 200–1.
46. G.G. Simpson, 'An Anglo-Scottish Baron of the Thirteenth Century: the Acts of Roger de Quincy, Earl of Winchester and Constable of Scotland' (Edinburgh University PhD thesis, 1965).
47. National Records of Scotland (NRS) RH 6/59.
48. Alexander Grant, 'Thanes and Thanages, from the Eleventh to the Fourteenth Centuries', in Grant and Stringer, *Medieval Scotland*, Appendix no. 17.
49. Young, 'The Earls and Earldom of Buchan in the Thirteenth Century', p. 197.
50. J. Stevenson (ed.), *Documents illustrative of the History of Scotland 1286–1306*, I (Edinburgh, 1870), p. 393.

51. Ian A.G. Shepherd, *Exploring Scotland's Heritage: Grampian* (1986), no. 29, p. 89.

52. Details of Comyn castles following Alan Young, 'The Comyns to 1300', in Oram and Stell, *Lordship and Architecture in Medieval and Renaissance Scotland*.

53. I am most grateful for Dr Alexander Grant's help with fourteenth-century material which has been invaluable in determining the main centres within the earldom.

54. *Cal. Docs Scot.* I, no. 2513; II, no. 187; *Calendar of Close Rolls* (1272–9), pp. 126, 136, 429, 529; *Calendar of Patent Rolls* (1266–72), p. 300; (1272–81), p. 423; (1281–92), p. 18.

55. *Calendar of Close Rolls* (1227–) (London, 1892–), p. 138 (hereafter *Cal. Close Rolls*).

56. *Calendar of Inquisitions Post Mortem and Other Analogous Documents* (H.III–) (London, 1904–), ii, no. 753 (hereafter *Cal. Inq. Post Mortem*).

57. *Placito de Quo Waranto* (Record Commission, 1818), p. 559.

58. NA Special Collections, Ancient Petitions, SC8/197, no. 9816.

59. Stevenson, *Documents* I, p. Iii.

60. NA SCI 16/93; NA SCI 21/158; *Cal. Docs Scot.* II, no. 215.

61. Stevenson, *Documents* I, p. Iii–iii.

62. *Cal. Docs Scot.* II, nos 107, 122, 123.

63. Ibid., nos 59, 62, 82, 90, 97, 152, 154, 160, 241; *Cal Docs Scot.* V, no. 38.

64. *Anglo-Scottish Relations*, p. 81 (my italics).

65. *Cal. Docs Scot.* II, no. 62.

66. *Foedera* II, pp. 1079–83.

67. Ibid., pp. 266–7.

68. *Chron. Fordun* II, pp. 304–5.

69. *Chron. Bower* (Watt) V, p. 427.

70. Andrew Wyntoun, *Orygynale Cronykil of Scotland* II, ed. D. Laing (Edinburgh, 1872–9), p. 266 (hereafter *Chron. Wyntoun* (Laing)).

71. G.W.S. Barrow, 'A Kingdom in Crisis: Scotland and the Maid of Norway', *Scottish Historical Review* 188 (October 1990), p. 126.

72. *Chron. Fordun* II, p. 305.

73. *Chronicle of Lanercost, 1272–1346*, trans. Sir Herbert Maxwell (Glasgow, 1913), pp. 39–43 (hereafter *Chron. Lanercost*).

74. Barrow, *Robert Bruce*, p. 17.

75. Ibid.

76. A.A.M. Duncan (ed.), *Formulary E Scottish Letters and Brieves 1286–1424* (University of Glasgow, Occasional Papers, 1976), no. 89.

77. *Melrose Liber*, no. 396, as cited in Barrow, *Robert Bruce*, p. 17.

78. Grant G. Simpson, *Handlist of the Acts of Alexander III, the Guardians and John* (1960–), pp. 44–6.

79. Stevenson, *Documents* I, pp. 26–7.

80. *Chron. Lanercost*, pp. 43–4.

81. Ibid., p. 44.

82. N. Reid, 'The Kingless Kingdom: the Scottish Guardianship of 1286–1306', *Scottish Historical Review* 172 (October 1982), p. 106; Geoffrey Barrow and

Ann Royan, 'James Fifth Stewart of Scotland, 1260(?)–1309, in K.J. Stringer (ed.), *Essays on the Nobility of Medieval Scotland*, p. 170.

83. Alan Young, *Robert the Bruce's Rivals*, pp. 96–100.
84. Barrow, *Robert Bruce*, p. 17.
85. *Exchequer Rolls* I, pp. 35–7.
86. Ibid., p. 39.
87. Ibid.
88. Ibid., p. 43.
89. *Chron. Bower* (Watt) VI, p. 9.
90. Stones, *Anglo-Scottish Relations*, pp. 85–6; see M. Prestwich, 'Edward I and the Maid of Norway', *Scottish Historical Review* 188 (October 1990).
91. Prestwich, 'Edward I and the Maid of Norway', p. 166.
92. Stevenson, *Documents* I, pp. 95–6.
93. For translation see Barrow, 'A Kingdom in Crisis', pp. 137–41 (my italics).
94. Barrow, *Robert Bruce* p. 28.

Chapter 4

1. *English Historical Documents* II, eds. David C. Douglas and George W. Greenaway (Oxford, 1981), p. 828.
2. Stones, *Anglo-Scottish Relations*, p. 103.
3. Ibid., pp. 107–11.
4. A.A.M. Duncan, 'The Process of Norham, 1291', in P.R. Coss and S.D. Lloyd (eds), *Thirteenth Century England* V (Woodbridge, 1995), p. 207, as cited in Dauvit Broun with A.B. Scott (eds) notes on 'The Scottish Poem' in *Liber Extravagans*, appended to *Scotichronicon* by *Walter Bower* hence *Chron. Bower* (Watt) IX, p. 115.
5. 'The Scottish Poem' in *Liber Extravagans*, *Chron. Bower* (Watt) IX, p. 77.
6. *Chron. Bower* (Watt) VI, pp. 51–3.
7. Barrow, *Robert Bruce*, p. 52.
8. See generally Amanda Beam, *The Balliol Dynasty 1210–1364* (John Donald, 2008), especially Introduction p. 108, for a valuable Balliol insight on this dramatic period.
9. Stones, *Anglo-Scottish Relations* p. 131.
10. *Chron. Bower* (Watt) IX, p. 116.
11. Barrow, *Robert Bruce*, p. 63.
12. *Acts. Parl. Scot* I, p. 453.
13. *Chron. Lanercost* (Maxwell), p. 115.
14. Stones, *Anglo-Scottish Relations*, p. 137.
15. *Chron. Lanercost*, pp. 115–16.
16. Stones, *Anglo-Scottish Relations*, pp. 141–3.
17. *Cal. Docs Scot*. II, no. 742; also see nos 839 and 848.
18. *Chron. Lanercost*, p. 145 (my italics).
19. For translation of the Treaty of Birgham/Northampton, G.W.S. Barrow, 'A Kingdom in Crisis: Scotland and the Maid of Norway', p. 139.
20. 'The Scottish Poem' in *Liber Extravagans*, *Chron. Bower* (Watt) IX, p. 81.

21. *Chron. Fordun* II, p. 322.
22. J.E. Fraser, 'A Swan From a Raven: William Wallace, Brucean Propaganda and *Gesta Annalia* II', *Scottish Historical Review* 80 (2002), pp. 6–9.
23. Stevenson, *Documents* II (1870), p. 190.
24. Ibid., pp. 167–9, 198; M. Prestwich, *Edward I* (London, 1988), p. 476.
25. Stevenson, *Documents* II, pp. 202, 212.
26. *Rotuli Scotiae* I, p. 506, as cited in Barrow, *Bruce*, p. 344, no. 23.
27. *Cal. Docs Scot.* II, no. 963.
28. *Chron. Guisborough*, as cited in Barrow, *Bruce*, p. 344, no. 23.
29. Stevenson, *Documents* II, p. 226.
30. Ibid., p. 207.
31. Peter of Langtoft in *English Historical Documents* III, ed. H. Rothwell (London, 1975), pp. 243–4.
32. *Chron. Fordun* II, p. 323.
33. Fraser, 'A Swan from a Raven' for good discussion pp. 14–19.
34. Ibid., p. 15.
35. A. King (ed. and trans.), *Sir Thomas Gray Scalacronica 1272–1363*, Surtees Society 209 (2005), pp. 228–9 (hereafter *Scalacronica* (King)).
36. *Chron. Fordun* II, p. 324.
37. D. Broun, 'A New Look at *Gesta Annalia* attributed to John of Fordun', in Barbara E. Crawford (ed.), *Church, Chronicle and Learning in Medieval and Early Renaissance Scotland* (Edinburgh, 1999), pp. 9–29, especially p. 27; A. Grant, 'The Death of John Comyn: What was going on?', *Scottish Historical Review* 86 (2007), pp. 189–99.
38. A. Grant, 'Bravehearts and Coronets: Images of William Wallace and the Scottish Nobility' in Edward J. Cowan (ed.), *The Wallace Book* (Edinburgh, 2007), p. 100; A. Grant, 'The Death of John Comyn', p. 219.
39. *Chron. Fordun* II, p. 324.
40. *Chron. Bower* (Watt) V, p. 18.
41. *Chron. Guisborough*, p. 306.
42. Barrow, *Robert Bruce*, p. 91.
43. *Cal. Docs Scot.* II, no. 742.
44. M. Ash, 'William Lamberton, Bishop of St Andrews 1297–1328', in G.W.S. Barrow (ed.), *The Scottish Tradition: Essays in Honour of R.G. Cant* (Edinburgh, 1974), p. 45; *Cal. Docs Scot.* II, no. 1017.
45. Barrow, *Bruce*, p. 347, note 9; *Cal. Docs Scot.* II, no. 1978.
46. *Cal. Docs Scot.* V, no. 220.
47. *Chron. Fordun* II, p. 324.
48. M. Lynch, *New History of Scotland* (London, 1995), p. 122.
49. Barrow, *Robert Bruce*, p. 114.
50. Stevenson, *Documents* II, p. 207.
51. In general see work of F. Watson, *Under the Hammer, Edward I and Scotland 1286–1307* I (East Linton, 1998), especially p. 116; also F. Watson, 'The Enigmatic Lion: Scotland, Kingship and National Identity in the Wars of Independence', p. 26; also Young, *Robert the Bruce's Rivals*, p. 174.

52. *Cal. Docs Scot.* II, no. 1592; Watson, *Under the Hammer*, p. 116; Barrow, *Bruce*, pp. 104–5.

53. *Liber Sancte Marie de Aberbrothoc* I (Bannatyne Club, 1848–56), no. 231 (hereafter *Arbroath Liber*).

54. Stones, *Anglo-Scottish Relations*, p. 167.

55. Ibid., p. 239.

56. Watson, *Under the Hammer*, p. 78ff; Barrow, *Bruce*, p. 109ff.

57. Barrow, *Robert Bruce*, pp. 110–14; A. Beam, *The Balliol Dynasty 1210–1364* (Edinburgh, 2008), pp. 185–6.

58. Barrow, *Robert Bruce*, p. 114.

59. Watson, *Under the Hammer* p. 170.

60. Ibid., p. 171.

61. *Chron. Bower* (Watt) VI, notes p. 419.

62. Prestwich, *Edward I*, p. 498.

63. *Chron. Fordun* II, p. 326, in general 325–8.

64. *Scalacronica* (King), p. 45; for description of the battle pp. 45–6.

65. Ibid., p. 221, note 10.

66. *Chron. Fordun* II, pp. 327–8.

67. *Acts. Parl. Scot.* I, pp. 454–5, as cited in Barrow, *Bruce*, p. 128.

68. Ibid.

69. Watson, *Under the Hammer*, p. 171.

70. *Chron. Fordun* II, p. 320.

71. *Scalacronica* (King), p. 45.

72. *Chron. Bower* (Watt) VI, p. 297.

73. Andrew Wyntoun, as cited in Watson, *Under the Hammer*, p. 170.

74. *Scalacronica* (King), pp. 46–7.

75. Stevenson, *Documents* II, p. 486.

76. *Scalacronica* (King), p. 47.

77. Rothwell (ed.), *English Historical Documents* III, p. 225.

78. Watson, *Under the Hammer*, p. 185; for detail see Watson, 'Settling the Stalemate: Edward's Peace in Scotland 1303–1305', in M. Prestwich, R. Britnell and R. Frame (eds), *Thirteenth Century England* (1997); Young, *Robert the Bruce's Rivals*, pp. 186–7.

79. F. Palgrave (ed) *Documents and Records Illustrating the History of Scotland* (London, 1837), p. 278.

80. Ibid., p. 287; G.O. Sayles 'The Guardians of Scotland and a Parliament at Rutherglen in 1300', *Scottish Historical Review* 24 (1927), pp. 245–50.

81. Barrow, *Robert Bruce*, p. 129.

82. Palgrave, *Documents*, p. 280.

83. Ibid., p. 276.

84. Prestwich, *Edward I*, pp. 497–8; see also pp. 207–17.

85. Stones, *Anglo-Scottish Relations*, pp. 241–59.

86. *Cal. Docs Scot.* II, no. 1741.

87. Stones, *Anglo-Scottish Relations*, pp. 241–3.

88. Palgrave, *Documents*, p. 293.

89. Barbour, *The Bruce* (Duncan), p. 79.

90. Beam, *Balliol Dynasty*, p. 191; Grant, 'The Death of John Comyn', p. 216.
91. Stevenson, *Documents* II, pp. 449–50.
92. Stones, *Anglo-Scottish Relations*, p. 159.
93. Beam, *Balliol Dynasty*, pp. 173–7, 186.
94. Ibid., pp. 187–9.
95. Excellent discussion of sources in Grant, 'The Death of John Comyn' though I do not agree with some important conclusions.
96. E.L.G. Stones and G.G. Simpson, *Edward I and the Throne of Scotland 1290–1296* (Oxford, 1978) I, p. 15; II, p. 138; I am grateful to Douglas Richardson for identifying 'Eleanor' as the first wife of John Comyn, Earl of Buchan, rather than the Balliol wife of John Comyn II, Lord of Badenoch. I am also thankful to Geoffrey Stell for alerting me to this valuable information.
97. Grant, 'The Death of John Comyn', pp. 202–7, 215–16.
98. 'The Scottish Poem' in *Liber Extravagans, Scotichronicon*, p. 79.
99. Ibid., pp. 116–17, notes pp. 242–4.
100. Ibid., notes pp. 257–60.
101. Grant, 'The Death of John Comyn', p100.
102. *Scalacronica* (King), p. 47.
103. Barbour, *The Bruce* (Duncan), p. 71; E.J. Cowan *For Freedom Alone: The Declaration of Arbroath* (East Linton, 2003), pp. 29–30; A.A.M. Duncan, 'The War of the Scots', *Transactions of the Royal Historical Society* (1992), p. 136.
104. Cowan, '*For Freedom Alone*', p. 30.
105. Watson, 'The Enigmatic Lion', p. 24.
106. R. Frame, *The Political Development of the British Isles 1100–1500* (Oxford, 1995), p. 193.
107. Beam, *Balliol Dynasty*, p. 318.

Chapter 5

1. Of the Inner Temple, Barrister. My profound thanks to Mrs A.I. Pexton Cumming; Professor K. Shoemaker, Law Faculty and Department of History, University of Wisconsin; my co-author, Dr A. Young; Professor A.D.E. Lewis, Law Faculty, UCL; Professor D. d'Avray, UCL; Dr N. Norbye UCL; Dr M. Robinson, Balliol College, Oxford; Dr A. Grant; Dr A. Borthwick, National Archives of Scotland; Dr Nigel Saul, RHC-London; Dr J. McDonald; HE Cardinal O'Brien; Dr Bruce McAndrew; Sir David Edward QC ; The Lord Lyon of Scotland; Lord Sumption OBE; and Lord Selkirk of Douglas QC. All errors and omissions are my own responsibility.
2. G.W.S. Barrow, *Robert Bruce and the Community of the Realm*, 4th edition (Edinburgh, 2005) *passim*. A recent dissenting view recognising that Bruce intentionally murdered Comyn is established in the impressive analysis by A. Grant in 'The Death of John Comyn: What Was Going On?', *Scottish Historical Review* 86 (October 2007), p. 176 *passim*, whose speculative conclusion regretfully does not follow from the premises of the overall solidly based factual analysis. Lord Sumption opined in an email September 2010 that

an analysis excluding intention on the part of Bruce in the killing of Comyn would be 'simply too convenient' for Bruce in the overall assessment of his behaviour at that time.

3. This murder had several consequences both immediate and long term: in the immediate short term Bruce thereby usurping the throne of Scotland and completely eliminating thereby other possible claimants such as Comyn. Grant, 'The Death of John Comyn', pp. 176, 213–14, argues that Comyn's senior dynastic position in terms of descent from Margaret, eldest daughter of David, Earl of Huntingdon, coupled with descent from Hextilda, granddaughter of Donald III Bane, is likely to have figured prominently in the calculations of Bruce as regards the murder of Comyn; and at pp. 221–2 the documentary evidence concerning the motives of Bruce as regards his accession to the throne of Scotland and his relationship to Edward I whose support he sought to obtain to that end. In contra W.D.H. Sellar 'Was it Murder? John Comyn of Badenoch and William Earl of Douglas', in C.J. Kay and M.A. Mackay (eds), *Perspectives on the Older Scottish Tongue: a Celebration of DOST* (Edinburgh, 2005), pp. 132, 136, 'Historians I think have sometimes found it difficult to explain why Bishop Wishart of Glasgow and Bishop Lamberton of St Andrews among others continued to give Bruce their full support apparently undeterred by the murder of Comyn Wishart absolving Bruce from this shortly after the event and Lamberton saying pontifical high mass at Bruce's inauguration as king later in 1306. The answer is clear. It was not murder . . . In the long run the canon law analysis was to be very influential in the later classification of homicide in many European jurisdictions including Scotland. But its impact on secular mores in the fourteenth and fifteenth centuries was limited.' With due respect to Sellar, coupled with my thanks to him for so kindly sending me the photocopy of his article, first, he does not cite any written evidence to substantiate his claim of an attempted absolution by Wishart; second, arguably, there is no explanation as to why Sellar chose not to undertake an application of the canon law in the instant case, given that canon law was applied in the instant case and not civil law as evidenced by the two documents cited herein in date of 1306 and 1308 respectively. Accordingly, and with due respect, Sellar has not made out his legal case that 'It was not murder'.

4. Barrow, *Robert Bruce*, p. 146.

5. For something of an evaluation of the acts and policies of King Robert see R. Nicholson, *Edward III and the Scots* (Oxford, 1965), in particular p. 7.

6. O.J. Reichel, *A Complete Manual of Canon Law* II (London, 1890), p. 322. The 'corpus juris canonici' or code of canon law is the name give to the systematised collection of laws begun by the monk Gratian in the middle of the twelfth century augmented during the next two centuries by volumes of decretals issued with papal sanction, approved by successive popes, commented upon and expanded by canons and text writers in the schools and generally received as a standard throughout the Western church until the great rebellion against authority in the sixteenth century. The four chief parts which properly form the code and were approved of as such by Gregory XIII in 1575 are: (1) the Decretum of Gratian; (2) the Decretals of Pope Gregory IX; (3) the Sext of

Boniface VIII; (4) the Clementines of Pope Clement V. Gratian, the author of
the Decretum, was a Benedictine monk, by birth a Tuscan, sometime an inmate
of the monastery of Classe near Ravenna and subsequently of St Felix at
Bologna.

7. 'Gratian was a canon lawyer from Bologna who lived in the twelfth century
and was a Camaldolese monk. Arguably Gratian's work was an attempt, using
early scholastic method, to solve seemingly contradictory canons from previous centuries. He quoted a great number of authorities, including the Bible,
papal and conciliar legislation, church fathers such as Augustine of Hippo, and
secular law in his efforts to reconcile the canons there were several codes of
canon law in the Roman Catholic Church; Gratian's work was an attempt,
using early scholastic method, to solve seemingly contradictory canons from
previous centuries. Gratian quoted a great number of authorities, including the
Bible, papal and conciliar legislation, church fathers such as Augustine of
Hippo, and secular law in his efforts to reconcile the canons, the first arguably
expressed in the Decretals of the second in the 1917 *Code of Canon Law* and
the third in the 1983 canon law. The *Decretum Gratiani* or *Concordia discor-*
dantium canonum (in some manuscripts *Concordantia discordantium*
canonum) is a collection of canon law compiled and written in the twelfth
century as a legal textbook by the jurist known as Gratian. It forms the first
part of the collection of six legal texts, which together became known as the
Corpus Juris Canonici. It retained legal force in the Roman Catholic Church
until Pentecost 1918, when a revised *Code of Canon Law* (*Codex Iuris*
Canonici) promulgated by Pope Benedict XV on 27 May 1917 obtained the
Force of Law. The name is fitting: Gratian tried to harmonise apparently
contradictory canons by discussing different interpretations and deciding on a
solution. This dialectical approach allowed other law professors to work with
the *Decretum* and to develop their own solutions and commentaries. These
legalists are known as the decretists.', A. Winroth, *The Making of Gratian's*
Decretum (New York, 2004), *passim*.

8. O.J. Reichel, *A Complete Manual of Canon Law*, vols I–II.

9. Rev. S.B. Smith, *Elements of Ecclesiastical Law*, vols I–III, 2nd edition (New
York, 1888), *nihil obstat*.

10. 'Sacrilege is in general the violation or injurious treatment of a sacred object.
In a less proper sense any transgression against the virtue of religion would be
a sacrilege. Theologians are substantially agreed in regarding as sacred that
and that only which by a public rite and by Divine or ecclesiastical institution
has been dedicated to the worship of God. The point is that the public authority must intervene; private initiative, no matter how ardent in devotion or
praiseworthy in motive, does not suffice. Attributing a sacred character to a
thing is a juridical act, and as such is a function of the governing power of the
Church. It is customary to enumerate three kinds of sacrilege: personal, local,
and real. St Thomas teaches (Summa, I–II, Q., xcix) that a different sort of
holiness attaches to persons, places, and things. Hence the irreverence offered
to any one of them is specifically distinct from that which is exhibited to the
others. Suarez (*De Religione*, tr. III, 1–3) does not seem to think the division

very logical, but accepts it as being in accord with the canons.' www. newadvent:org/org/cathen/13321a.htm

11. Barbour, *The Bruce* (Duncan) poses the problem in the context of whether or not to consider at least certain of the chronicles such as that of Barbour to be primarily a literary work which arguably reduces substantially the likely factual rigour of the document in terms of historic evidence aside from the fact that Barbour was not a contemporary witness to any of the events described or narrated in his work. Barrow, *Robert Bruce*, p. 312, observes: 'To some extent our view of Bruce will always depend upon the credence we give to Barbour. If we choose to ignore Barbour altogether as we may, we shall be left with a jejeune assortment of glimpses in record and chronicle and a few authentic utterances. These might carry more weight than Barbour but they would not add up to a portrait.' With due respect, surely a few authentic utterances are more valuable than a factually inaccurate portrait.

12. My thanks to Sir David Edward QC for having put me on the path of documents at the National Archives of Scotland relevant to this chapter as well as to HE Cardinal O'Brien for his very kind introduction to the Vatican Archives.

13. Excommunication: 'A form of ecclesiastical censure by which a person is excluded from the communion of believers, the rites or sacraments of a church, and the rights of church membership, but not necessarily from membership in the church as such. Some method of exclusion belongs to the administration of all Christian churches and denominations, indeed of all religious communities. Roman Catholicism distinguishes between two kinds of excommunication, that which renders a person *toleratus,* tolerated, and that which renders him *vitandus,* one who is to be avoided. The second and more severe form requires—except for certain crimes that incur it automatically—that the culprit be announced by name in public as *vitandus,* in most cases by the Holy See itself; this is reserved for the gravest offenses. Both kinds of excommunication bar the excommunicated person from the sacraments of the church as well as from Christian burial.' *Encyclopedia Britannica* www.britannica.com [accessed 13.11.12].

14. Papal bull: 'In Roman Catholicism, an official papal letter or document. The name is derived from the lead seal (*bulla*) traditionally affixed to such documents. Since the twelfth century it has designated a letter from the pope carrying a *bulla* that shows the heads of the apostles Peter and Paul on one side and the pope's signature on the other. By the thirteenth century the term *papal bull* referred to only the most important documents issued by the pope. These included canonisations of saints, dogmatic pronouncements, Henry VIII's dispensation to marry Catherine of Aragon (his brother's widow), the restoration of the Society of Jesus in 1814 and the announcement (25 December 25 1961) of the forthcoming Second Vatican Council. *Encyclopedia Britannica* www.britannica.com/EBchecked/topic/84314/bull-papal [accessed12.11.12].

15. For the purposes of this chapter the date provided by H.J. Lawlor, 'The Absolution of Robert Bruce', *Scottish Historical Review* 19 (1922), pp. 324, 326: 'The date of this letter is obviously incorrect; for Pope Clement III died in 1191. But if we regard *dementis* iii as a *lapsus calami,* and substitute for it

ementis v, we get the date 23rd July, 1310, which is consistent with other
indications in the letter.'

16. My thanks to Dr Marigold Norbye, Department of Greek and Latin, UCL,
for her kind assistance with the translation as well as to Professor D. d'Avray,
Department of Greek and Latin, UCL, for his most helpful observations
concerning the purpose of the bull which is primarily that of a commission
to investigate the foundation in fact of the excommunication *latae sententiae*
prior to the issuing of a declaration thereof. Full text in English: 'Clement,
bishop and servant of servants, to the venerable brothers the Archbishop of
York and the Bishop of Carlisle, greetings and apostolic blessing. It has come
to our notice through a reliable report that Robert, Earl of Carrick, with a
few of his followers from that area, having come armed to the church at the
place of the Friars Minor of Dumfries, in the diocese of Glasgow, violated
with temerity the immunity of the said church by committing within it sacrilege by homicide against the indults and permissions of the privileges
conceded to the said brothers by the Apostolic See to the peril of his soul and
to the scandal of many people: for this it is declared that he has incurred the
sentence of excommunication. Since therefore if the things mentioned before
(i.e. the premises) rest on truth, we do not want to nor should we pass by
under dissimulation, we give order to your Fraternity through Apostolic
writings that if it is evident to you that the said earl and other supporters of
his from this area have incurred the sentence of excommunication because of
the premises or any part of them you denounce this same earl by name and
the other persons supporting him in this part in your churches in presence of
people having tolled the bells and lit the candles as excommunicates and that
you have this announced throughout the lands and parts of England,
Scotland, Ireland and Wales and in other places which you consider expedient, and that they should be avoided by all very narrowly, until such times as
the earl and the above mentioned supporters will have duly satisfied concerning these things and will have deserved to obtain the benefice of an absolution owed to them. And indeed tying with the knot of excommunication all
those who support follow and give refuge/shelter to the said earl (unless by a
warning sent in advance they will have desisted from favouring or befriend-
ing the said count and from following or harbouring him), you should in the
same way announce them publicly as being excommunicate and have it also
announced in all places which you consider expedient. And placing the lands,
castles and villages of these people under ecclesiastical interdict and ensuring
that this (interdict) be observed inviolately through our authority until such
time as they shall have desisted from following and harbouring the same earl
and shall have obtained the benefice of absolution concerning these things by
our good will and order. Papal Bull 1306 Given at Bordeaux on the 15th
calends of June (18 May in the Roman Calendar) in the first year of our
pontificate [18.5.1306].'

17. My thanks to Professor A. Lewis, Law Faculty, UCL, for his kind assistance
with the translation as well as legal reflections notably as regards the limitations of what might be termed procedurally based legal truth. Full text in

English: 'Letters for the absolution of King Robert Bruce 1310: Berengar, by Divine Grace cardinal priest of the title of SS Nereus and Achilleus to the man of religion, the abbot of the Benedictine monastery of Paisley, diocese of Glasgow [greetings]. A petition sent to us states that he, once persuaded [by the devil], with several accomplices, killed John and Robert Comyn, knights, and others joined against him, in the church of the Friars minor in Dumfries, but since he, with his accomplices, because of the murderous enmity and war and other considerations could not approach the Holy See, or even his diocesan bishop or his vicar, to make humble supplication on behalf of himself and of his accomplices . . . by the same See to be mercifully provided. We therefore who freely undertake for faithful Christians penitential discipline by the authority of the lord pope, commit to your discretion, that if it subsequently be that the said Robert and his said accomplices make sufficient satisfaction to the church aforesaid, you may absolve him and his said accomplices from that excommunication which they happen to have incurred [on that account] and from that same guilt of lay killing in accordance with the church's accustomed form and having carefully heard their confession and considered their guilt you may impose salutary penance and other matters which are lawfully to be imposed under the same aforesaid authority. Given at [Ascoli] Piceno [around] August in the fifth year of the pontificate of Clement [V].'

18. Subsequent to his enthronement on 27 March 1306.
19. *Catholic Encyclopedia* www.newadvent.org [accessed 30.5.13], 'Immunities'. The *Catholic Encyclopedia*, also referred to as the *Old Catholic Encyclopedia*, is an English-language encyclopedia published in the USA. The first volume appeared in March 1907 and the last three volumes appeared in 1912, followed by an index volume in 1914 and later supplementary volumes.
20. According to the *Catholic Encyclopedia* www.newadvent.org [accessed 30.5.13]: 'We must remember that with reference to reservation or the *right* to absolve, excommunications are divided into four classes: excommunications specially reserved to the *pope*; excommunications simply reserved to the *pope*; excommunications reserved to the *bishop* (ordinary); and, finally, excommunications that are not reserved (*nemini reservat*).' It is submitted that following the *Catholic Encyclopedia* the matters involve herein fall within the category of matters specially reserved to the adjudication by the pope himself pursuant to the explanation in the *Catholic Encyclopedia*, namely: 'Those who themselves or through others, invade, destroy, or detain cities, lands, places, or rights of the Roman Church, those who hold possession of, disturb, or detain its sovereign jurisdiction, and all who give aid, counsel, or countenance to these offences.' The rights here are those alluded to in the papal bull which concern the interdict against defiling holy objects, i.e. the violation of the civil immunity: ' That is, in arriving armed to the church at the place of the Friars Minor of Dumfries in the diocese of Glasgow violated with temerity the immunity of the said church by committing within it sacrilege by homicide.' King Robert not only 'violated the immunity' but necessarily a right as arguably the immunity was a right possessed by the Roman Church and for this reason it is specifically stated in the papal bull of 1306.

21. H.J. Lawlor, 'The Absolution of Robert Bruce', *Scottish Historical Review* 19 (1922), pp. 324, 326 (my italics).

22. H.T. Riley (ed.), *Registra Johannis Whethamstede* II (London, 1873), pp. 347, 352: '*Le samedi (avaunt que ce) cette lettre fust faite, le counte de Carrike vient à Glascu et levesque le dona absolucion pleyniement . . . et le fist jurer qil esterroit al ordinance de la clergie d'Escoce et lasoitter come . . . est bien . . . purchaser son heritage en totes les maneres qil pout.*'

23. Ibid., p. 347.

24. Smith, *Elements of Ecclesiastical Law*, p. 230, para 3063, observes: 'When is a censure *ipso jure* null and void? (a) want of jurisdiction in the superior.' Effectively any attempt by Bishop Wishart to usurp the authority of the pope by endeavouring to grant an absolution to Robert Bruce would have resulted in purported absolution being void.

25. According to the *Catholic Encyclopedia* www.newadvent.org [accessed 21.5.13]: 'Excommunication', it would seem that the letter authorises the abbot to do two things: first, authority to grant absolution from the excommunication and then second, to grant absolution from the sins of homicide and murder. The *Encyclopedia* observes: 'It is to be noted at once that, though the same word is used to designate the sacramental sentence by which sins are remitted and that by which excommunication is removed, there is a vast difference between the two acts. The absolution which revokes excommunication is purely jurisdictional and has nothing sacramental about it. It reinstates the repentant sinner in the Church; restores the rights of which he had been deprived, beginning with participation in the sacraments; and for this very reason, it should precede sacramental absolution, which it thenceforth renders possible and efficacious. After absolution from excommunication has been given *in foro externo*, the judge sends the person absolved to a confessor, that his sin may be remitted; when absolution from censure is given in the confessional, it should always precede sacramental absolution, conformably to the instruction in the Ritual and the very tenor of the formula for sacramental absolution.'

26. Reichel, *A Complete Manual of Canon Law* II, p. 289.

27. Ibid., p. 292, note 198. The authority is Lucius III in *Decret. Lib.* III, tit. II: C7.

28. Sellar, 'Was it murder?', pp. 132–8.

29. Reichel, *A Complete Manual of Canon Law* II, p. 292, note 198. The authority is Lucius III in *Decret. Lib.* III, tit. II: C7.

30. Reichel, *A Complete Manual of Canon Law* II, p. 292.

31. Ibid.

32. Ibid.

33. Reichel, *A Complete Manual of Canon Law* II, p. 40: 'A crime is defined as any open and manifest excess which calls for condemnation and punishment in public interest.'

34. Reichel, *A Complete Manual of Canon Law* II, p. 58.

35. *Catholic Encyclopaedia* www.newadvent.org

36. O.J. Reichel, *A Complete Manual of Canon Law* II, p. 230.

37. Ibid.

38. Smith, *Elements of Ecclesiastical Law* III, pp. 26–7
39. Ibid.
40. Ibid.
41. Ibid., p. 26.
42. Ibid., p. 27.
43. Ibid., p. 215
44. Reichel, *A Complete Manual of Canon Law* II, p. 322.
45. Ibid.
46. Smith, *Elements of Ecclesiastical Law* III, p. 215.
47. Sellar, 'Was it Murder?', pp. 132–8.
48. Reichel, *A Complete Manual of Canon Law* II, p. 65.
49. Ibid., p. 63.
50. Ibid., p. 255.
51. Ibid, p. 255.
52. Rymer, *Foedera* I, p. 46, AD 1306 Edv I: '*Johannis Comyn: De caede Johannis Comyn per Robertum de Brus et de intendendo Adomaro de Valentia locum tenenti Regis et Capitaneo contra Rebelles 1306*'.
53. Grant, 'The Death of John Comyn', pp. 176, 177–8.
54. Reichel, *A Complete Manual of Canon Law* II, p. 255.
55. At this point in time there do not appear to have been any records which subsist and which contain among other things in the UK the decision of the archbishop and the bishop – private email in date of 13 May 2013 per Dr A. Borthwickl, National Archives of Scotland, Edinburgh.
56. Reichel, *A Complete Manual of Canon Law* II, p. 230.
57. Ibid.
58. Grant, 'The Death of John Comyn', p. 176 at 178–9.
59. Ibid. p.176, note 17, observes: 'Rymer (ed.), *Foedera* I (2), p. 987; the papal bull presumably repeats the wording of Edward's accusation: "... because lately Robert de Brus, former earl of Carrick, in whom we had full trust, contemptuous of his homage and fealty given under oath to us, along with certain malefactors, partisans and accomplices, wickedly and treasonably killed (*interfecit*) the noble John Comyn of Badenoch, our faithful man, and certain others in our fealty, in the church of the Friars Minor of Dumfries in Scotland. And not content with such an outrageous and wicked crime, but heaping on more wickednesses, he hostilely disturbed our peace, which we had publicly proclaimed should be firmly observed in our land, following the homages and fealties that its inhabitants gave us, by making war against them; and he strove to usurp the lordship of that land to himself by force".' With due respect to Grant it is not clear in what sense the papal bull can be said to repeat the working of Edward's accusation at least if the bull is that of 1306. One notes specifically that in the bull of 1306 there is mention that Bruce entered the church armed which of course attracted in itself excommunication *latae sententiae* on the basis of it constituting a sacrilege. This fact is absent from the complaint of Edward I.
60. Ibid., Papal bull of 1306.
61. Grant, 'The Death of John Comyn', pp. 176, 224.

62. Professor A. Lewis, Emeritus Professor of Comparative Legal History, UCL.
63. Dr K. Shoemaker, Professor, Law Faculty and Department of History, University of Wisconsin.
64. Reichel, *A Complete Manual of Canon Law* II; *A Complete Manual of Canon Law* I, 'Penance', p. 140.
65. Reichel, *A Complete Manual of Canon Law* II; *A Complete Manual of Canon Law* I, p .167.
66. Smith, *Elements of Ecclesiastical Law* III, p. 253.
67. Reichel, *A Complete Manual of Canon Law* II; Reichel, *A Complete Manual of Canon Law* I, p. 167.
68. From Lord Douglas of Selkirk QC, email, October 2012: 'King Robert is said to have expressed up to the moment of his own death, to his close followers (perhaps his friend Sir James Douglas) his profound regret for having murdered John Comyn. In truth, however, such an eventual expression of piety serves only to underline that whilst the king intended to kill Comyn he did not foresee being troubled throughout his life and, particularly, at the moment of his own death, by the moral repugnance of his act.'
69. Sellar, 'Was it Murder?', pp. 132, 136.
70. Letter of Edward I: Rymer, *Foedera* I, p. 46, AD 5 April 1306 Edv I: '*Johannis Comyn: De caede Johannis Comyn per Robertum de Brus et de intendendo Adomaro de Valentia locum tenenti Regis et Capitaneo contra Rebelles 1306*'.
71. Notwithstanding that he seems not to have obtained either a magister or doctorate in theology at the Sorbonne, it would certainly have been appropriate for Bishop Wishart to advise King Robert on canon law given his significant ecclesiastical role, as bishop, in applying the system.
72. Grant, 'The Death of John Comyn', pp. 176, 180–2, after a thorough exegis of the chronicles decisively destroys the colported legend of betrayal of Robert Bruce to Edward I by John Comyn III.
73. Young, *Robert Bruce's Rivals*, *passim*.

Chapter 6

1. Barbour, *The Bruce* (Duncan), p. 334.
2. Ibid., p. 80.
3. *Chron. Bower* (Watt) V, p. 323.
4. Barbour, *The Bruce* (Duncan), p. 458.
5. Fraser, *The Red Book of Menteith*, p. 18.
6. James Ferguson of Kinmundy, KC, Sheriff of Forfarshire, 'The House of Comyn (1124–1314–1914)', *Buchan Field Club*, vol. XI, p. 53.
7. *The Charters of David I* (1124–1153), ed. G.W.S. Barrow (Woodbridge, 1999), in addition to the *Regesta Regum Scottorum* (Acts of the Kings of Scotland) Edinburgh University series: *The Acts of Malcolm IV* (1153–1165), ed. G.W.S. Barrow (1960); *The Acts of William I* (1165–1214), ed. G.W.S. Barrow with the collaboration of W.W. Scott (1971); *The Acts of Alexander III* (1249–1286), eds Cynthia Neville and Grant G. Simpson (2012); and *The Acts of Robert I* (1306–1329), ed. A.A.M. Duncan (1988). Also available are the

Regesta Regum Scottorum, Handlists for *The Acts of Alexander II* (1214–1249), ed. J.M. Scoular (1959) and *The Acts of Alexander III, the Guardians and John*, ed. G.G. Simpson (1960).

8. Cowan, 'For Freedom Alone', p. 18.
9. See especially, D. Broun, 'A New Look at *Gesta Annalia* Attributed to John of Fordun', in Barbara E. Crawford (ed.), *Church, Chronicle and Learning in Medieval and Early Renaissance Scotland*, (Edinburgh, 1999), pp. 9–30.
10. *Chron. Bower* (Watt) V, note pp. 448–9, also pp. 235–6, 242–3, 281.
11. A.A.M. Duncan, 'Sources and Uses of the Chronicle of Melrose, 1165–1297', p. 163.
12. Ibid., p. 172.
13. *Chron. Bower* (Watt) V, p. 448.
14. R. Frame, *The Political Development of the British Isles 1100–1300* (Oxford, 1990).
15. Ibid.
16. Simpson 'Kingship in Miniature', p.131; Young, *Robert the Bruce's Rivals*, pp. 11, 210.
17. Young, *Robert the Bruce's Rivals*, pp. 143, 147; Cowan, 'For Freedom Alone', p. 20.
18. Cowan, 'For Freedom Alone', p. 31.
19. Morton, *Wallace*, p. 31.

Bibliography

Primary Sources

RECORD MATERIAL

Acts of the Parliaments of Scotland, eds T. Thomson, and C. Innes (Edinburgh, 1814–1875).

Calendar of Chancery Rolls (1277–1326) (Various) (London, 1912).

Calendar of Charter Rolls (1226–) 6 vols (London, 1903–1919).

Calendar of Close Rolls (1227–) (London, 1892–).

Calendar of Documents relating to Scotland, I–V, eds J. Bain *et al.* (Edinburgh, 1881–1986).

Calendar of Entries in the Papal Registers relating to Great Britain and Ireland: Papal Letters, eds W. H. Bliss and others (London, 1893).

Calendar of Inquisitions Post Mortem and Other Analogous Documents (H.III–) (London, 1904–).

Calendar of Patent Rolls (1216–) (London, 1893–).

Documents Illustrative of Sir William Wallace, his Life and Times (Maitland Club, 1841).

English Historical Documents, vol. II (1042–1189), eds David C. Douglas and George W. Greenaway (Oxford, 1981).

English Historical Documents, vol. III (1189–1327), ed. Harry Rothwell (London, 1975)

Exchequer Rolls of Scotland, eds J. Stuart and others (Edinburgh, 1878–1908).

Foedera, Conventiones, Litterae, e Cuiuscunque Generiis Acta Publica, ed. T. Rymer, 4 vols (Record Commission edition, London, 1816–1869).

Liber Cartarum Prioratus Sancti Andree in Scocia (Bannatyne Club, 1842).

Liber Sancte Marie de Aberbrothoc, 2 vols (Bannatyne Club, 1848–1856).

Palgrave, F. (ed.), *Documents and Records Illustrating the History of Scotland*, 2 vols (London, 1837).

Regesta Regum Scottorum I (Acts of Malcolm IV 1153–65), ed. G.W.S. Barrow (Edinburgh, 1960); II (Acts of William I, 1165–1214), ed. G.W.S. Barrow (Edinburgh, 1971).

Regesta Regum Scottorum V (Acts of Robert I 1306–1329), ed. A.A.M. Duncan (Edinburgh, 1988).

Regesta Regum Scottorum IV, Pt I (The Acts of Alexander III) eds C. Neville and G.G. Simpson (2013).

Regesta Regum Scottorum (handlists): Acts of Alexander II, ed. J.M. Scoular (Edinburgh, 1959); Acts of Alexander III, the Guardians and John, ed. G.G. Simpson (Edinburgh, 1960–).

Stevenson, J. (ed.), *Documents illustrative of the History of Scotland 1286–1306*, 2 vols (Edinburgh, 1870).

Stones, E.L.G. (ed.), *Anglo-Scottish Relations 1174–1328: Some Selected Documents* (London, 1963).

NARRATIVE SOURCES (CHRONICLES, ANNALS, ETC.)

Anderson, A.O. (ed.), *Early Sources of Scottish History, 500–1286*, 2 vols (Edinburgh, 1922, reprinted 1990).

Anderson, A.O. (ed.), *Scottish Annals from English Chroniclers 500 to 1286* (London, 1908, reprinted 1990).

Barbour, J., *The Brus*, ed. A.A.M. Duncan (Edinburgh, 1997).

Fordun, John of, *Johannis de Fordun, Chronica Gentis Scotorum*, 2 vols, ed. W.F. Skene, (Edinburgh, 1871–2).

Chronicle of Walter of Guisborough, ed. H. Rothwell (Camden Society, vol. LXXXIX, London, 1957).

King, E. (ed.) *Blind Hary's Wallace, William Hamilton of Gilbertfield* (Edinburgh, 1998).

Chronicle of Lanercost, 1272–1346, trans. Sir Herbert Maxwell (Glasgow, 1913).

The Chronicle of Melrose, trans. J. Stevenson, in *Church Historians of England* (London, 1835–8).

Paris, M., *Chronica Majora*, 7 vols, ed. H.R. Luard, (Rolls Series 57, London, 1872–83).

Liber Pluscardensis, ed. F.J.H. Skene, 2 vols (Edinburgh, 1877–80).

Scalacronica by Sir Thomas Gray, trans. and ed. A. King (Surtees Society, vol. 209, 2005).

Scotichronicon by Walter Bower, general editor D.E.R.Watt, 9 vols (Aberdeen and Edinburgh, 1987–).

Wyntoun, Andrew, *Orygynale Cronykil of Scotland*, 3 vols, ed. D. Laing (Edinburgh, 1872–9).

Secondary Sources

BOOKS

Appleby, J.C. and Dalton, P., *Government, Society and Religion in Northern England 1000–1700* (Stroud, 1997).

Barrell, A.D.M., *Medieval Scotland* (Cambridge, 2000).

Barron, E.M., *The Scottish War of Independence* (Inverness, 1934).

Barrow, G.W.S., *The Kingdom of the Scots* (London, 1973).

Barrow, G.W.S., *Robert Bruce*, 3rd edition (Edinburgh, 1988).

Barrow, G.W.S. (ed.), *The Scottish Tradition, Essays in Honour of R.G. Cant* (Edinburgh, 1974).

Beam, A., *The Balliol Dynasty 1210–1364* (Edinburgh, 2008).

Birch, Walter de Gray, *History of Scottish Seals* (Stirling, 1905–7).

Bjorn, C., Grant, A. and Stringer, K.J. (eds.), *Nations, Nationalism and Patriotism in the European Past* (Copenhagen, 1994).

Bjorn, C., Grant, A. and Stringer, K.J. (eds.), *Social and Political Identities in Western History* (Copenhagen, 1994).

Broun, D., Finlay, R. and Lynch, M., *Image and Identity: The Making and Re-Making of Scotland through the Ages* (Edinburgh, 1998).

Brown, K.M. and Tanner, R., *Parliament and Politics in Scotland 1235–1560* (Edinburgh, 2004).

Brown, M., *The Wars of Scotland 1214–1371* (Edinburgh, 2004)

Clanchy, M.T., *England and its Rulers 1066–1272*, 2nd edition (Oxford, 1998).

Cooney, N., *The North East and the Scottish Wars of Independence* (Aberdeen Town and County History Society (Aberdeen, 2008).

Coss, P. (ed.), *Thomas Wright's Political Songs of England* (Cambridge, 1996).

Cowan, E.J., *'For Freedom Alone': The Declaration of Arbroath, 1320* (East Linton, 2003).

Cowan, E.J. and Finlay, R.J., *Scottish History: The Power of the Past* (Edinburgh, 2002).

Cowan, E.J., *The Wallace Book* (Edinburgh, 2007).

Cumming-Bruce, M.E., *Family Records of the Bruces and Cummings* (Edinburgh, 1870).

Davies, R.R., *Domination and Conquest: The Experiences of Ireland, Scotland and Wales, 1100–1300* (Cambridge, 1990).

Duncan, A.A.M., *The Kingship of the Scots 842–1292* (Edinburgh, 2002).

Duncan, A.A.M., *Scotland, the Making of the Kingdom* (Edinburgh, 1975).

Fawcett, R. and Breeze, D., *Inchmahome Priory* (Edinburgh, 1986).

Fisher, A., *William Wallace* (Edinburgh, 1986).

Frame, R., *The Political Development of the British Isles, 1100–1400* (Oxford, 1990).

Fraser, W., *The Red Book of Menteith* (Edinburgh, 1880).

Godsman, J., *King-edward, Aberdeenshire: The Story of a Parish* (Banff, 1952).

Goldstein, J., *The Matter of Scotland: Historical Narrative in Medieval Scotland* (Lincoln and London, 1993).

Grant, A., *Independence and Nationhood: Scotland 1306–1469* (London, 1984).

Grant, A. and Stringer, K.J. (eds), *Medieval Scotland: Crown, Lordship and Community: Essays Presented to G.W.S. Barrow* (Edinburgh, 1993).

Hailes, Lord, Sir David Dalrymple, *Annals of Scotland from the Accession of Malcolm III to the Accession of the House of Stewart*, 3 vols (Edinburgh, 1819).

Horne, J. (ed.), *The History of Kirkintilloch* (Kirkintilloch, 1910).

Jackson, R. and Wood, S. (eds), *Images of Scotland*, The Journal of Scottish Education, Occasional Papers No. 1, Northern College (Dundee, 1997).

Lynch, M., *Scotland: A New History* (Edinburgh, 1991).

MacGibbon, D. and Ross, T., *The Ecclesiastical Architecture of Scotland* (Edinburgh, 1887–92).

Mackenzie, A.M., *The Kingdom of Scotland* (Edinburgh, 1948).

McNeil, P. and MacQueen, H., *Atlas of Scottish History to 1707* (The Scottish Medievalists and Department of Geography, University of Edinburgh, Edinburgh, 1996).

Morton, G., *William Wallace: Man and Myth* (Stroud, 2001).

Nicholson, R., *Edward III and the Scots* (Oxford, 1965).

Nicholson, R., *The Edinburgh History of Scotland: The Later Middle Ages*, 2 vols (Edinburgh, 1974).

Oxford Dictionary of National Biography (Oxford, 2004).

Powicke, M., *The Thirteenth Century* (Oxford, 1962).

Pratt, J.B., *Buchan* (Aberdeen, 1859).

Prestwich, M., *Edward I* (London, 1988).

Reichel, O.J., *A Complete Manual of Canon Law*, 2 vols (London, 1890).

Reid, N. (ed.), *Scotland in the Reign of Alexander III, 1249–1286* (Edinburgh, 1990).

Reynolds, S., *Kingdoms and Communities in Western Europe 900–1300* (Oxford, 1997).

Richardson, J.S. and Simpson, M.E.B., *The Castle of Balvenie, Banffshire* (Edinburgh, 1961).

Riley, H.T. (ed.), *Registra Johannis Whethamstede* II (London, 1873).

Simpson, W.D., *Dundarg Castle*, Aberdeen University Studies no. 131 (Aberdeen, 1954).

Smith, Rev. S.B., *Elements of Ecclesiastical Law*, 3 vols, 2nd edition (New York, 1888).

Stell, G., *(Exploring Scotland's Heritage: Dumfries and Galloway* (Edinburgh, 1986).

Stevenson, J.H. and Wood, M., *Scottish Heraldic Seals* (Glasgow, 1940).

Stones, E.L.G. and Simpson, G.G., *Edward I and the Throne of Scotland 1290–1296* (Oxford, 1978).

Stringer, K.J., *Earl David of Huntingdon 1152–1219: A Study in Anglo-Scottish History* (Edinburgh, 1985).

Stringer, K.J. (ed.), *Essays on the Nobility of Medieval Scotland* (Edinburgh, 1985).

Watson, F., *Under the Hammer: Edward I and Scotland 1286–1307* (East Linton, 1998).

Wood, S., *Wallace, Bruce and the Wars of Independence* (Glasgow, 1999).

Young, A., *William Cumin: Border Politics and the Bishopric of Durham 1141–1144*, Borthwick Paper 54, University of York (York, 1978).

Young, A., *Robert the Bruce's Rivals: The Comyns 1212–1314* (East Linton, 1997, 1998).

Young, A. (and Stead, M.), *In the Footsteps of Robert Bruce* (Stroud, 1999, 2010)

Young, A. (and Stead, M.), *In the Footsteps of William Wallace* (Stroud, 2002, 2010)

BOOK CHAPTERS AND JOURNAL ARTICLES

Ash, M., 'William Lamberton, Bishop of St. Andrews, 1297–1328', in Barrow, G.W.S. (ed.), *The Scottish Tradition* (Edinburgh, 1974) pp. 44–55.

Barrow, G.W.S., 'The Idea of Freedom in Late Medieval Scotland', *Innes Review* 30 (1979), pp. 26–32.

Barrow, G.W.S., 'The Scottish Clergy and the War of Independence', *Scottish Historical Review* 41 (1962), pp. 16–26.

Barrow, G.W.S., 'Wales and Scotland in the Middle Ages', *Welsh Historical Review* 10 (1980–1), pp. 302–19.

Barrow, G.W.S., 'Badenoch and Strathspey, 1130–1312: 1. Secular and Political', *Northern Scotland* 8 (1988), pp. 1–15.

Barrow, G.W.S., 'A Kingdom in Crisis: Scotland and the Maid of Norway', *Scottish Historical Review* 188 (October 1990), pp. 120–41.

Broun, D., 'A New Look at *Gesta Annalia* Attributed to John of Fordun', in Crawford, B.E. (ed.), *Church, Chronicle and Learning in Medieval and Early Renaissance Scotland* (Edinburgh, 1999).

Brown, M., 'Henry the Peaceable: Henry III, Alexander III and Royal Lordship in the British Isles, 1249–1272', in Weiler, Bjorn, K.U. and Rowlands, Ifor W., *England and Europe in the Reign of Henry III (1216–1272)* (Aldershot, 2002).

Cowan, E.J., 'The Wallace Factor in Scottish History', in Jackson, R. and Wood, S. (eds), *Images of Scotland*, The Journal of Scottish Education, Occasional Paper No. 1, Northern College (Dundee, 1997).

Dixon, P., 'From Hall to Tower: The Change in Seigneurial Houses on the Anglo-Scottish Border after c.1250', in Coss, P.R. and Lloyd, S.D. (eds), *Thirteenth Century England* IV (Proceedings of the Newcastle upon Tyne Conference, 1991).

Dunbar, J., 'The Medieval Architecture of the Scottish Highlands', in Maclean, L. (ed.), *The Middle Ages in the Highlands* (Inverness Field Club, 1981).

Duncan, A.A.M., 'Sources and Uses of the Chronicle of Melrose 1165–1297', in Taylor, S. (ed.), *Kings, Clerics and Chronicles in Scotland 500–1297* (Dublin, 2000).

Duncan, A.A.M., 'The Earldom of Atholl in the 13th Century', *Scottish Genealogist*, vol. 8, no. 2 (April 1960).

Duncan, A.A.M., 'The Early Parliaments of Scotland', *Scottish Historical Review* 45 (1966), pp. 36–58.

Duncan, A.A.M., 'The Nation of Scots and the Declaration of Arbroath', *Historical Association* G.75 (London, 1970).

Duncan, A.A.M., 'The War of the Scots', *Transactions of the Royal Historical Society* (1992), pp. 125–51.

Ferguson, J., 'The Old Castles of Buchan', *The Buchan Field Club*, vol. 10 (1909).

Ferguson, J., 'The Old Baronies of Buchan', *The Buchan Field Club*, vol. 10 (1909).

Ferguson, J., 'The House of Comyn (1124–1314–1914)', *The Buchan Field Club*, vol. 11 (1915–17).

Fisher, A., 'Wallace and Bruce', *History Today*, February 1989, pp. 18–23.

Fraser, J.E., 'A Swan From a Raven: William Wallace, Brucean Propaganda and *Gesta Annalia* II', *Scottish Historical Review* 81 (2002), pp. 1–22.

Goldstein, R.J., 'The Scottish Mission to Boniface VIII in 1301: A Reconsideration of the Context of the "Instructiones and Processes"', *Scottish Historical Review* 70 (1991), pp. 1–15.

Grant, A., 'Bravehearts and Coronets: Images of William Wallace and the Scottish Nobility', in Cowan, E.J. (ed.), *The Wallace Book* (Edinburgh, 2007).

Grant, A., 'The Death of John Comyn: What was Going On', *Scottish Historical Review* 86 (October 2007), pp. 176–224.

Lawlor, H.J., 'The Absolution of Robert Bruce', *Scottish Historical Review* 19 (1922), pp. 324, 326.

Lewis, J., 'Inverlochy Castle', *Discovery and Excavation Scotland* (1989).

Malcolm, C.A., 'The Office of Sheriff in Scotland: Origins and Early Development', *Scottish Historical Review* 20 (1922–3), pp. 130–41, 223–311.

McQueen, A.A.B., 'Parliament, the Guardians and John Balliol, 1284–1296', in Brown, K.M. and Tanner, R.J. (eds), *Parliament and Politics in Scotland, 1235–1560* (Edinburgh, 2004).

Mitchell, J., 'An Historical Account of the Comyns Earls of Buchan', National Library of Scotland MSS2099 (nineteenth century).

Oram, R., 'An Overview of the Reign of Alexander II', in Oram, R. (ed.), *The Reign of Alexander II, 1214–49* (Leiden, 2004).

Prestwich, M., 'Colonial Scotland: The English in Scotland under Edward I', in Mason, R.A. (ed.), *Scotland and England, 1286–1815* (Edinburgh, 1987).

Prestwich, M., 'England and Scotland During the Wars of Independence', in Jones, M. and Vale, M. (eds), *England and Her Neighbours 1066–1453: Essays in Honour of Pierre Chaplais* (Hambledon, 1989), pp. 181–97.

Prestwich, M., 'Edward I and the Maid of Norway', *Scottish Historical Review* 69 (October 1990), 157–73.

Reid, N., 'Crown and Community under Robert I', in Grant, A. and Stringer, K.J. (eds), *Medieval Scotland, Crown, Lordship and Community* (Edinburgh, 1993), pp. 203–22.

Reid, N., 'Margaret "Maid" of Norway and Scottish Queenship', *Reading Medieval Studies* 8, (1982), pp. 75–96.

Reid, N., 'The Kingless Kingdom: The Scottish Guardianship of 1286–1306', *Scottish Historical Review* 61 (1982), pp. 105–29.

Richardson, H.G. and Sayles, H.O., 'The Scottish Parliaments of Edward I', *Scottish Historical Review* 25 (1928), pp. 300–17.

Round, J.H., 'The Origins of the Comyns', *Ancestor* 10 (1904).

Round, J.H., 'Comyn and Valoignes', *Ancestor* 11 (1922), pp 104–19.

Sayles, G.O., 'The Guardians of Scotland and a Parliament at Rutherglen in 1300', *Scottish Historical Review* 24 (1927), pp. 245–50.

Sellar, W.D.H., 'Was it Murder? John Comyn of Badenoch and William Earl of Douglas', in Kay, C.J. and Mackay, M.A. (eds), *Perspectives on the Older Scottish Tongue: a Celebration of DOST* (Edinburgh, 2005).

Simpson, G.G., 'Why was John Balliol called "Toom Tabard"', *Scottish Historical Review* 41 (1968), pp. 196–9.

Simpson, Grant G., 'Kingship in Miniature: A Seal of Minority of Alexander III, 1249–1257', in Alexander Grant and Keith J. Stringer (eds), *Medieval Scotland: Crown, Lordship and Community* (Edinburgh, 1993), pp. 134–5.

Simpson, W.D., 'Slains Castle', *Transactions of the Buchan Field Club* 16 (1940).

Smallwood, T.M., 'An Unpublished Early Account of Bruce's Murder of Comyn', *Scottish Historical Review* 54 (1975), pp. 1–10.

Stell, G., 'The Balliol Family and the Great Cause of 1291–2', in Stringer, K.J. (ed.), *Essays on the Nobility of Medieval Scotland* (Edinburgh, 1985).

Stones, E.L.G., 'The Submission of Robert Bruce to Edward I c.1301–2', *Scottish Historical Review* 34 (1955), pp. 122–34.

Stones, E.L.G., 'English Chroniclers and the Affairs of Scotland 1286–1296', in Davis, R.H.C. and Wallace-Hadrill, J.M. (eds), *The Writing of History in the Middles Ages* (Oxford, 1981).

Watson, F., 'The Enigmatic Lion: Scotland, Kingship and National Identity – the Wars of Independence', in Brown, D., Finlay, R. and Lynch, M. (eds), *Image and Identity* (Edinburgh, 1998).

Watson, F., 'The Demonisation of King John', in Cowan, E.J. and Finlay, R.J. (eds), *Scottish History: the Power of the Past* (Edinburgh, 2002).

Watt, D.E.R., 'The Minority of Alexander III of Scotland', *Transactions of the Royal Historical Society* 5th series, 21 (1971), pp. 1–23.

Webster, B., 'Review Essays: Anglo-Scottish Relations, 1296–1389: Some Recent Essays', *Scottish Historical Review* 197 (April 1995), pp. 99–108.

Young, A., 'The Political Role of Walter Comyn, Earl of Menteith, during the Minority of Alexander III in Scotland', in Stringer, K.J. (ed.), *Essays on the Nobility of Medieval Scotland* (Edinburgh, 1985), pp. 131–49.

Young, A., 'Noble Families and Political Factions', in Reid, N. (ed.), *Scotland in the Reign of Alexander III, 1249–1286* (Edinburgh, 1990), pp. 1–30.

Young, A., 'The Earls and Earldom of Buchan in the Thirteenth Century', in Grant, A. and Stringer, K.J. (eds), *Medieval Scotland: Crown, Lordship and Community* (Edinburgh, 1993), pp. 174–99.

Young, A., 'The Bishopric of Durham in Stephen's Reign', in Rollason, D., Harvey, M. and Prestwich, M. (eds), *Anglo-Norman Durham, 1093–1193* (Woodridge, 1994), pp. 353–68.

Young, A., 'The North and Anglo-Scottish Relations in the Thirteenth Century', in Appleby, J.C. and Dalton, P. (eds), *Government, Society and Religion in Northern England, 1000–1700* (Stroud, 1997), pp. 77–89.

Young, A., 'The Comyns and Anglo-Scottish Relations (1286–1314)', in Prestwich, M., Britnell, R. and Frame, R. (eds), *Thirteenth Century England* VII (Woodbridge, 1997).

Young, A. 'The Comyns to 1300', in Oram, R. and Stell, G. (eds), *Lordship and Architecture in Scotland, 1100–1650* (Edinburgh, 2005).

Index